TWAYNE'S WORLD AUTHORS SERIES
A Survey of the World's Literature

GERMANY

Ulrich Weisstein, Indiana University

EDITOR

Hermann Broch

TWAS 485

HERMANN BROCH

By ERNESTINE SCHLANT

Montclair State College

TWAYNE PUBLISHERS
A DIVISION OF G. K. HALL & CO., BOSTON

Copyright permission has kindly been given by Pantheon Books, a
Division of Random House, New York, to quote from *The Sleep-
walkers* and *The Death of Virgil*; and by Little, Brown, and Co.,
Boston, to quote from *The Guiltless.*
Mrs. Annemarie M.-G. Broch, Mr. H. F. Broch de Rothermann,
and the Suhrkamp Verlag, Frankfurt/Main, hold the copyrights for
all of Broch's writings in German. They granted the author per-
mission to use these texts and to translate them into English.
The Winkler Verlag, Munich, gave permission to quote from Paul
Michael Lützeler's book *Hermann Broch—Ethik und Politik.*

Library of Congress Cataloging in Publication Data

Schlant, Ernestine.
   Hermann Broch.

   (Twayne's world authors series; TWAS 485: Germany)
   Bibliography: p. 183-89
   Includes index.
   1. Broch, Hermann, 1886-1951—Criticism and interpretation.
PT2603.R657Z859   828'.9'1209   77-19354
ISBN 0-8057-6326-0   3

To Bill

Contents

About the Author

Ernestine Schlant was born in Germany and started her academic training at the University of Munich. She continued her education in the United States and received her Ph.D. in Comparative Literature from Emory University, Atlanta, Georgia. She has taught at Spelman College in Atlanta, the State University of New York at Stony Brook, and is now an associate professor of German at Montclair State College in New Jersey. She also worked for two years as assistant producer in film production.

Her publications include a book on the philosophy of Hermann Broch, articles on Broch, Kafka, East German literature, and the American film. She co-authored several textbooks for students of German and translated Kate Millett's *Sexual Politics* into German.

Preface

Hermann Broch's reputation as a writer rests on two novels, *The Sleepwalkers* and *The Death of Virgil*. On the basis of these two novels alone he must be included among the foremost novelists of the twentieth century. Yet Broch's *oeuvre* is more comprehensive. In addition to further literary work (*The Unknown Quantity, The Mountain Novel, The Guiltless*) he developed a "theory of humanity," which he subdivided into the study of mass psychology and mass hysteria, and into a theory of politics and law, culminating in a theory of democracy; and he based the entire structure on a theory of knowledge.

While articles, dissertations, and books on the novels proliferate, few scholars have seen the intimate connection between Broch's literary and political/philosophical writings. This situation is exacerbated as far as the general public is concerned. Broch is not an "easy" writer, and access to his writings requires concentration and patience. Perhaps the new German paperback edition of his collected works will lead to a more thorough understanding through a better presentation and exposition of his ideas in their full context.

For the English-speaking public, acquaintance with Broch is even more difficult. Only three of his novels have been translated (*The Sleepwalkers, The Death of Virgil,* and *The Guiltless*), and of the political philosophical writings only those few have been published in English that were done during Broch's lifetime, primarily in the 1940s. To date there is available only one slim volume in English that discusses more than a single work and serves as an introduction to Broch's *oeuvre* as a whole.[1] The present study is motivated by the desire that Broch's writings may find a wider circle of readers among laymen and scholars alike, and that it will contribute to place Broch's achievements in the position of prominence they so amply deserve.

ERNESTINE SCHLANT

Montclair State College

Acknowledgments

I would like to express my appreciation to the National Endowment for the Humanities. The Summer Stipend in 1972 allowed me to do research in the Broch archives at the Beinecke Rare Books Library at Yale University, where Broch's unpublished manuscripts are located. Montclair State College has generously granted me research release time over a number of semesters. In particular W. B. Fleischmann, Dean of the School of Humanities, and John D. Moore, Chairman of the German Department, have enthusiastically endorsed all my requests. I enjoyed the same support from the staff of the Montclair State College Library, particularly Joyce Schaefer's of the Interlibrary Loan Division, who never tired in providing or acquiring the material I needed.

I owe special thanks to H. F. Broch de Rothermann for his interest in this study and for all the information he provided to make this presentation of his father's life and work more complete. Mrs. Lilly Kahler of Princeton generously shared her Broch memorabilia with me, and Christa Sammons of the Beinecke Library greatly facilitated access to Broch's legacy. Paul Michael Lützeler, who, to my knowledge, has done the most extensive and thorough research into the early Broch and into Broch's years in exile, allowed me to draw on his findings even before they were published.

Winifred Donahue and Kathy Woodhull were always there when I needed their typing skills. Robert Shelton read the manuscript with great care and attention to details. Some of the most enjoyable moments in the process of completing this manuscript came when my daughter Stephanie ruthlessly corrected my punctuation. Yet more than anybody else, my husband Bill contributed to this text through his patience with my erratic work schedule and his encouragement and invaluable suggestions in the final stages of assembling the manuscript.

Where no translations of Broch's work are available in print, my own translations are used, followed by reference to the German source.

Chronology

1886   Hermann Broch born November 1 in Vienna.

1903   Graduates from the Staats-Realschule; later attends the Vienna Webschule.

1905– Concludes his training as a textile engineer in Mühlhausen/
1906   Alsace.

1908   Joins parental business.

1908– *Notizbücher Kultur 1908–1909* and first essays published (in
1914   part) in *Der Brenner*.

1909   Marries Franziska de Rothermann.

1910   Birth of only child, Hermann Friedrich. Autodidactic studies of current philosophical issues.

1914– Exempted from military service because of poor health. Ad-
1918   ministers a Red Cross reconvalescent home in Teesdorf. Publishes essays, reviews, and one novella in *Summa*.

1918– Participates in commissions to maintain peace among workers
1919   during the revolutionary period. Publishes political essays in *Die Rettung* and *Der Friede*.

1922   Divorce.

1925– Attends courses at the University of Vienna, primarily with
1930   members of the "Vienna Circle."

1927   Sells the textile plant in Teesdorf over family opposition.

1931– Publishes *Die Schlafwandler*.
1932

1933   *Die Unbekannte Grösse.*

1934   May 15, première of *Die Totenklage* at the Schauspielhaus in Zurich.

1936   Completes first version of the *Bergroman*.

1937   Preliminary drafts for *Der Tod des Vergil*.

1938   March 13–31, imprisonment in Alt-Aussee subsequent to the *Anschluss*; emigrates via Scotland. October 9, arrives in the United States.

1939– Receives Guggenheim fellowship to continue work on *Der*
1940   *Tod des Vergil.*

1939– Rescue activities in New York on behalf of Jewish emigrants.
1945

CHAPTER 1

Growing up in the Vienna of the "Gay Apocalypse"

HALFWAY through our century and two years before his death in 1951, Hermann Broch expanded what was to be a short introduction to the work of Hugo von Hofmannsthal into a study of *fin-de-siècle* Vienna. The introduction provided him with the opportunity to survey the political structure, the social and economic events, and the cultural heritage of which he and Hofmannsthal were part. Born in 1874, Hofmannsthal was twelve years Broch's senior; yet biography and autobiography merge in the exploration of an era which Broch was to term the "gay apocalypse," referring to Vienna's doomsday insouciance of the turn of the century (GW, VI, 76).

The Austrian empire, in which Broch and Hofmannsthal grew up, was one of the oldest European monarchies. Toward the end of the eighteenth century, the Josephinian reforms had breathed into this absolutist state a spirit of enlightenment, characterized by such rights as freedom of worship for Protestants and Jews, freedom of movement, and free choice of occupation. However, the legacy of Metternich and his diplomatic successes at the end of the Napoleonic wars reestablished repression and introduced censorship and a reactionary police system. This situation became still more exacerbated after the economic depression of 1847 and the revolution of 1848, and left its imprint upon the citizenry in the form of political apathy. However, following the precedents set by national liberation movements all over the continent in the early part of the century, the many nationalities contained in the vast Austrian empire yearned for self-determination. The result was a state of "permanent crisis" that engulfed the final years of the Habsburg monarchy. Cultural nationalism, with its insistence on national languages and indigenous cultural traditions, turned into political nationalism. Although Habsburg pacified Hungary in 1867 by establishing the Dual Mon-

13

archy, it was not prepared to make similar arrangements for its many
other nationalities. In the almost seven decades of his reign, until his
death in 1917, emperor Francis Joseph was the one symbol which
kept the empire from disintegrating. Broch viewed him as the
prototype of an abstract monarch, implying that his title and crown,
rather than his political power, provided the last cohesiveness for
increasingly divergent interests: "In 1848 it became clear without a
doubt that without the crown the Austrian conglomerate was without
substance, that the state's staying power—the most important requi-
site for its existence—was concentrated in the crown; in brief, that
the crown alone represented the basis of the state. Thereby the crown
was invested with the function of totality, a kind of involuntary 'L'état
c'est moi' . . ." (GW, VI, 90).

Yet amid this state of permanent crisis occurred an unprecedented
economic boom. After the stock market crash of 1873 the Austrian
economy followed an upward trend which extended almost without
setbacks to the threshold of World War I. The economic prosperity
went hand in hand with an increasingly weakened political structure,
with greater restiveness among the many nationalities, and a feeling
of political powerlessness on the part of the general populace. This
combination created a cultural resurgence of the most impressive
dimensions which set the tone for many decades. Only Paris, among
the European capitals, could compare with Vienna in the wealth of its
artistic and intellectual life. In literature, Vienna had its representa-
tives of decadence and of the art-for-art's-sake movement, such as
Hermann Bahr, Stefan Zweig, Arthur Schnitzler, Hugo von Hofmannsthal, and the "Young Vienna" group. With Gustav Klimt and
the Secession of 1893 it contributed its share to the decorous style of
Art Nouveau, and through Egon Schiele it paved the way for
Kokoschka and Expressionism. Simultaneously, this was the Vienna
of Freud's *Interpretation of Dreams* (1900), the *Psychopathology of
Everyday Life* (1904), the *Three Contributions to the Sexual Theory*
(1905), and of Musil's *Young Törless* (1906). It was the Vienna of
Strauss waltzes and Lehár operettas, as well as of the music of Gustav
Mahler, Arnold Schönberg, Anton von Webern, and the young Alban
Berg. The architect Adolf Loos wrote his essay "Ornament and
Crime" in 1908. Vienna had one of the world's leading medical
schools. At the university, the physicist Ludwig Boltzmann taught
until 1906, the physicist-philosopher Ernst Mach exerted his
positivistic influence, and the foundations were being laid for the

post–World War I Vienna Circle. Finally, Vienna could boast of the most enlightened journalism on the continent.

In the late nineteenth century, Austria followed the path of other industrializing nations: a booming economy entailed a rapid expansion of the number and size of cities. Vienna, more than any other city in the empire, showed the underside of economic prosperity in its slums and the incipient socialist movements. Yet the arts did not reflect these social and political problems. Naturalism with its commitment to a critical view of society and the indictment of social, political, and economic ills—a thriving movement in other European countries—found no roots in Austria. Accustomed to political helplessness and conditioned by the most effectively operating bureaucracy in Europe, the Austrian writers took the road of internalization and fled into the private universe of a Symbolist and Impressionist aestheticism. While artists in France, for example, compensated for the exploration of the inner life with a commitment to external causes, while Zola balanced the withdrawal into the ivory tower, and Naturalism balanced Symbolism, Austrian artists, philosophers, and scientists pursued single-mindedly the investigation of the inner lives of their heroes and patients. Perhaps nowhere else in Europe was the sense of an ending anticipated and analyzed as strongly as in Austria at the turn of the century; yet the impending disintegration was only explored philosophically and psychologically. The accent remained strictly on the individual. According to Carl Schorske, "not only Vienna's finest writers, but her painters and psychologists, even her art historians, were preoccupied with the problem of the individual in a disintegrating society."[1]

The combination of political impotence and enonomic prosperity created a public whose taste, mitigated by Victorian standards, ran in the direction of easy consumerism, epitomized in the coffee houses with their *Sachertorte,* the wine restaurants with the *Heurige,* and the amusement park *Prater.* Such gay enjoyment in an environment of restive nationalities and a politically crumbling empire invited the most acerbic criticism from the few concerned observers, foremost among whom was Karl Kraus. Nearly half a century passed before Broch, in 1948, fully realized that "all that was left was the cheapest imitation of the Comic Opera, leveled down to pure idiocy with its partly charming, partly stale romanticism. The uninspired cynicism of the plain, that is, exclusively decorative amusement began to spread, and the appropriate carrier of its immortality was the 'Waltzer' genius of Strauss" (*GW*, VI, 83). The long road Broch had traveled by the end of his life can be measured against the background from which he had to extricate himself. As a young man he had shared the atmosphere in which the state of permanent crisis had dulled the citizens' awareness of the magnitude of events taking place around them. It was the norm that "the middle-class, and above all the young middle-class, Viennese hardly recognized the seriousness of the situation that was developing before their very eyes. Zweig reports that, when he and his friends read the newspapers, they passed over the Boer War, the Russo-Japanese War, and the Balkan crises, in much the same way that they disregarded the sports pages."[2]

No one in *fin-de-siècle* Vienna countered the decadence or the explorations of the individual psyche by focusing on a view of the individual as part of his society. Under the pervasive influence of Nietzsche's philosophy, alternatives to the interest in delicate psychological mechanisms became available, but the emphasis on the individual remained, indeed gained momentum in the strong-willed and powerful *Übermensch* ("Superman"). In the same vein, the erotic movement and the various trends of vitalism were obvious retreats from social awareness into an apotheosis of the individual. The compensatory longing of the tired and bored who yearn for the powerful and extraordinary began to reveal its irrational core. Taking refuge in an ideology of the strong provided no solution, only a sad commentary on a society that formulated and accepted its own disintegration.

I   *"Destined to become a spinner, weaver, and cotton-mixer"*

This was the Vienna in which Hermann Broch grew up. He was born on November 1, 1886, as the oldest of two sons. His brother Friedrich was born three years later. Joseph Broch, the father, had come to Vienna as a young man from Olomouc in Moravia. He made his fortune in the textile business, and married Johanna Schnabel, descendant of a wealthy and old Viennese Jewish family. Though perhaps more successful financially, Joseph Broch was not unlike many other Jews who had left the provinces to try their luck in the big city. Indeed, he fitted perfectly into a pattern which, in the words of his son, was established in the preceding century. A constantly increasing movement of Jewish merchants from the ghettos of Bohemia and Moravia to Vienna began at the end of the eighteenth century, "initiated with the Josephinian tolerance edicts and unimpeded, much less discontinued, by their revocation" (*GW*, VI, 106).[3]

To the same degree that Joseph Broch's life followed the path of many Jewish compatriots, there also ensued similar conflicts between father and son. What has been said in the case of Karl Kraus and others holds equally true for Hermann Broch: "Here was a family constellation that was typical at the turn of the century: the sons of Central European Jewish businessmen—often self-made men, strong and self-willed, heads of patriarchially organized families— turned to literature. Cases in point are Franz Kafka, Stefan Zweig, Siegfried Trebitsch, Felix Salten and Franz Werfel."[4] Arthur Schnitzler and Hugo von Hofmannsthal were fortunate in that their fathers furthered their sons' literary interests. Most other young writers of similar background had to overcome great paternal objections. The list of generational conflicts would be even longer if one included in the nonliterary arts and the sciences names such as Freud, Mahler, and Weininger. Yet where, for example, Franz Kafka insisted, at tremendous cost to himself, on choosing his own profession and identity, Broch followed for the first forty years of his life the path his father had prescribed, "destined even before birth to become a spinner, weaver, and cotton-mixer" (*GW*, X, 329). When Kafka died in 1924 at the age of forty-one, Broch, who was three years his junior, had not even begun work on his first novel.

In 1903, young Broch graduated from the Staats-Realschule, which stressed the natural sciences and French. He enrolled in the Vienna Institute for Weaving Technology (Webschule) and also took courses in insurance mathematics at the Vienna Technological University. In his "Autobiographie als Arbeitsprogramm" ("Autobiography as Work Program") (*GW*, IX, 37), written about 1940, and in letters with autobiographical information, Broch never mentions that during the winter semester 1904–1905 he audited courses at the University of Vienna.[5] His enrollment in these courses is interesting insofar as it reflects interests which lay in mathematics and philosophy, not in business. Nevertheless, Broch's professional training was continued first at the Webschule in Vienna and then at the Technikum in Mulhouse in Alsace, where he was graduated in 1906 with the degree of textile engineer. His propensity for mathematics found a practical application in the invention of a cotton-mix machine which he developed with a colleague and patented in 1908. The twenty-year-old Broch must have been quite impressed by his sojourn in Alsace; a quarter of a century later he drew on the memories of this period for the setting of the third part of *The Sleepwalker* trilogy.

After graduation, Broch worked for about a year in his father's textile plant at Teesdorf near Vienna, and in factories in Bohemia. In September, 1907, he took a two months' trip to the United States, which his father viewed partly as a recognition of his achievements and partly as a continuing education in the cotton industry of the southern United States. The trip seems to have left no impression on the twenty-one-year-old Broch. After his return he remained obedient to his father's desires and joined the army as a volunteer officer's candidate. He eventually became a lieutenant. During the same time, he entered his father's business in the official capacity of director and assumed increasing responsibilities in the plant. In 1907, during a train ride, he met Franziska de Rothermann, daughter of a Dutch-Hungarian sugar-beet producer, and for the next two years a stormy courtship ensued. Both families resisted the alliance for religious as well as social reasons. Yet after Broch's conversion to catholicism and his discharge from the military, the couple was married in December, 1909. One year later their only child, Hermann Friedrich, was born.

By 1910, Broch looked at first glance the fulfillment of middle-class aspirations. He was a well trained young engineer with a patent to his credit. He had recently married a woman with a substantial dowry, and was soon to be a father. He seemed the natural successor to his father in the family business. Despite disagreements over financial and managerial matters Joseph Broch had reason to be proud of his oldest son. These controversies were part of their relationship and were heightened after Hermann's marriage by conflicts between the elder Mrs. Broch and her daughter-in-law. Yet family squabbles about money were a common aspect of bourgeois life. According to the standards of business mentality, other matters caused graver concern: young Broch continued to be interested in philosophy and the natural sciences. During the next few years he acquired an extensive library, studied late into the night, and tried to make up for a lack of formal training at the university. In the two years preceding his marriage, in addition to business responsibilities, military duties, and courtship, he had begun to collect notes on the culture of his era, *Kultur 1908–1909 (Culture 1908–1909)*.[6]

These notebooks are interesting insofar as they document Broch's intellectual origins, which were very much in the mainstream of contemporary popular intellectual thought. Quite obviously, Broch had to come to terms with the prevalent philosophical fashions before he could embark on a system of his own. The extent to which his thought remained rooted in the popular philosophical concepts of his era (for example, the recognition of strong irrational components in the human psyche, the insistence on individualism, the idealist position of the supremacy of ethics over economics as socially formative forces) will be discussed later. The names Broch mentions during these and subsequent years, and the selective absorption of their influences, show his acquaintance with the movements of vitalism and neo-Kantianism, with the work of Nietzsche, Schopenhauer, Kierkegaard, Weininger, and, most importantly, with that of Karl Kraus. Paul Michael Lützeler describes it like this:

He [Broch] becomes aware of the contours of the impeding catastrophes in the Europe predating World War I, but it would be premature to say he had any analysis of his own to offer for the causes of this "Civilization and its Discontent." It is true, in his aphorisms of 1908 and 1909 he analyzes the enormous superficiality of the Viennese cultural life more thoroughly than most of his contemporaries. Yet in his aggressive polemics against this cultural to-do and against modern civilization in general he stays on the surface. He attacks only the educated bourgeoisie and the arts it sponsors; the entire complex of the socioeconomic structure and the political situation is left out of consideration.[7]

Broch's lack of interest in the sociopolitical complex was not merely a personal shortcoming. It reflected the climate of the era in which he grew up, where "a passionate commitment to politics was hampered by a failure to grasp the true realities of the political situation" and where a "legacy of tutelage and inexperience" created a generation which grew up "in an environment which paid exceptional deference to the arts and set great store by cultural refinement. As the political power of the bourgeoisie (which had always been limited) waned in the 1880's, the function and meaning of art changed: it became a refuge from political impotence."[8]

II *Starting out in the mainstream of popular philosophical thought*

Broch's intellectual career began as an essayist with a penchant for philosophy. In 1912 he submitted the "Notizen zu einer systematischen Ästhetik" ("Notes toward a Systematic Aesthetic") to Ludwig von Ficker, the publisher of the journal *Der Brenner* in Innsbruck. This biweekly periodical printed the works of many contemporary artists, such as Trakl, Rilke, Else Lasker-Schüler, and Theodor Däubler and also opened its pages to Theodor Haecker, the Swabian Kierkegaard scholar. Wittgenstein entrusted part of his patrimony to Ficker to distribute among worthy artists (the choice fell on Rilke and

Trakl) and remained in close contact with Ficker. At the same time, "Ficker was the only editor in Austria who would even mention the work of Karl Kraus, let alone concede its importance."[9] Broch's choice of *Der Brenner* is therefore significant, since it may be assumed that he was familiar with the journal before he selected it for his own publications.[10] Ficker rejected Broch's first philosophical ruminations; yet he did publish subsequent essays and a poem during 1913 and 1914. He also invited Broch, as a sign of his esteem, to contribute a statement on Karl Kraus, to be published with those of Else Lasker-Schüler, Richard Dehmel, Frank Wedekind, Thomas Mann, Peter Altenberg, Georg Trakl, Adolf Loos, Stefan Zweig, Alfred Mombert, Willy Haas, Franz Werfel, and Oskar Kokoschka in the "Antwort auf eine 'Rundfrage über Karl Kraus' " ("Answer to a 'Questionnaire Concerning Karl Kraus' ") in *Der Brenner* of June 15, 1913.

About the rejected essay of 1912, Broch admitted in a letter to Ficker, dated May 18, 1913: "To come back to the 'Notes:' they cannot boast of any clarity. . . . they are anything but 'too scientific,' rather too loose . . ." (*GW*, X, 253). Yet, as a document of Broch's development, the article is interesting in many ways: it resumes some of the ideas of the earlier aphoristic notes, *Culture 1908–1909*, and indicates the direction of Broch's subsequent studies. In addition to Karl Kraus, Broch mentions Otto Weininger, whose book *Geschlecht und Charakter* (*Sex and Character*) of 1903 exerted a formidable influence on "toute Vienne."[11] Broch disagrees with Weininger when he defines the properties of the aesthetic (*GW*, X, 225), and shows that he has read Schopenhauer, probably as a result of Weininger's indebtedness to Schopenhauer's "Metaphysik der Geschlechtsliebe" ("Metaphysics of Sexual Love").[12] The close connection he sees between aesthetic, erotic, and mystical ecstasy is here still treated in a straightforward manner. Soon it will become the target of irony in Broch's literary writings, when the attempted shortcuts at transcendence are mocked. Examples are "Eine methodologische Novelle" ("Methodological Novella") of 1918 and numerous incidents in the novels from *Die Schlafwandler* (*The Sleepwalkers*) to *Die Schuldlosen* (*The Guiltless*).

Yet it is Kant whose impact on Broch's thinking is most pronounced in this essay. Broch enters the Kant-Schopenhauer controversy[13] aligning himself with Kant and opposing Schopenhauer's absolutist/irrational classifications such as "energy," "God," "natural law." He states: "All these concepts require a 'faith,' an absoluteness; it is the merit of Kant's philosophy to avoid such absoluteness. The 'thing-in-itself' is *not* identical with Schopenhauer's 'will' " (*GW*, X, 217). In the same essay, thoughts on aesthetic symmetry and equilibrium as well as on the spatialization of time are found for the first time; they still occupy him twenty years later, in the important essays of the 1930s.

Of equal importance are references to the architect Adolf Loos, though his essay "Ornament and Crime" of 1908 is not mentioned by name. Broch deplores the absence of ornamentation as it is advocated by Loos[14] and relates it to Kandinsky's *Über das Geistige in der Kunst (On the Spiritual in Art)* of 1912 (*GW*, X, 235). Here, thoughts are tentatively expressed which find their systematic formulation in the theory of the disintegration of values, notably presented in *The Sleepwalkers*, further elaborated in some of the essays of the 1930s, and reiterated in the Hofmannsthal essay at the end of his life. The young Broch ventures to forecast:

Therefore, I consider it inappropriate to predict the advent of a great new art due to the incapacity to create ornaments, and due to conceiving beauty in the useful, in the machine. Even in the breakthrough of the spiritual I can only see a necessary conclusion. I see a period of decadence ahead, much rather than of great art; a decadence which will replace the naive and serious pathos of the old style with beautiful skepsis. (*GW*, X, 236)

This cluster of problems will occupy Broch for the rest of his life, though in time he will reverse his evaluation of these issues.

The first article by Broch, which *Der Brenner* published in 1913, was "Philistrosität, Realismus, Idealismus der Kunst" ("Philistrosity, Realism, Idealism in Art"), ostensibly a review of Thomas Mann's *Tod in Venedig (Death in Venice)*. In this early essay, one of Broch's idiosyncrasies is already revealed: under the guise of a specific topic (such as the review of a book, Freudian psychology, music, etc.), he veers off to develop his own theories of a more general nature, for which the topic at hand serves at most as pretext. He then has to remind himself, almost forcefully, of the subject which occasioned his formal disquisition and ties the two fields together rather abruptly. In the essay on *Death in Venice*, there are no startling insights into Mann's novella, but Broch mentions for the first time the "Platonic Idea" in its complex associations. As the cornerstone of Broch's theory of knowledge, the "Platonic Idea" permeates all philosophical categories. It is therefore quite curious that he never refers to specific passages in Plato or quotes him in any direct way.[15] On the basis of Broch's own references, his source for the "Platonic Idea" is Schopenhauer, specifically Book 3 of *Die Welt als Wille und Vorstellung (The World as Will and Idea)*. In 1912, Broch had criticized Schopenhauer's equation of the "will" with Kant's "thing-in-itself." One year later, he declares the Kantian "thing-in-itself" synonymous with Schopenhauer's "Platonic Idea," thereby overriding Schopenhauer's more tentative approximation of the two concepts: "The basic thought of Schopenhauer's aesthetics: artistic vision is the capacity to divine in the objects their 'Platonic Idea,' the 'thing-in-itself'; artistic creation means to manifest this divination concretely" *(GW, X, 242)*.[16]

Broch never saw the epistemological confusion which resulted from his uncritical appropriation of Schopenhauer. In terms of the system which he developed in later years this inaccuracy appears insignificant; in terms of Broch's methods of absorbing the intellectual heritage, it points to an impatient eclecticism pursuing its own goals. When Broch finally began to systematize his epistemology in 1948, his exclusive attention to the cognitive processes led him away from an inquiry into the relation between object and subject of cognition. The young Broch's *Kant-Erlebnis*, the intense first awareness of Kant's philosophy, concentrated on the epistemological investigation into the boundaries of reason; Schopenhauer's "Platonic Idea" assumed the unquestioned status of an ideational totality in which the world of phenomena can never be more than a succession of symbols. The "thing-in-itself," as Kant interpreted it, was for Broch never of any concern.

The short essay "Ethik" ("Ethics") of 1914 is the last article written before the outbreak of World War I and published in *Der Brenner*; it documents the next step in Broch's coming to terms with prevalent intellectual currents. The essay substantiates the impact of Weininger, whom Broch calls "the most passionate moral philosopher after Kant" *(E, 689)*, and refutes Schopenhauer in favor of Nietzsche, "who arrives in his critique of knowledge at incomparably deeper insights than Schopenhauer, but who has apparently taken over his [Schopenhauer's] Kant interpretation . . ." *(E, 687)*. More important, however, is the fact that in this essay Broch begins to search for a frame of reference in which the view of a disintegrating society could be objectified. As soon as he saw Kant's search for the boundaries of reason as an ethical task, he had found that combination of concepts which was to become the guideline for all his future philosophizing.

Discussions of the Kantian boundaries of reason were common enough among the neo-Kantians and, in fact, "were a dominant feature of Viennese intellectual and cultural debate from 1890 on."[17] In the essay "Philistrosity, Realism, and Idealism in Art" of 1913, Broch had already broached this subject, but had rejected the possibility of deriving an ethics from the Kantian epistemology. He had said: "The Kantian, the idealistic philosophy, is an analysis of boundaries, and to derive an aesthetic, moral philosophy from this skeptical analysis is, one hundred years after Kant, no longer feasible" (*GW, X, 243*). One year later his attention shifted from the aesthetic implications of Kant's "exactly determined *ignorabimus*" (*GW, X, 244*) to ethics. The exploration of the boundaries of reason is now viewed as a supremely personal task which it is the responsibility and duty of each individual to pursue. Once the connection between the investigation of the boundaries of reason and the ethical implications of this exploration was established, Broch could see this search in a historical context; and he could arrive at his theory of value, which is an attempt to place the Viennese sense of disintegrating values in an objective perspective.

He took the first step toward this theory when he demanded that the exploration of the boundaries of reason should be carried out by the individual in the loneliness of his "I". Above all, the philosopher takes upon himself this "most terrible cognition, the loneliness of the spirit, without any modification, without any hope, in an act of overcoming the self which to me seems the essence of the philosophical" (*E*, 685). To accept this mission requires heroism; and, indeed, Broch saw Kant's philosophy as the culmination of heroic skepticism. In a second step, the historical perspective was achieved insofar as this loneliness and the philosopher's heroism were understood as *recent* necessities. Kant becomes a historical phenomenon, and his philosophy, with the emphasis on "the loneliness of the I," is seen as a response to the disintegration of social and religious bonds.[18]

Broch's mystification of the "I" and its loneliness can be seen as a direct result of the cult of individualism and the feeling of disintegration, projected into his interpretation of Kant. Although Broch saw this "loneliness of the I" and the concomitant ethical-cognitive task as recent historical phenomena, he did not admit that such a view of history was heir to a specific intellectual tradition. The reduction of the individual to the core of spiritual loneliness could be explained as symptomatic of the process of disintegration. Yet the theory of disintegration is itself an historic phenomenon, similar to other "rise-

and-fall" views of history. The prevalence of these theories during Broch's formative years, from Nietzsche's hypothesis of the "eternal recurrence" to Spengler's *Untergang des Abendlandes (Decline of the West)* (1918–1922) left few alternatives to an aspiring young intellectual whose primary source of inspiration and information were current topics. Broch's intellectual struggles, particularly during the last two decades of his life, can be viewed as an attempt to rid himself of these powerful conditionings.

During the next few years, Broch realized that the concentration on the formal aspects of the cognitive processes and the exploration of the boundaries of reason did not suffice to provide sufficient ethical directives. Following the "laws of the I" (*Gesetzlichkeit des Ichs, E,* 686) would lead to the autonomy of the individualistic approach and negate any communal responsibility. Here are the roots of some inconsistencies in the thought of the early Broch. On the one hand, the pursuit by the individual of his own cognitive explorations is understood as the most important and ethically most "redeeming" activity; on the other hand, the individual autonomy of each such pursuit is condemned as contributing to an "anarchy of values" (as Broch was to call it a few years later) and as furthering the disintegration of communal values. Broch's suggested escape from this impasse was the institution of a "central value" which should infuse each individual endeavor with directives and a goal, and contribute to a reintegration of values. Instead of pursuing the "laws of the I" for their own sake, exploration should occur in the service of a common, humanistic goal. It was almost twenty years after World War I, in the face of Hitler Germany and as an exile to the United States, that Broch elaborated on the nature of this goal: it was to be the preservation of human dignity and human life, anchored in a constitutional framework and protected by law.

In one final step, Broch rounded out the skeleton for his philosophical system when he identified this humanistic ideal, an unattainable goal as he admitted, with the Platonic Idea. Not unlike the Neoplatonic theory of emanations, Broch's system can be visualized as a hierarchy dominated by the Platonic Idea, an absolute totality which manifests itself in time and history in sequential order. In our secularized, fragmented era, in which the Platonic totality is no longer symbolized in God, a quasi-divine image of man and the humanistic ideal of bettering man's lot in this life should become the new symbol around which to congregate. Advancing from a state of nonawareness and propelled by the cognitive drive (and hence obeying the innate, most human, and most humanizing faculty), the individuals are scattered according to their cognitive progress along this steep road to the ultimate and always unattainable goal. Broch believed that he was creating an incontestably logical system in which the scientific-formalistic exploration of the boundaries of reason was placed in the service of an idealistic humanism; instead, he contributed a new version of the myth of Faustian striving and the redemptive powers inherent in the pursuit of the communal-humane goal. The novels, in particular *The Sleepwalkers* and *Der Tod des Vergil* (*The Death of Virgil*), can be considered monumental fictional enactments of the two major cornerstones of Broch's philosophy. The different characters in *The Sleepwalkers* will be exemplifications of the pursuits of the "laws of the I" and of their violations. The ambivalence of Broch's concept of ethics (autonomy of cognitive striving as opposed to its subordination under the Platonic Idea) will become most obvious in the evaluation of the characters of Huguenau and Eduard von Bertrand. *The Death of Virgil* focuses on epistemology mythologized: the great difficulties of the cognitive voyage and the many pitfalls will not deter Virgil from seeking ultimate self-redemption in the process of exploring the boundaries of reason.

II *Eclecticism as training ground*

Scholars of Broch's early development have pointed to his derivative and eclectic approach. This eclecticism and the rephrasing of prevalent intellectual currents in the pre–World War I Vienna reflect Broch's desire to come to terms with the issues raised in his particular society. And since this society offered a splendid array of some of the twentieth century's most influential artists, philosophers, and scientists, attention to the current issues provided an excellent training ground for an industrialist who had no systematic education in philosophy. In fact, one could express surprise that the *embarras de choix* confronting the young autodidact did not distract him into the dead end of aestheticism, of vitalism, or of unmitigated irrationalism, but that he found his way, in a relatively short period of time, to an idealistic humanism. That Broch felt he had to come to terms with the philosophical factions and fads of the pre–World War I Vienna was again an attitude typical of his intellectual climate. The same holds true for his tendency to see and define situations against a holistic background. In the Vienna of that period, none of the disciplines was pursued in the spirit of specialization and compartmentalization so characteristic of subsequent decades. The "interdependence of the different Viennese arts and sciences" was an unquestioned assumption of a cultural milieu where "everyone in the educated world discussed philosophy and regarded the central issues in post-Kantian thought as bearing directly on his own interest, whether artistic or scientific, legal or political," and where terms taken from "the Kantian tradition, notably from the 'antiphilosopher' Arthur Schopenhauer" pervaded the "drawing rooms of Vienna."[19]

CHAPTER 2

World War I and the Aftermath

WORLD War I broke out on July 28, 1914, when Austria declared war on Serbia. The mobilization in Germany followed on August 1. The general populace and most intellectuals welcomed the war with fervent enthusiasm. Among the few voices that pleaded for peace was that of Karl Kraus, who had for years spoken out against the coming catastrophe. Under the influence of Kraus' ethical intransigence[1] and shortly before the outbreak of the war, Broch wrote a lengthy poem, *Cantos 1913*, interspersed with prose texts.[2] It combined acerbic criticism of the prewar Victorian society with a view of history in which progress is measured by the diminution of human suffering. It culminates in the sardonic verses:

> Kling Klang Gloria,
> Wir ziehen in die Schlacht,
> Wir wissen nicht, warum wir's tun,
> Doch Mann an Mann im Grab zu ruhn
> Vielleicht Vergnügen macht.[3]

> Ding, dang, gloria
> Off to battle we go;
> We do not know why we go,
> Perhaps it will be fun
> To lie man next to man
> In the grave.

The poem remained unpublished at the time of its composition, probably because events rapidly overtook the fears expressed in it. In this poem, Broch sketched for the first time a consistent philosophy of history indebted to the then prevalent cyclical view of history, but modified by a possible redemption through a deliberate, humane application of the advances in cognition. In Broch's idealistic system, progress of knowledge, that is, obedience to the Kantian exploration of cognitive boundaries, becomes the driving force of history. Broch's affirmation of the primacy of mind and of intellect as historically determining factors remained unmitigated, and in the course of his life found constant and renewed confirmation in his literary, philosophical and political writings. In the *Cantos 1913*, Broch combined his view of history as progressive knowledge with what may be called his humanistic imperative (a modification of the Kantian categorical imperative), namely, the responsibility to act "humanely." "Do not make science responsible;/it invents the electric needles, which can/be used to heal as much as to torture,/for progress as much as regress while/alone responsible is the demonic stupidity,/the stupidity of all of us."[4] The fact that man can act "stupidly" is not simply a personal characteristic, but is rather due to historical situations in which phases of uncertainty provoked by cataclysmic breakthroughs into new levels of knowledge alternate with those of spiritual certainty. Broch described one of these phases in the *Cantos 1913*. The passage can stand as a paradigm for his view of history. "Born in turmoil, after the medieval/humanity and dispersed, born/in war and terror, introduced by/the burning of heretics and witches, accompanied by/expulsions and misery of the most unheard of/and previously unthinkable dimensions,/the Baroque overcame all this,/emancipated itself into Enlightenment, and has created/a humanity all its own . . ." of which "we, the world citizens, are still/the happy beneficiaries."[5] The cultural pessimism of the notebooks *Culture 1908–1909* is now absorbed into an historical view of society which will be more profoundly elaborated in *The Sleepwalkers*, but is already clearly sketched in this early version. In reference to his own era, Broch states:

And they do not see that knowledge had suddenly burst the frame which the Baroque had imposed on it as absolute—this occurred at the turn of the century—and that consequently everything contained within this frame is implicated, not least the absolute value of humanity under whose auspices the Victorian epoch had been able to diminish the sufferings of mankind. For one aspect goes with the other and everything belongs inescapably together. The imperturbable mathematical construction, the imperturbable Newtonian space, both of them till recently absolutes, have fallen victim to the new basic research, and to the new physics; how could it be avoided that the progress of humanity, too, would be shaken in its foundations? Yet is it therefore again necessary to have witch trials, to have a Thirty Years' War, to have devastating misery, before the new humanity can find its modes of expression?[6]

Guided by the holistic thinking of his era, Broch had no doubts that breakthroughs in thinking, exemplified in the sciences, necessitated breakthroughs in the other spheres of human endeavor, notably in ethics and politics. Yet he was unwilling to accept the necessity of cataclysms for these periods of transition. He argued against the cyclical recurrence of "witch trials" and "the Thirty Years' War" with an appeal to man's capacity to accomplish these transitions without bloodshed. Broch's view of history as a progressive improvement of the lot of mankind, based upon breakthroughs in knowledge and characterized by the diminution of human suffering, is an idealistic construct which ignores all socioeconomic factors. No wonder that in the years to come his practical suggestions for implementing this utopian theory met with little success.

The outbreak of the war in 1914 put a temporary end to Broch's activities as an essayist. Declared unfit for military duty,[7] he ran a convalescent home for the Red Cross in Teesdorf near Vienna, where the family plant, which he continued to operate, was located. His acquaintance with military hospitals at the end of World War I is vividly rendered in the third part of *The Sleepwalker* trilogy. In his spare time, he continued his studies. During the last two years of the war, he published reviews, essays, and one novella in *Summa,* Franz Blei's short-lived periodical.[8] Of these writings, "Zum Begriff der Geisteswissenschaften" ("Concerning the Concept of the Humanistic Sciences") and "Konstruktion der historischen Wirklichkeit" ("Construction of Historical Reality"), of 1917 and 1918, are the most significant; both document Broch's continued immersion in Kant. "Concerning the Concept of Humanistic Sciences," ostensibly an inquiry into Dilthey's methodology, is an exposition of materialism-positivism as opposed to Broch's idealism. Judging by the names Broch mentions in this essay, it is apparent that he has considerably advanced his studies: he agrees with the neo-Kantian Paul Natorp, paraphrases the phenomenologist Edmund Husserl, quotes Kant, cites Bernhard Bolzano and disapproves of Heinrich Rickert, Wilhelm Dilthey, Wilhelm Windelband, and Auguste Comte on the basis of their positivistic methodology. "Construction of Historical Reality," appearing in the last issue of *Summa,* continues thoughts tentatively sketched in the "Ethics" essay of four years earlier.

"A Methodological Novella," which also appeared in *Summa* in 1918, is Broch's first published literary work (apart from a sonnet in *Der Brenner* in 1913). The novella, besides being a scathing critique of philistine, petit-bourgeois mentality, is a translation into fiction of the Kantian "boundaries of cognition" and, within those boundaries, of the "conditions of possible experience." The theoretical and experimental approach to fiction is here more obvious than in any of Broch's subsequent literary writings. In a slightly altered version this novella was integrated into the novel *The Guiltless*, written more than thirty years later, in 1949.

For Austria, more than for any other European country with the exception of Russia (which had abolished the house of Romanov in the Russian Revolution of 1917), the end of the war signaled a complete break with its past. *Die letzten Tage der Menschheit (The Last Days of Mankind)*, Karl Kraus's monumental answer to the "gay apocalypse," were at hand. On November 3, 1918, Austria signed an armistice amid the dissolution of the empire into independent nationalities. Vienna, long the center of a vast empire with a thriving bureaucracy, found itself a capital with no hinterland. Austria was reduced to her German-speaking parts, which clamored for *Anschluss* ("annexation") to the Reich. Over the next few years, constant strife and skirmishes along the newly emerging borders occurred, for which the peace treaty of St. Germain (accepted by the Austrian Parliament on September 10, 1919) provided no permanent settlement. The Habsburg dynasty, the oldest on the continent, had ceased to exist as a political force. A provisional national assembly stood in for the house of Habsburg until the elections of February, 1919, determined a coalition government of Social Democrats and Christian Socialists with Karl Renner, the Socialist leader, as chancellor. The success of the Russian Revolution of 1917 raised the hopes that an old era had come to an end and a new and better one was dawning. The considerable number of Communist takeovers of city administrations in Germany during, and after the end of, World War I was eclipsed by events in Hungary and Bavaria, where Soviet Republics were declared on March 21, 1919, and April 7, 1919, respectively. For a few months, Austria was literally caught between two Soviet Republics as Béla Kun's government sought to foment strong discontent in the young Austrian Republic, with the purpose of further expanding the Communist territorial gains. In this brief period, workers' and soldiers' councils played an influential role in Austrian politics. The Western allies threatened to cut off supplies to Austria if a Soviet Republic was declared.

Broch entered into these controversies with the essay "Konstitutionelle Diktatur als demokratisches Rätesystem" ("Constitutional Dictatorship as Democratic Council System"). It was published on

April 11, 1919, in *Der Friede*, a few days after the declaration of the Bavarian Soviet Republic. Coming from the author of the statement "possessions do not possess me" (*GW*, X, 257), the article pleads, not surprisingly, for a specific form of council systems—a form in which the "democratic participation" of all workers stipulates the inclusion of employers, intellectuals, and managers. In what might be considered a liberal argument, Broch reasoned against the exclusive dictatorship of the proletariat on the grounds that it violated the democratic ideal. From a pragmatic point of view he portrayed the disastrous consequences—exemplified in the Russian Revolution—that accompany the liquidation of the economic leadership, whose skill and knowledge are essential for the transition into an equitable socialist society. The bloodbaths of the Russian Revolution substantiated Broch's fears that periods of transition are steeped in "witch trials." In the spirit of the *Cantos 1913* he proposed a transition which was slower, though protective of human life, and which would occur within the limits of a body of laws designed to assure a peaceful change. Broch summarized the most significant considerations in favor of a socialist evolution as opposed to a Communist revolution in an argument that would later solidify into the cornerstone of his theory of politics: the preservation of life and the avoidance of cataclysmic events are more important than victories drenched in blood. The strength of his feelings was obvious when he stated: "Consonant with the spirit of socialism, it has to be pointed out over and over again that every rape of freedom per se, committed by man against man, that every insult of human dignity is and remains the most execrable crime."[9]

At various points in the article, Broch found himself in agreement with the position of the Austro-Marxists. With the end of the war, Austro-Marxists achieved positions of prominence in the Austrian government (Karl Renner was elected chancellor, Otto Bauer secretary of state, and Julius Deutsch secretary of the military). Their statements and writings could no longer go unnoticed, and Broch, as avid as ever to participate in current intellectual controversies, contributed his share of thoughts. As a first step, he had addressed an "open letter" to Franz Blei, written in response to the riots in front of Parliament on November 12, 1918,[10] in which he spoke sharply against mass hysteria and mass manipulation. A more detailed and thoughtful account of socialism as the future form of government was presented in the article under discussion, "Constitutional Dictatorship and Democratic Council System."

Broch seemed well enough acquainted with the works of the Austro-Marxists;[11] in fact, in 1922 he wrote a review of two books by his friend Max Adler, *Marx as Thinker* and *Engels as Thinker*.[12] But there is no evidence that he ever studied the original texts of either Marx or Engels. Here, as in the studies preceding World War I, Broch participated in current debates without examining the layers of interpretation intervening between the original sources and the prevalent discussions. Nothing in his environment challenged him to undertake such a task; the many divergent factions of Austro-Marxism rather invited personal variations of the commonly accepted tenets. Broch was in profound agreement with the Austro-Marxists on several accounts: he was a convinced pacifist; he pleaded for a peaceful transition into the socialist state; and he rejected the violent cataclysms of the Russian Revolution. This attitude implied, of course, a willingness to admit compromises as interim stages on the road to the socialist society. Of equal importance for Broch's agreement with the Austro-Marxists was their common attempt to reconcile Marx with Kant.[13] Although the Austro-Marxists' efforts were not equal to Broch's single-minded Kantianism, they both agreed on a strongly ethical dimension as a prime, independent force in society. When the socialist Thomas Masaryk, president-to-be of the newly founded Czechoslovakian Republic, proclaimed that "society is not only organized technically and economically but also ethically—law and morals are real, social factors . . . Marx and Engels have never taken this sufficiently into consideration,"[14] he reprimanded Marx and Engels for a presumable lack of an ethical dimension. Broch, on the other hand, was impressed by the "logical and philosophical purity" of Marxism and attributed it to the "idealistic purity of the Marxian point of view."[15] . . . Masaryk and Broch may have disagreed on the presence or absence of a moral-idealistic element in Marxian writing, but they both agreed on the need for such a component in the social fabric.

In the same essay, "Constitutional Dictatorship as Democratic Council System," Broch voiced some theoretical opinions on dictatorship and the nature of the state. As he was prone to do in most of his subsequent political writings, he used hackneyed phrases to express his idiosyncratic reflections. This practice has resulted in grave misinterpretations. When Broch proclaimed that "every healthy state is dictatorial" (or, late in his life spoke of "totalitarian humanism"), he was not speaking as a Fascist. Rather he fell victim to the same ambivalence that was apparent in his definition of "ethical": the formal and structural definition needed to be supplemented by a specific content in order to assume value status. Words such as "dictatorial" or "dictatorship" were used by Broch formally, devoid of content. "Dictatorial" then means assertion of the "will to power"[16] of the idea on which a particular state is founded. Democracies, for example, are "dictatorial" when they assert their democratic ideals against engulfment by other forms of government. Thirty years later, in the period of the Cold War, Broch found that democracies are not "dictatorial" enough in the assertion of their ideals against communism. He urged democracies to use the "totalitarian" methods of propaganda and punishment in cases of violation of the democratic ideals in order to compete more successfully with fascist and communist governments.

The ultimate goal for the system of councils and the process of socialization was, according to Broch, the de-politization of society. But de-politization, in his view, did not mean a turning away from political concerns and activities. Instead it carried the hope that politics, as a force governing the people's behavior, would eventually become superfluous. Indeed, the de-politicized society bears striking resemblance to the Marxist classless society. (At this time, there were several points of agreement between the Marxist view of society and Broch's position. Only with the advent of the Cold War following the end of World War II—more than a quarter of a century later—did Broch occasionally interpret Marxism as a narrowly applicable economic theory, totally misapprehending its intricate dialectic.) Broch did not find it difficult to abandon the capitalistic system, but sought a conciliatory and evolutionary position in which the accomplishments of the past, including the cultural, technical, and scientific achievements, could be salvaged into the new era. Led by his own indifference to the capitalistic use of assets (such as the textile plant in Teesdorf), he assumed the same attitude in others. Such a gross misjudgment of human character showed the fallacy of generalizing personal convictions (even when formulated within the context of the Kantian imperative and "good will") and hinted at the impossibility of instituting this future society by the means he suggests.

Yet in this essay Broch came as close as he ever would to connecting practical considerations of political expediency with the utopian goal of society. He suggested:

The division of the legislative power into a democratic parliament and a democratic system of councils is, for the time being, the only means to satisfy the demand and the deep need of the Social Democracy to maintain democracy during the simultaneous, purposive dictatorship of the Socialist Idea. The principle of justice, inherent in democratic thinking, is now the only one which can prevent violation, terror, and civil war and which can protect the proletariat from concomitant further physical and psychic, economic and cultural pauperization. The fact that, in the future, the democratic parliament will have to abdicate in favor of the democratic system of councils, just as the monarchy abdicated in favor of parliamentarism, does not prevent their temporary coexistence. The goal of the system of councils is the complete de-politization of mankind and can only be achieved when all political dregs have been drained.[17]

With the aborted Communist *Putsch* in Vienna on June 15, 1919, and the collapse of the Soviet Republic of Hungary in August of the same year, the workers' and soldiers' councils lost their influential role in Austrian politics. (The Bavarian Soviet Republic had been defeated even earlier in the year.) The young Austrian democracy, not unlike its German neighbor, remained a precarious structure. The state of permanent crisis in Austrian politics during the decades before World War I had given way to a state of permanent turmoil on the social and economic plane which continued long after the fighting stopped.

In a statement written in exile around 1942 ("Autobiography as Work Program"), Broch remembered the decade of World War I in this manner:

In 1908, I started working in the industry, and although my interests [in philosophy] in principle had not changed, I now had to apply them to new fields. In retrospect, I cannot regret this as much as I did at the time, since during these years I gained, on the one hand, many insights into the working of the economy which I would hardly have acquired in any other way and, on the other hand, learned much about the relation between industry and the workers as well as about social mechanics. I continued to learn when, in the second half of the war and during the subsequent restless times of the revolution, I held various official and semiofficial positions, as for example in commissions to maintain peace among the workers, etc. I also participated in the new formulation of the rights of the workers and finally in the efforts to combat unemployment. Due to her particularly difficult circumstances, Austria offered, so to speak, a better focused, if smaller, picture of the total economic and social world situation, and therefore these activities were extremely instructive. (*GW*, IX, 39)

I   Dichtung—*the answer to cognitive impatience?*

The decade of the 1920s seems to have been the most crucial in Broch's life. He broke the patterns and bonds which had identified him both socially and economically, and had established his role vis-à-vis his family. He separated from his wife after twelve years of marriage in 1921 and was divorced in 1922. He stopped writing essays. Between 1919 and 1922, he poured out a constant stream of inconsequential book reviews, then shrouded himself in silence. Only two reviews authored in those years deserve special mention, since they connect with Broch's political thought and his deliberate and specific rejection of materialism. "Die erkenntnistheoretische Bedeutung des Begriffes 'Revolution' und die Wiederbelebung der Hegelschen Dialektik. Zu den Büchern Arthur Lieberts" ("The Epistemological Significance of the Concept 'Revolution' and the Revival of Hegelian Dialectics. On the Books of Arthur Liebert") was published in the *Prager Presse* on July 30, 1922; and the review of two books by Max Adler, *Marx als Denker (Marx as Thinker)* and *Engels als Denker (Engels as Thinker)* appeared in the prestigious *Kant-Studien* of 1922.

As Broch was to mention later in his life, the 1920s were the period in which he worked out his philosophy of history, which, however, was never published. For all the silence, these years are the incubation period, at the end of which Broch presented his first major novel, *The Sleepwalkers.*

During the first half of the decade, he still followed an intense and hectic work schedule, expanded the family business, and managed to steer the plant with uneven success through the economic ups and downs of the inflationary postwar period. By his own account,

I was nominated to several official positions for the express purpose of dealing with such problems; I belonged to the Board of Directors of the Austrian Industrial Association; I was permanent Justice of the Governmental Arbitration Court which had been established to settle disputes between industry and labor—a rather complicated task in the revolutionary years of 1922 and 1923. In addition, I was a member of the Labor Board set up by the government to fight unemployment. [18]

In 1925, almost twenty years after he first attended courses at the University of Vienna and approaching his fortieth year, Broch abandoned his autodidactic studies and registered at the university. He concentrated heavily on mathematics, with philosophy (primarily logic and epistemology) taking second place, followed by physics. During the nine semesters Broch studied at the university, he took eight lecture courses and seminars with Moritz Schlick and six with Rudolf Carnap. He continued his studies until 1929–1930, when work on *The Sleepwalkers* asserted itself as more important.[19]

In 1927, he took a momentous step: he sold the textile plant over the strong protest of his family.[20] Even though the financial offer may have been advantageous, the decision must have been excruciating; the political situation was unstable (witness the July 15, 1927, demonstrations and riots) and the future uncertain. The arrangements of the distribution of the money from the sale of the factory left Broch without income. (The money was divided into four equal shares among father, mother, his brother Fritz, and Broch, who consigned his share to his former wife and their son.) For the rest of his life, financial worries and energy spent to meet the barest living expenses became part of his daily fare. Although no longer running a factory, as the oldest son, he still felt responsible for his family. After the stock market crash and the financial world crisis in 1929, the monies dwindled; and the new owner of the Broch plant committed suicide when he found himself unable to maintain the financial obligations he had assumed with the ownership of the plant.

In retrospect, it is easy to see that Broch's return to the University of Vienna set the direction for the rest of his life. Yet Broch's goal in resuming these studies is not quite clear. In a letter dated August 12, 1949, he reminisced that he had wanted to complete his doctorate. He recalled (remembering the dates incorrectly): "During my time in industry, I continued my intensive occupation with mathematics and philosophy, especially epistemology. From 1929 to 1932 I audited (since I had only the Realschule degree) mathematics and some philosophy (Schlick) at the University of Vienna. I wanted to get my doctorate, but then the literary writings (*Sleepwalkers* 1929, etc.) got in my way" (*GW*, VIII, 360). Yet can literary activities simply "get in one's way?" Broch had written, if not voluminously at least persistently, during the past two decades. With few exceptions (the poem "Mathematisches Mysterium" ["Mathematical Mysterium", 1913], the *Cantos 1913*, and the "Methodological Novella", 1918), he had, however, avoided literature. In his matriculation book at the university, philosophical and mathematical lectures abound, but there are none that have to do with literature, either creatively, philosophically, or historically.[21] This observation is important, since it testifies to Broch's primarily theoretical and philosophical interests, which he did not repress when he wrote novels. On the contrary, it seems that his literary writings are exemplifications or enactments, in a different medium, of concerns and ideas which he had developed over many years. That he could express them in a literary manner which today ranks him with the major writers of the twentieth century, while his philosophical stature remains negligible, may attest to the fact that we are here confronted with a personality whose interests and intellectual propensities militated against his talents.

The primacy of Broch's philosophical interests is evident even in his reasons for turning from philosophy to literature. His renewed study of philosophy had confirmed his previous suspicions: the sciences, including philosophy, had become positivistic in the sense that they followed the logic of their own systems without regard for outside values. These intellectual disciplines perpetuated the disintegration and anarchy of values that Broch attempted to overcome through the infusion of a central value. The logical positivists of the Vienna Circle relegated the search for values to metaphysics, and in turn refused to acknowledge metaphysics as a legitimate field of philosophical inquiry. As Wittgenstein put it so succinctly at the conclusion of the *Tractatus:* "What one cannot speak about, on that one must keep silent."[22]

Positivism became for Broch synonymous with the autonomy of any system which pursued its goals without reference to a common value center, and with the refusal to acknowledge intellectual inquiries that could not be pursued with a scientific methodology. While Broch viewed the "spirit of positivism," on the one hand, as responsible for the disintegration of values, he had to admit, on the other, that it obeyed the Kantian postulate to explore the boundaries of cognition. Therefore, even in its most rigorous single-mindedness, it gave proof of man's cognitive drive and considerably contributed to the progress of knowledge. Broch pushed his own logic to the paradoxical conclusion that although positivism destroyed the Platonic totality it was nevertheless a manifestation of that totality by virtue of its cognitive faculties. He could not even exclude Kant's critical epistemology from his definition of positivism and conceded that Kant was "in the widest meaning of the word a positivist."[23]

Broch saw it as his mission to overcome the autonomy of the

positivistic systems and the ensuing anarchy of values by infusing them with a commonly accepted ethical goal. He admitted readily that the choice of this goal was historically conditioned, and arrived at the conclusion that the modern era has to place the ideal of man and of mankind in lieu of a god or of gods, as other ages had done. The imposition of this arbitrary (though admittedly beautiful) goal opens another aspect of Broch criticism. For who can deny that the "logic of the system" would work as well if the central value were the glorification of racial supremacy or that of any other antihumane political ideology? In the years to come, Broch was to elaborate on the dire consequences of advocating supremist goals rather than humanistic ideals as the central, "Platonic" value, and he adamantly insisted that only humanistic values can provide answers to the economic, social, political, religious, and artistic problems of our times. Yet he could not thereby avoid the dangers inherent in such a dualistic and ultimately irrational system, for the most intricate logical structure cannot satisfactorily answer the question: "why humanism instead of barbarism?"

That which "one cannot speak about" came, in subsequent years, to be of the most burning interest to Broch. Philosophy must escape being a positivistic science. It must be dedicated to a humanistic holism. Influenced by the concept of the Platonic Idea as an all-encompassing totality, Broch saw no contradiction in admitting that the exploration of the Kantian boundaries of reason included the investigation of extrarational spheres. This opinion culminated many years later in a "theory of intuition" as part of his epistemology. Seeing himself surrounded by a vacuum of values for which the metaphysical uprootedness and lack of ethical directives seemed the most striking evidence, Broch understood the search for values as a legitimate quest, just as fears and anxieties and "irrational emotions" deserved serious consideration. If philosophy declared itself incapable of dealing with these magnitudes, then the investigation had to proceed by other means: only *Dichtung*, the creative literary activity, seemed capable of unifying the disparate, autonomous fields of human endeavor and of upholding an anthropocentric humanistic world view in which man's metaphysical and nonrational needs were acknowledged. Broch had no intention of "irrationalizing" cognition or human relationships; but since he saw manifestations of the irrational everywhere, he wanted to reveal the mechanisms of these powerful substrata operating in the life of each individual. In a retrospective explanation of his turn from philosophy to literature he offers two reasons:

Dichtung is legitimized by the metaphysical evidence which fills man and to which *Dichtung* penetrates when all other rational means of thought prove to be insufficient for this task: *Dichtung* has always been cognitive impatience, and a perfectly legitimate impatience at that.

The was the first reason for my turn to the extrascientific, literary mode of expression; yet there was another reason, actually a more rational one: the immediate ethical impact. . . . Ethical effectiveness is to a large extent due to enlightenment; and for such activities the work of literature is a far better means than science. This was the second reason for my turn to literature. (*GW*, IX, 45–46)

The motives underlying Broch's turn to literature in the late 1920s already contain the seeds for his eventual withdrawal. Ultimately he realized that literature was not an adequate vehicle to carry out the tasks he had assigned to it.

CHAPTER 3

The Mechanics and Metaphysics of Sleepwalking

BROCH had begun work on *The Sleepwalkers* by 1929, the year of the stock market crash, and continued writing during increasing economic crises and unemployment. He finished the novel in 1931–1932,[1] as Engelbert Dollfuss became head of the Austrian government and Hilter's rise to power was imminent.[1] The novel was Broch's analysis of the modern historical situation characterized by disintegrating value systems. In this respect, *The Sleepwalkers* can be considered Broch's monumental effort to structure the personal as well as social, political, and historical ambience in which he had grown up. Twenty years after his first tentative sketches in the notebooks of *Culture 1908–1909*, Broch presented a coherent, interlocking theory of the causes and possible alternatives to a disintegration of values.

Despite the heavy doses of philosophy which make the novel "difficult" reading, Broch seemed not quite at peace with the thought of having written a novel instead of a philosophical treatise. In letter after letter from that period he explained why literature rather than philosophy had become the more appropriate vehicle for the task to which he had committed himself. Explanations merge into self-justifications, as shown by the following passage from a letter to Frank Thiess, written soon after the publication of *The Sleepwalkers*, in April, 1932:

. . . you know my thesis concerning the present condition of philosophy: philosophy as such, as far as it does not become mathematics, can no longer "prove" anything—though as "science" it would be obliged to do so—and in view of this situation philosophy has withdrawn into mathematical concerns. However, this does not do away with the tremendous metaphysical remnants, they exist; the questions and problems exist, they are more urgent than ever, but the basis for their proof must be looked for elsewhere. It can be found only in the irrational, the poetic. If there exists a task for the poetic, and since Goethe it does exist, it lies in making these mystic remnants accessible as proofs. (*GW*, VIII, 67)

For about ten years of his life, roughly the period from the inception of *The Sleepwalkers* until his emigration in 1938, Broch expressed the hope that literature might be the vehicle to carry on the ethical duty, to voice the (scientifically) inexpressible, thereby assuming the task of sustaining man's metaphysical dimensions. Soon after the completion of *The Sleepwalkers*, in some of the essays of 1932–1933, in *The Death of Virgil*, published in 1945, and again in the large epistemological fragment of 1948, "Über syntaktische und kognitive Einheiten" ("On Syntactical and Cognitive Units"), Broch discussed the symbol as alone capable of conveying within a rational structure the cognition of the irrational.[2] Translated into Broch's theory and practice of the novel, this meant that a rational presentation was of the utmost importance even when nonrational phenomena were concerned. At this time, it was one of Broch's expressed ambitions to advance into the nonrational (of which the irrational would be part) and "illuminate" it by means of a scientific methodology. Broch had been in contact with positivism for too long not to be convinced of the need for a scientific methodology, no matter what the field of inquiry. In fact, it was this combination of a scientific methodology applied to a nonrational, that is, metaphysical, realm that made him wish that Kant's critical philosophy had culminated in a critique of metaphysics; a wish that he saw being fulfilled in Husserl's phenomenology.[3] *The Sleepwalkers* can thus be viewed as Broch's defiant answer to the logical positivists of the Vienna Circle and as his first major attempt to shape through words that which "one cannot speak about."[4]

I   *Sleepwalking—a state of history*

The Sleepwalkers falls into three parts: "1888—Pasenow or Romanticism"; "1903—Esch or Anarchy"; and "1918—Huguenau or Matter-of-Factness."[5] At first glance, the three parts present three distinct units, each of them commanding a separate style. It has been suggested that "Pasenow" is reminiscent of Fontane's realism and his relativistic perspective,[6] "Esch" of naturalism (by virtue of the choice of milieu and characters), and "Huguenau" of expressionism due to the apocalyptic-utopian emotionalism and the disjointed presentation. Yet Broch is not interested in re-creating styles practiced at specific historical periods in order to present "authentic" imitations; he uses them as a critique of the style and, by extension, of the period. By limiting himself to historically conditioned modes of perception and expression, he demonstrates the limits of that period, as well as why and how the characters in the novel were confined by experience and language within the horizons of their epoch. Insensitivity to this metacritical frame results in misinterpretation when, for example, Broch is seen as promulgating the very attitudes and ideas which he inspects critically and rejects with reasons stated. "Huguenau" for example, is a critique of messianic expressionism rather than its recreation.

The continuity and interrelatedness of the three parts is assured through a complex web of symbols and images, through the metamorphoses of recurring images, and the use of leitmotivs. While working on *The Sleepwalkers,* Broch repeatedly mentioned the importance of the "rational-irrational polyphony" and imputed the delay in the completion of the novel to the difficulty of achieving a balanced architecture.[7] Above all, however, his theory of value holds the three tableaux together, places them in a meaningful relationship to each other, and provides, through the sequence of disintegrating value systems, a philosophy of history.

The three episodes span the reign of Emperor William II, beginning with his ascension to the throne in 1888 and ending with his abdication in November, 1918.[8] Although each episode encompasses a relatively static historical period from spring to fall of the same year, the consecutive tableaux suggest movement and provide the intended historical perspective.[9] For each temporal shift, there is a corresponding shift in geography and in social class. From Berlin and the surrounding Mark Brandenburg, the heartland of Wilheminian Prussia with its Junker class, the move is to Mannheim and Cologne with is urban proletarian petit-bourgeoisie; and from there, in the last part, to a small town on the Mosel River with a stable middle class, impoverished wine growers, and temporary inhabitants brought there through the war and gathered around the army hospital. It may well be that "the movement in the trilogy from Prussia through the Rhineland to the Mosel valley represents a symbolic progression from Eastern romantic mysticism to Western rationalism";[10] but then, rationalism must be understood as the driving force of positivism, and therefore of the disintegration of the formally cohesive social bonds. The hypertrophy of rationalism is then exemplified by the revolution—revolution being, in the Brochian context, the ultimate consequence of the fragmentation of values, leading via anarchy to total freedom, and concomitantly to the outbreak of the irrational. The location of the "nameless, medieval little town" in the vicinity of Trier may be an allusion to Karl Marx, who was born there in 1818, exactly one hundred years before the events of "Huguenau." That "Huguenau" takes place on Marxist territory is further suggested by the one-day pseudorevolution at the end of the novel, when the medieval city hall, the last architectural remnant of an "integrated" age, goes up in flames and the prison gates are thrown open.

The hero of the first part of the novel is Joachim von Pasenow, second son of a family belonging to the landed gentry in Western Prussia. In accordance with tradition, he is destined for a military career, while his older brother Helmut must take over the estate. Although Helmut would prefer the military and Joachim the country life, neither of them can think of alternatives to the tradition of which they are part. Helmut is killed in a duel and thus dies the "death in the field of honor" properly reserved for the military. This alleged usurpation of Joachim's military role forces Joachim to quit the service and take over the management of the estate. As the elder von Pasenow's eccentricities develop into insanity, he in turn sees Joachim's new role as an usurpation of the dead Helmut's career.

The archetypal triangle situation of the Pasenow males (a father blessing one son, Helmut, while cursing the other, Joachim) is complemented by an even more common triangle: a young man, Joachim, is torn between two women. According to Victorian convention, one is fair, proper, and virginal, as her name indicates: Elisabeth. The other is dark, exotic, and erotic: Ruzena. Joachim is the easy victor without battle in the male triangle. It is much more difficult for him to extricate himself from the dark charms and explosive demands of the show girl Ruzena and to enter into the expected marriage with Elisabeth, daughter of a neighboring estate owner and member of the same social class.

The first part of the novel emphasizes the conventionality, indeed triviality, of events. The protagonists, however, lack this perspective, and experience their lives and the events surrounding them as complex and ambivalent.[11]

On occasion this ambivalence causes excitement, but more often fear, to which the characters respond by withdrawing into habitual and conventional patterns of behavior and thought. The openness inherent in ambivalence, and the sensation of incipient freedom from the habitual, signal the moment when breakthroughs into new systems become possible. That these moments are rarely taken advantage of—indeed, cannot be taken advantage of due to the social, psychological, and cognitive "boundaries" of the individual—demonstrates the restrictive interaction between man and his society, or more precisely, between man and the specific historical period in which he lives.

At the beginning of the novel, Joachim seems well established in his military career. A few months and several cataclysmic events later (after the death of his brother, his affair with Ruzena, and his father's insanity), the first part of the trilogy ends on Joachim and Elisabeth's wedding night, their future secure as landed West Prussian gentry.

Esch, the hero of the second part, follows a similar pattern. Like Joachim, he is thirty years old, experiences an extreme and intense period of dislocation (geographically as well as spiritually and financially), and settles into marriage at the conclusion of the cataclysmic events. Having lost his job as a bookkeeper in Cologne, Esch finds employment as a store clerk in the Mannheim dockyards. He rents a room from the customs inspector Balthasar Korn, who wants him to marry his sister, Erna. At a Cabaret, Esch encounters Ilona, who poses for the knife-thrower Teltscher-Teltini. Esch quits his job to "redeem" Ilona from her dangerous act and organizes ladies' wrestling matches. When the enterprise fails, he returns to Cologne and marries Mutter Hentjen, a tavern keeper from his past, in the late fall of the same year, 1903.

The helplessness which Joachim felt is here intensified into frustration and rage. For Esch, an "impetuous man" (SW, 183, 539), the ambiguities of existence are radicalized into either/or propositions since he is much less protected by social convention and upbringing than Joachim. Esch views himself as an orphan, "free" of parents (SW, 185); born in Luxemburg, a "free" country (SW, 175), he is "free" to go wherever jobs take him.[12] When the world does not make sense (as, for instance, when he is fired from his job), the lack of a system of conventions, which could absorb his fears, causes him to fly into rages. His actions illustrate Broch's view that the loss of guiding value systems entails immediate translation of spontaneous impulses into action. The anger and rage, which lead to the beatings of Mutter Hentjen, are not indications that Esch is a vicious person, but rather demonstrate that his unchecked emotions need to be "tamed" into rational systems in which events "make sense." There is an obvious parallel between Freud's theory of civilization as sublimation of potentially dangerous eruptions of the id and Broch's view of civilization, in which spontaneous, nonrational impulses are absorbed and thereby defused in value systems (and the more comprehensive the value system, the fewer the instances of "free," that is, nonrational, elements in it.).

Although the disintegration of value systems has progressed considerably from Joachim to Esch, Esch still relies on one system to explain events: bookkeeping. Radicalized, he experiences the daily incongruities as metaphysical injustices; and the bookkeeping, designed to set accounts straight, correspondingly assumes cosmic dimensions. Since a balancing factor is needed to set the accounts straight, Esch wants to sacrifice himself in order to "redeem" the world of its injustices. This "sacrifice" is conceived as an archaic fertility rite, where fertilizing the barren earth (Mutter Hentjen and Ilona both do not have children) will initiate a new cycle of cosmic order. Broch deliberately combines bookkeeping and sexuality as redemptive forces to characterize Esch. In Esch, he dissects the anatomy of the irrational before it is channeled into rational systems.

In Broch's opinion, the irrational is the most personal, since it has not yet been structured by extraneous systems. The refurbishing of this enormous reservoir with continuously erupting irrational impulses is due to man's innate awareness and fear of death. (Indeed, Broch maintains that the sense of time and, with it, of death is one of the characteristics which make man human and distinguish him from the animal.) It is for the sake of investigating areas such as this, that Broch turned from philosophy to literature, from positivism to metaphysics. Yet the irrational sphere that contains man's knowledge about death cannot be clearly segmented from the rational, since even the most archaic attempts to exorcise this fear are expressed in some kind of rational structures. For this reason, religion is interpreted as a primary attempt to cope with death. And for the same reason, the breakdown of value systems releases impulses which cannot remain free (that is, irrational), but immediately fuse into a "private theology." This "private theology" is an individual's makeshift solution to structure the personal universe.

An example is provided in the scene in which Esch first sees Ilona pose for the knife-throwing Teltscher-Teltini. Esch's physical and metaphysical aspirations fuse in an act of mental acrobatics that is equal to Teltscher-Teltini's knife-whirling artistry.

Esch could almost have wished that it was himself who was standing up there with his arms raised to heaven, that it was himself being crucified, could

almost have wished to station himself in front of that gentle girl and receive in
his own breast the menacing blades. . . . Indeed the thought of standing up
there alone and forsaken where the long blades might pin one against the
board like a beetle, filled him with almost voluptuous pleasure. . . . It was
the fanfare of the Last Judgment, when the guilty were to be trodden
underfoot like worms; why shouldn't they be spitted like beetles? Why,
instead of a sickle, shouldn't Death carry a long darning-needle, or at least a
lance? (SW, 179–80)

Here, Esch is only beginning to warm up to the system of cosmic
checks and balances, yet his misapprehended redeemer fixation is
Broch's excellent device to demonstrate the use of imagery and
symbols epistemologically. It shows the extent and the limitations of
the character's emotional and intellectual capacities and underlines
Broch's conviction that even the irrational forces can manifest themselves only in a personal and historical guise. Esch combines Christian imagery and symbols (devoid of their "logical context," that is,
their function within the Christian value system) with the logic of
bookkeeping to shape his own religion—a mystical mathematics
which is at most capable of accommodating a "protestant" sectarianism.

At this point, it may be appropriate to focus upon the distinction
between the cognitive and epistemological function of a symbol.
When Esch speaks about the Anti-Christ, he indicates the limits of
his cognitive system, the boundaries of his cognitive faculties; hence
"the Anti-Christ" serves to describe Esch in his cognitive context.
The epistemological theory that encompasses this "phenomenon
Esch" explains why Esch is caught at this cognitive level at this
historical point. It embeds the individual incident in an historical
analysis of the past, and shows why Esch is incapable of choosing any
other alternative that might point into the future.

In keeping with the requirement that each historical period is
limited by its particular "style of thought," Broch presents each
protagonist in the epistemologically appropriate pattern. The
triangle relationships in which Joachim is caught are easily recognizable and border on a cliché, emphasizing that Joachim moves very
much in conventional patterns, even when he experiences them as
acute personal crises. Within one specific historic period and within
one specific social class, only a limited range of experiences is
possible. This practice exemplifies in fiction Broch's understanding of
the Kantian "conditions of possible experience."

Since Esch lives in an environment where traditional structures have considerably eroded and the irrational is no longer absorbed into existing value systems, he unknowingly reenacts primordial events where sexual practices become religious rites meant to establish a cosmic order. At the same time, Esch's being-in-history occurs in the form of an interaction with archaic, barely recognizable irrational shadows. Broch chooses prehistorical fragments of myths in order to explicate Esch's battle in which he confronts, with mystic ardor and sectarian zeal, the most sinister female triad imaginable. The constellation of Mutter Hentjen, Ilona, and Erna represents the negativity of all mother-goddess myths. Dead, immovable, barren, Mutter Hentjen presides behind her counter and under the picture of her dead husband over a dark tavern. Under this aspect, she is Persephone, queen of the dead, raped and brought to the netherworld by her husband (Hades). No amount of symbolic mathematics on Esch's part his demand that she remove Herr Hentjen's picture from behind the bar or his desire to make her pregnant—can return her to fertility and life. But she is also an archaic Aphrodite; the Aphrodite of brothels, the patroness of saleable love, who knows how to avail herself of her sexuality. She despises the men in the restaurant, but is compassionate with the waitresses who serve the men's desires.[13] Anger and rage are her most prevalent moods (*SW,* 167–70), suppressed into stiffness when she presides over her dark, cavernous world.

Ilona is the second figure in this negative trinity. She has much in common with Mutter Hentjen. The two women, who never meet, are described in similar terms: both are indifferent, mute, immovable, with heavy bodies and expressionless, puffy faces; both have been "killed" in their encounter with men (*SW,* 185–86) and cannot have children. But Ilona is less restrained than Mutter Hentjen, who is literally and symbolically held together by her tight corset and stiff coiffure. Ilona is on intimate terms with death and mutilation, posing in the posture of crucifixion night after night for the whirling knives of the cabaret performer Teltscher-Teltini. Bloodthirsty avenger and victim in one, she embodies the sinister Kali–aspect of a merciless archaic code:

She bore a scar on her neck and she felt that the man to whom she had been unfaithful that time had been justified in trying to kill her. If Korn had been unfaithful to her, however, she would not have killed him, but merely thrown vitriol at him. Yes, in matters of jealousy such an apportionment of punishment seemed to her fitting, for if one possessed another, one would want to destroy, but if one merely employed another one could content oneself with making the object unfit for use. . . . Once a man had killed himself because of her; it had not touched her very deeply, but she liked to remember it. (SW, 327)

Erna Korn is the spinster sister of Balthasar Korn, with whom Ilona has an affair while in Mannheim. Erna appears as the very opposite of Ilona: a calculating tease, skinny, quick, talkative, and nasty, but she, too, bears the negative marks of what constituted the virginal aspect in a positive triad. She and Ilona are presented as "sisters," complementing as "daughters" the mother aspect of Mutter Hentjen. Esch's confrontation with this archaic female triad in modern guise points to the danger inherent in the breakdown of value systems: "private theologies" pave the road toward a rebarbarization of previously overcome stages of social and religious evolution.

Erna is marketing her (long lost) virginity as a commodity for the highest bidder; and finally catches the "chaste Joseph" Lohberg, owner of a cigar store. Here an epiphenomenon spins off the central mythological constellation of the female triad, insofar as Erna, the shrewd nonvirgin, becomes pregnant by Esch, making the "chaste Joseph" believe he is the father. The shift from the female triad to the mother–holy infant myth alludes to a historical progression; in the *Bergroman (Mountain Novel)* Broch will make a more detailed use of this technique of indicating successive time frames. Seen here in the context of Esch's erotic mysticism, the unborn child becomes the hope for opposing the Anti-Christ and redeeming the world. This cruel parody of the holy family serves as an indication of Esch's attempt to organize the world in religious terms, but at the same time criticizes his delusions. The transfer of orthodox religious doctrine and imagery to a secular, petit bourgeois, profane setting produces a freakish hybrid, meaningful only to Esch. What clearer verdict could be spoken over Esch's misconceptions?[14]

The *éminence grise* of *The Sleepwalkers'* first two parts is Eduard von Bertrand.[15] Acquainted with Joachim von Pasenow when they both attended military school, he quit military service to become an export-import merchant. Fifteen years later, he is the president of the Mannheim shipping company where Esch finds temporary employment. Free from convention and from the emotional lethargy that characterizes Joachim, Bertrand represents to Joachim excitement as well as danger, the very qualities inherently connected with "freedom." Joachim's ambivalent, even contradictory attitudes are crystalized in his reactions to Bertrand, whom he sees, on the one hand, as "agent provocateur," mocking his attachment to tradition, and on the other hand, as a physician, helping Joachim straighten out his affair (which means terminating the affair with Ruzena in a "gentlemanly manner" by paying her off).

The difference in social class between Esch and Bertrand is too great for them ever to meet on approximately equal terms. Yet after Esch's redeemer aspirations fail, Bertrand becomes for him the cause of everything that is wrong. And since Bertrand's alleged homosexuality is the only bit of hearsay evidence Esch can get hold of, he fastens his sexual-mystic indignation on this source of cosmic putrefaction. In a surreal dream sequence, he travels to Bertrand's retreat in Baden-weiler and confronts him in a garden of Eden-Gethsemane, acting Judas to an Anti-Christ whose suicide will not redeem the world and balance the cosmic records.

Bertrand is relativized in the first two parts of the novel through the subjective perspectives of the characters (Joachim, Ruzena, Esch, etc.) who project their dreams and unconscious fears on him. Because of their helplessness and incompetence in worldly matters, he seems of superior mind and character. In the third part of the novel, the theory of value will interpret the occurrences of the entire novel in an historical frame. It is here that the verdict over Bertrand and his kind is spoken. Broch emphasized Bertrand's elusive quality in his role as reflector and catalyst of events (though Bertrand's range, too, is limited to the specific historical periods in which he acts). In a letter to his publisher of June 24, 1930, Broch guards against too concrete a rendition of this protagonist: "After much thought and many experiments, I have come to the conclusion that the figure of Bertrand must not be 'made flesh' any further. This too is a preparation of what is to follow: this figure, though still acting and speaking normally despite a slight turn toward the abstract, is nowhere 'described' in the proper sense of the word" (*GW*, VIII, 23).[16]

In "Huguenau," a third "possible experience" of the same basic pattern is offered: the period of dislocation starts in early spring and ends in late fall with the protagonist's return to a more stable environment, exemplified as in the two previous instances, in marriage. In this final instance, the interim quality of the period under inspection is even further stressed: Huguenau is on vacation. The vacation starts when he deserts the army in Flanders in the spring of 1918 and ends as he returns to his native Colmar, town of the Isenheim Altar, equipped with proper military papers, in November of the same year. He spends his "vacation" in a small Mosel town in the vicinity of Trier, where he meets with Joachim von Pasenow, the town's military commander, and Esch, now a local newspaper publisher. He establishes credibility by posing as the agent of an imaginary conglomerate, interested in buying Esch's newspaper. When this "adequte child of his time" (*GW*, VIII, 26) is caught in the outbreak of unrest at the conclusion of the war, he feels free, in the ensuing chaos, to enact the archetypal Oedipus situation: he kills Esch and seduces/coerces Frau Esch. After this climactic episode, content and without misgivings, he returns to the life of an industrious and successful petit bourgeois. En route, he delivers Major von Pasenow, who had literally lost his mind when his car turned over and burned during the minirevolution, to a military hospital in Cologne.

"Huguenau" consists of about three hundred pages—almost as long as the first two parts together. It is composed of a number of narratives that run parallel to the major plot and portray Hannah Wendling, a young doctor's wife in the town; the orphan Marguerite, drifting in and out of the Esch household; the mason Gödicke who had been buried in the trenches; the doctors, nurses, and convalescent soldiers at the hospital. In addition, ten essays on the disintegration of values and the "Story of the Salvation Army Girl" in Berlin, apparently unconnected with the events in the little Mosel town, are interspersed. The fragmentation of a previously continuous narrative "enacts" the theme of the novel from the structural point of view. The conventional requirements of the novelistic genre are exploded as bits and pieces of narrative, essays, lyrical prose and poetry, drama, and samples of specialized prose such as business letters and newspaper articles, follow each other in unmediated directness.

In keeping with his theory that each historical era has unique characteristics, Broch showed how even this seeming chaos is informed by one overriding concept. He explained this to Daisy Brody in a letter of July 23, 1931, a few months before the publication of "Huguenau:"

The book consists of a series of stories which are all variations of the same theme, i.e. man's confrontation with loneliness—a confrontation due to the disintegration values . . . These individual stories, interwoven like tapestry, present various levels of consciousness: they rise out of the wholly irrational (story of the Salvation Army Girl) to the complete rationality of the theory (disintegration of values). The other stories take place between these two poles on staggered levels of rationality. (*GW*, VIII, 57)

Broch did not mention that "the staggered levels of rationality" in the novel as a whole also implied a time factor, that is, a progression in time toward disintegration. Yet such an "historically limiting factor," in which certain events are possible only within a specific historical parameter, again acknowledged Broch's interpretation of the Kantian "boundaries of reason." Since the delineation of these boundaries of reason preoccupied Broch in all his intellectual endeavors, it should not surprise that he wanted to show in fiction, too, limitations inherent in the medium. He formulated this endeavor in the "narrator as idea." Deeply impressed by James Joyce's *Ulysses*[17] and its "scientific objectivity," he drew upon the theory of relativity to explain Joyce's technique and implicitly his own aspirations as a novelist. In analogy to the theory of relativity, where "an ideal observer and an ideal act of observation must be included in the field of observation" (*GW*, VI, 197), he realized "that one cannot simply place an object under a lightbeam and describe it, but that the subject of representation, hence the 'narrator as idea,' and no less language, with which the object of representation is described, are part of the means of representation" (*GW*, VI, 197).[18]

The "narrator as idea" is Broch's contribution to the theory of the novel in the twentieth century. In distinction to the traditional techniques of narrative perspective (omniscient, first person, personal perspectives, etc.) the "narrator as idea" is present in any device[19] which draws attention to the fact that the novel is a deliberate, "scientific" construct, expressing not only narrative content but cognizance of stylistic and technical limitations as well as those of perspective. With the presentation of the "narrator as idea" Broch made a major contribution to the arsenal of novelistic techniques.

II   *Romanticism is not always romantic*

It is now in order to explain the terms "romanticism," "anarchy," and "matter-of-factness" in Broch's rather idiosyncratic usage, and to discover how "sleepwalking" is a characteristic common to all these states. This calls for a brief summary of Broch's Platonism. As pointed out previously, it is Broch's thesis that during disintegrative periods the Platonic Idea loses its position as all-informing value center. While the integrative movements into periods of "high culture" are to be commended and the disintegrative periods to be deplored, the historical progression is constituted by the systolic as well as the diastolic movement. Yet where does the impetus for the movement

come from, and what forces contribute to an integration under the
rule of the Platonic Idea? And how can that Idea, if indeed it
embodies totality, ever allow for disintegration? In order to substan-
tiate his view of history, Broch draws on thoughts sketched almost
twenty years earlier in the *Cantos 1913*. Historical forces are propelled by breakthroughs in cognition. These advances of knowledge
lead to problems which cannot be answered within the old system;
they assume an existence of their own outside the established order
and are pursued for their own sake.[20] The same ambivalence appears
here that runs through Broch's entire system and stems from his
two-step absorption of Kant. On the one hand, based upon the
autonomous exploration of the boundaries of reason, the pursuit of
knowledge even for its own sake is an ethically laudable endeavor. On
the other hand, this intellectual pursuit expresses a positivistic
attitude, that is, a disregard for the Platonic Idea: it leads to fragmentation and must therefore be fought. Yet while positivism is being
fought, it must still be acknowledged as a perverted manifestation of
the Platonic totality (since cognition is not possible outside this
totality). This self-constructed double bind will only be overcome
with the imposition of the absolute though unattainable humanistic
goal which all cognition must serve. Since the Platonic Idea can
manifest itself in history only symbolically and in the garb of changing
value centers, this means that the central value of a unified system
(such as God in the Catholic Church during Broch's hypothetical
Middle Ages) is in itself historically relativized and subject to change.
Broch later draws the conclusion that in our times, when God can no
longer be recognized as a central and generally binding value,
another, though no less encompassing, value must be posited. This
value he sees in man, or rather in the protection and preservation of
human life. In *The Sleepwalkers* this step is not taken. Where the
characters do not regress into "private theologies" (as do Pasenow,
Esch, Mary), they are (Huguenau) or fancy themselves to be (Bertrand) value free.

The secularization of the value system does not eliminate the
presence of the irrational components, culminating in the fear of
death. Once a system deals with these metaphysical factors, exactly
those which philosophy has abrogated, it is called "religious," irrespective of the degree of its secularization. For Broch, the term
"religious" is, hence, devoid of any doctrinaire content. "Religious
means: coming to terms with death. Transforming the world into a

spiritual cosmogony, hence placing it in the care of the Platonic logos
. . ." (*GW*, X, 276). The consequence Broch derives from this concept of the Platonic Idea and its totality for the novel in our times are of great weight. He demands no less than that the novel, during times of spiritual waste and fragmentation, become "religious" and assume the task of upholding a totality in which the irrational is not suppressed or ignored but absorbed. Goethe is for Broch the first poet striving on purely secular grounds for this totality. In our own century, Broch sees Goethe's achievement approximated only by Kafka, Thomas Mann, James Joyce, and, with reservations, André Gide and Musil. This novelistic attempt at "totality of cognition" (*Gesamterkenntnis*) Broch calls the "polyhistorical novel" (*GW*, VIII, 60), and he explains its purpose and function to his publisher, Daniel Brody, in a letter of August 5, 1931. The statement can be read as a commentary on his own work:

You know my theory, that the novel and the new form of the novel have taken over the task to absorb those parts of philosophy which, to be sure, correspond to metaphysical needs but which today count, according to the present state of research, either as "nonscientific" or, to speak with Wittgenstein, as "mystic." The era of the polyhistorical novel has begun. It is, however, inadmissible to accommodate this polyhistorism in the book in the guise of "educated" speeches or to use scientists as protagonists. The novel is poetry [*Dichtung*], hence occupied with the primal motivations of the soul, and to make an "educated" class the carrier of the novel is absolute irresponsibility [*Verkitschung*]. (*GW*, VIII, 60)

Broch's idiosyncratic interpretation of the words "romanticism," "anarchy," and "matter-of-factness" can now be seen in terms of his view of historical development. Romanticism is an attitude of "bad faith" which occurs when a person flees from the disintegrative pull upon his existence into a rigidly closed system. A system becomes closed when it is unable to accommodate cognitive advances or absorb the constantly surfacing new impulses which are "irrational" precisely because they are "free" and have not yet been processed. Examples for the pressure to abide by the conventions of the closed system and the comfort derived from it are Joachim's marriage to Elisabeth, Esch's conversion from a so-called "freethinker" (*Freidenker*) to a Protestant sectarian, Huguenau's nonchalant return to the security of a petit bourgeois family—and business man. In order to retain its position of dominance, the system must pretend that it can answer to all cognitive advances and subsume the irrational impulses: it posits itself as absolute. Yet, "when the secular exalts itself as the absolute, the result is always romanticism" (SW, 20). During disintegrative periods, each person partakes of different value systems at the same time, is romantic in one respect and matter-of-fact in another without realizing the inconsistency in his attitude. Introduced into the labyrinth of the character's subjective universe and understanding his inconsistencies within the frame of the narrative, the reader can avoid the mistakes of believing as "absolute" what is relative to the character only.

The example of Eduard von Bertrand may serve to elucidate this point. He is the successful, worldly businessman who represents in the minds of Joachim, Elisabeth, and Ruzena a freedom from convention that is unsettling and alluring at the same time. Yet when Bertrand speaks with Elisabeth, Joachim's future bride, he shows beneath his sophisticated front a romantic attitude, demonstrating that he has to elevate secular love to an "absolute," since it presents a challenge from the irrational with which he cannot cope. As always in instances where the security of convention is left behind and the metaphysical-irrational impulses are free to emerge, the language automatically becomes steeped in religious fervor. Bertrand says to Elisabeth: "I believe, and this is my deepest belief, that only by a dreadful intensification of itself, only when in a sense it becomes infinite, can the strangeness parting two human beings be transformed into its opposite, into absolute recognition, and let that thing come to life which hovers in front of love as its unattainable goal, and yet is its condition: the mystery of oneness. The gradual accustoming of oneself to another, the gradual deepening of intimacy, evokes no mystery whatever" (SW, 100).

By converting "earthly love" into a religion, Bertrand acts "romantically." He needs to make love an absolute because he cannot admit some of its components: the aspects of physical love. In his conversation with Elisabeth he says: "To court a woman means to offer oneself to her as the living biped that one is, and that's indecent . . ." (SW, 97). Or: "When the man will kneel before you whom I'm jealous of at this moment, the man who will offer you with that antiquated gesture his physical proximity; then the memory of, let us say, an aseptic form of love may help to remind you that behind every pseudo-aesthetic gesture in love there is hidden a still grosser reality" (SW, 97–8).[21] Divorced from its earthly components, Bertrand's concept of love becomes a lie which he feeds to himself and to others. (At the same time, his reported homosexuality in the "Esch" part finds a retrospective foundation.)

The verdict over men, or rather over attitudes like those of Bertrand, is spoken in the last part of the trilogy when Bertrand is identified as an "aesthete" who knows the difference between right and wrong (in distinction to Joachim, Esch, etc., who do not), but does not act on that knowledge. According to the definition given in the novel, ". . . the aesthete . . . does not distinguish good from evil: in that lies his fascination. But he knows very well what is good and what is evil, he merely chooses not to distinguish them. And that makes him depraved" (SW, 541). With respect to the system of the romantic, the distinction between a "mere" romantic and a romantic aesthete lies in the degree of consciousness and the conscious distortion which accompanies each "romantic" act. This is summarized in the novel in the following manner: " 'Ah,' says the romantic, putting on the cloak of an alien value system, 'ah, now I am one of you and am no longer lonely.' 'Ah,' says the aesthete, putting on the same cloak, 'I am still lonely, but this is a lovely cloak.' The aesthete represents the principle of evil within the romantic system" (SW, 540). [22]

When this interpretation of romanticism is applied to the Wilhelminian era, the relativized commentary states: "And because, when the secular exalts itself as the absolute, the result is always romanticism; so the real and characteristic romanticism of that age was the cult of the uniform, which implied, as it were, a superterrestrial and supertemporal idea of uniform . . ." (SW, 20). The characters who, unlike Bertrand, simply act out rather than reflect upon this romanticism, experience the closed system in which they take refuge as stiff and rigid. In this instance among many, Broch transposes the metaphorical description of the system directly into the novel: the uniform is a "hard casing," braced "with straps and belts" (SW, 21), protecting the wearer against the anarchy lurking beneath this second skin. When young Joachim sees a portrait of his grandfather wearing, not a stiff white shirt, but a lace jabot, he reflects: "But then in his time men had had a deeper and more intimate faith and did not need to seek any further bulwark against anarchy" (SW, 23). In the further development of the novel (and on into *The Death of Virgil* of almost fifteen years later), stiffness and rigidity become independent qualities, emerging in persons, gestures, attitudes, and settings alike, always indicative of a closed dogmatic value system. Mutter Hentjen in the "Esch" part, for example, becomes stiff or frozen when she feels her appearance threatened (*SW*, 164); and she has developed a mannerism of touching her "stiff and correct" coiffure, a "hard and little sugar-loaf" (*SW*, 163, 162), to support herself in a profession she does not like.

Conversely, when a system opens up to hitherto unknown possibilities, the descriptions abound in a variety of versions of "soft" and "softness." This applies above all in the act of love, and the description is frequently accompanied by the images of gliding or floating, of losing firm boundaries and outlines. This is epistemologically a most significant state, since it allows for the possibility of expanding one's own value system. At the same time, however, it is a period of extreme anguish which needs to be forgotten because it deprives the person of the accustomed security. The love scene between Joachim and Ruzena, for example, (*SW*, 36–40) is viewed in these terms. Ruzena, the call girl, is "enchanted by the conventionally stiff courtesy with which Joachim had treated her . . ." (*SW*, 36) because she too, is romantic, in the sense that she longs to belong to an established system. These characterizations are fictional transcriptions of Broch's philosophical tenets, but, at the same time, they are accomplished moral and psychological portraits. On their walk "the sky hung softly," "the rain sank quietly . . . and rustled softly," "a soft misty veil rose," and Ruzena "whispered softly" (*SW*, 37–38), while Joachim felt "being floated away, as though the longing which filled him were a soft, light outflowing of his heart, a breathing flood longing to be merged in the breath of his beloved, and to be lost . . ." (*SW*, 37). When they undress, the repertoire of these concepts is repeated: "But the sharp-cornered starched plastron of his shirt, cutting against her chin, still irked her . . . and squeezing her face between the sharp angles . . . and now they felt release and freedom, felt the softness of their bodies . . ." (*SW*, 39).

Progressive disintegration leads from romanticism to anarchy. This occurs when the dogmatic system to which the romantic has subjected himself can no longer satisfy the needs which bound him to it in the first place. The system is then no longer capable of answering the fears and needs of the metaphysical loneliness. The less these fears are "bound" into a system, the more freely they manifest themselves in irrational acts, that is, acts which are independent of a system. The "logic of the irrational" blatantly asserts itself. Anarchy is the seemingly chaotic state in which the freedom from systems is experienced with panic and the individual tries, with all his might and according to his own "logic," to reestablish value systems. For a physical person such as Esch, who lacks any social or intellectual constructs such as the military or business ethics, the only means of contributing toward an integrated world is his own body, more specifically, sex. From the anarchic perspective which is determined by eruptive irrational impulses, by vehemence, brutality and impetuosity[23] the romantic is very rational, tamed, and contained in his system, irrespective of the validity and cost of belonging: "The lonelier a man becomes, the more detached he is from the value-system in which he lives, the more obviously are his actions determined by the irrational. But the romantic, clinging to the framework of an alien and dogmatic system, is—it seems incredible—completely rational and unchildlike" (*SW*, 541).

In the third part of the trilogy, Esch's erotic mysticism is channeled into religious sectarianism when several members of the small town, among them Esch, the mason Gödicke, who had been buried in the trenches and has literally "risen from the dead," and Joachim von Pasenow, institute Bible sessions. For Esch, the anarchic "freethinker" and the "free" spirit of the second part of the trilogy, this refuge constitutes a regression (emphasized in the description that he carries his "head in the neck") (*SW*, 295),[24] but for Joachim von Pasenow, it signifies a subjective-lyrical release from strict dogmatic religiosity. In a letter written during the composition of *The Sleepwalkers* (July 27, 1930), Broch passes a clear verdict not only over Joachim's and Esch's mystic fervor, but over all attempts at mystic-erotic transcendence, and places the mystic search in the historical context: "This sterile reversion to the mystic, perhaps most clearly visible in the Russian philosphers of the prewar period— visible also in the Russian youth (and in the literature) around 1905 which took refuge in the erotic-mystic—is part of the necessary, epistemologically caused course of intellectual history, and Pasenow and Esch are representative of it" (*GW*, VIII, 28).

The progression from anarchy to matter-of-factness reaches the nadir of the disintegration of values. Each act stands by itself. Huguenau is a man on this path. While Esch still struggled desperately to subsume independent acts into a self-made cosmogony and where much of his impetuosity, frustration, and violence were due to the inadequacy of his inventions, Huguenau is free to act out taboos and fantasies without being under the compulsion to "make sense" of the world or to bring sense to it by his actions. When he deserts the army, embezzles money, kills Esch, and coerces Frau Esch to have intercourse with him, he does not think of these acts as crimes in defiance of social and religious value systems. He simply does not think at all.

In the character of Huguenau, the Janus nature of Broch's ethics approaches its most dangerous and reprehensible representation. In 1930 and 1931, when Broch worked on "Huguenau," the Kantian "loneliness of the I" and the consequences of the pursuit of the autonomy of the "I" as a formalistic cognitive device exerted an unmitigated impact upon Broch's thinking. Detailed reflections on the need for an absolute human value center and its necessity as a directive force to channel the anarchically "unbound" freedom appeared only later. For this reason, Huguenau is viewed rather approvingly as the appropriate representative of his times. In an early letter (July 19, 1931) to his publisher, Broch explains Huguenau in terms of his theory. He states as a kind of preamble: "The 'freedom' which alone counts in the truly ethical realm does not pay attention to traditional values; the concept of autonomy, in which this freedom has its logical foundation, has nothing to do with moral attitudes: surely, this autonomy is not yet the fulfillment of the ultimate divine value, but it is *the only form* in which it can come to pass. (All this is prepared to a large extent in Kant; also, of course, in Plato and Augustine; but I can omit documentation.)" (*GW*, VIII, 26). After placing Pasenow and Esch in their respective contexts,[25] Broch continues:

Only Huguenau is the truly "value-free" person and therefore the adequate child of his times. He alone is able to endure, he alone lives in the "autonomy of these times," which harbor a revolutionary struggle for freedom. . . . He is ethical only by virtue of the form of the autonomy, but otherwise completely amoral. Certainly he has not yet reached the freedom of the new divinity, of the new faith, and he does not even strive for it or long for it, although here and there a spark of the incipient possibilities flashes up in him. In this, he is like these times, which have not yet found their faith, which will not find it for a long time, and only have intimations of it here and there. But it is the vital form, the "form of freedom," in which alone the new content can grow. He stands at the beginning of this road (a road of whose existence Esch has an intimation in the anarchy of values—at the conclusion of the second part— after contact with Bertrand, without, however, having the possibility of ever walking that road). (*GW*, VIII, 26)

When Broch calls Huguenau "the adequate child of his times," he does not use the word "child" lightly. Huguenau's affinities with the child Marguerite are quite pronounced. They share a matter-of-factness, an interest in machines, a lack of family ties, and an unemotional, almost casual greed for money. Huguenau approaches Marguerite sexually in the manner of a child curious to explore the physical makeup of the other sex; he commits the Oedipus crimes not in order to usurp the husband-father-lover role but out of the jealousy of a child who wants undivided attention and asserts his own desires at all costs. Huguenau's repeated insistence on his role as a child in the Esch-Frau Esch-Huguenau triangle emphasizes his position of insouciance. He acts "irresponsibly" and "selfishly" as only undisciplined children can.[26]

If romanticism, anarchy, and matter-of-factness are three successive stages in the process of the disintegration of values, why and how is sleepwalking a denominator common to all these states?[27] Sleepwalking signals the departure from the accustomed value system and implies specific cognitive conditions. When Joachim follows Ruzena to her room, when Esch fantasizes about America, when Bertrand exchanges the stiff uniform for soft English cloth and travels around the world, hunting for the pathos of alienation, or when Huguenau walks away from the trenches safely as under a "glass bell," they all embark on a venture into the unknown. Sleepwalking can occur in any of the historic phases of escalated disintegration when one leaves the security relative to his times. In all instances, sleepwalking is not a conscious activity but occurs in a "dreamlike" state in which desires and fears are so primordial that they blot out socially imposed restrictions. Since sleepwalking indicates a break with customary value systems, it is also an enactment of desires forbidden within the existing value system and, therefore, relegated to the realm of dreams and fantasies. In Joachim's case, the breaking away is a trivial and common affair, and he is only too glad when Bertrand (in this instance the gentle and kind midwife), "delivers" him from this dream turned nightmare. In Esch's case, the fantasies about cosmic justice and freedom crystallize in the dream sequence of the voyager and in his imaginary confrontation with Bertrand. Huguenau, too, is sleepwalking throughout his "vacation trip." Even when he must rely on rational organization and logical persuasion (as, for example, when he convinces the town dignitaries to invest in the imaginary conglomerate or when he buys Esch's newspaper), the basis for his calculations remains the dreamlike security of a sleepwalker. And in his case, even more blatantly than in those of Joachim and Esch, the enactment of fantasies indicates freedom from the rational structure of value systems.

Only Eduard von Bertrand, the passive hero, offers a modification of sleepwalking. He deliberately searches out what the others only gropingly and unthinkingly attain: a state of freedom from the rational impositions of convention. Cases in point are his sexual freedom (homosexuality) and his lack of geographical confinement. Where for Esch the voyage becomes the symbol of an open system, Bertrand's constant traveling is the conscious imitation of such freedom. As symbol it retains a disquieting, propelling quality, as imitation it lacks the dreamlike, compulsive, irrational driving force. Bertrand is an imitation sleepwalker. He thinks he can attain freedom by imitating its form; he becomes "an aesthete and so he had to kill himself" (SW, 539).

In Huguenau (who kills others) and Eduard von Bertrand (who kills himself) Broch presents two extreme positions which he will reject explicitly and radically in his later work. The autonomy of "unbound" values and the pursuit of "free," that is, irrational actions will be interpreted in the context of positivism. In the essays of the 1930s, following the publication of The Sleepwalkers and in The Death of Virgil of the early 1940s, "aestheticism" as a deliberate imitation becomes the target of the most scathing criticism. While the figure of the aesthete continues to appear—and to be judged—frequently and in different versions throughout Broch's novels, the enactment of positivistic attitudes is not repeated. (The only minor exception will be Zerline in The Guiltless.)

Sleepwalking, then, is the state in which an individual, no longer protected by established patterns of behavior or thought, ventures into new lands (for example, Joachim's affair with Ruzena; Esch's fantasies about emigrating to America; Huguenau's desertion from the army). Sleepwalking can be viewed as an individual psychodrama on an unconscious level played against the social and historical background. It is a state of openness in which the desires and fears of the protagonists are enacted without inhibition. Due to its sheer irrationalism, sleepwalking can never become the basis for a new integration of values. Unless it can be channeled into rational structures and larger systems, it remains an unbound, value-free, anarchic force.

III   Abstraction and Judaism

In The Sleepwalkers Broch proposes to analyze the modern era. He elects as his tool of analysis the theory that cognitive breakthroughs are emanations of the Platonic Idea creating the events of history. He visualizes these cognitive advances as movements away from the established system, carrying with them new possibilities. Yet history remains, according to Broch's theory, curiously tied to two mutually exclusive views. On the one hand, history as progress in time is the intricate, though ever repeated, movement between two poles, that of totally integrated eras and that of the "atomization of values." On the other hand, however, the cognitive breakthroughs constitute a qualitative forward movement. The question asked in *Cantos 1913* has, almost twenty years later, still not found an answer: must the linear, open progression of cognitive breakthroughs inevitably be bent into the cyclically closed system of relapses into "witch trials" and "Thirty Years' Wars" or—in the vocabulary of *The Sleepwalkers*—into the "zero point of the atomization of values?"

The characters in the novel are transfixed at the crossroads of a cognitive incapacity to decide. At the same time, they are proponents of the specific historical period in which they live, which means that even their utopias and ideals are limited by the specific historical limiting factor. Their incapability is a reflection on Broch, who had not yet arrived at directives leading out of this impasse. (The jolt necessary for planned action was provided in the second half of the 1930s with Mussolini's war in Ethiopia, the impotence of the League of Nations, and Hitler's persecution of the Jews.) In *The Sleepwalkers*, Broch can define his position only through negative examples, that is, through attitudes *not* to follow. This is particularly evident in the "Epilogue," where leader–and redeemer–expectations conclude the novel. These projections are not intended as desirable alternatives for the future, but are viewed as part of the historical symptoms that make the "sleepwalkers" look for refuge in closed systems. Broch's lack of positive suggestions is even more clearly stressed in the open questions of his letters: ". . . the *new problem:* what direction does the longing for enlightenment and salvation take in times of disintegration and dissolution of old value systems? When the longing can no longer fuse into these systems? Can a new ethos emerge out of the sleep and the dream of the vilest everyday?" (*GW*, VIII, 18).

Broch presents the theory of the disintegration of values not only mimetically in the various protagonists of *The Sleepwalkers*, he also uses it to interpret historical data. In these instances, an extremely idiosyncratic, not to say confusing, use of terminology finds itself at odds with orthodox historiography. It does not surprise that Broch, with his idealistic background, emphasizes the spiritual and intellectual components of history and views the economic and social changes as contingent upon them. Equally predictable is Broch's interest in the disintegration of religious systems. In fact, *The Sleepwalkers* can be read as a history of the disintegration of *the* Western religious value system—Catholicism. In this context, Protestantism is designated as "the first great sect-formation in the decay of Christianity" (*SW*, 523). (Christianity is treated as synonymous with Catholicism, which, in its prime, represented the total presence of the Platonic Idea in history.) That this decay was irreparable became evident in the efforts of the Counter-Reformation when Catholicism had to appeal to "heathenish folk-customs" and aspired to an "ecstatic unity," thereby substituting the personal and subjective, that is, Protestant experience, for the spontaneous "mystic symbolic unity of the Gothic." Indeed, Protestantism signaled the invasion of the positivistic spirit into the field of religion. Protestantism in its "radical inwardness of the religious experience" did no longer "absorb the non-religious values, it only tolerated them." Although unwilling to absorb non-religious values, it still needed to provide ethical directives, with the result that "the most characteristically Protestant idea is the categorical imperative of duty" (*SW*, 524). Yet even this Kantian phase is only transitory in a development toward ever more formidable abstraction, with the relegation of more and more spheres into non-religious minisystems.

For in excluding all other values, in casting himself in the last resort on an autonomous religious experience, he [the Protestant] has assumed a final abstraction of a logical rigour that urges him unambiguously to strip all sensory trappings from his faith, to empty it of all content but the naked Absolute, retaining nothing but the pure form, the pure, empty and neutral form of a "religion in itself," a "mysticism in itself." (*SW*, 525)

At this point in the development of Protestantism occurs a surprising turn of events: similarities with Judaism are uncovered. Judaism becomes for Broch the epitome of abstract modernity, the ultimate consequence of Protestant radicality, and a direct continuation of its end phase, Kantian "theology." In effect, the Jew comes close to fitting the definition of "positivist":

The Jew, by virtue of the abstract rigour of his conception of infinity, is the really modern, the most "advanced" man *kat' exochen:* he it is who surrenders himself with absolute radicality to whatever system of values, whatever career he has chosen; he it is who raises his profession, even though it be a means of livelihood taken up by chance, to a hitherto unknown absolute pitch; he it is who, unconditionally and ruthlessly following up his actions without reference to any other system of values, attains the highest summit of spiritual enlightenment or sinks to the most brutal absorption in material things. . . . (SW, 526)

Broch's theory of the religious systems as symptoms of the disintegration of values is acted out in the Berlin sections of *The Sleepwalkers*. The story of Marie, the girl from the Salvation Army, is told over large stretches in verse or lyrical prose. Since the lyric is the most subjective mode of literary expression, this form indicates extreme relativism and Marie's longing for an ecstatic unity. Marie's god is an extremely personal and sectarian god who instills meaning in a life which has eliminated from its concerns all that cannot be brought into consonance with the faith. The Salvation Army is militant in its attempt to proselytize. Its organization is that of the military (in itself a partial system), and its members wear uniforms (yet uniforms in themselves are a warning signal as to the weakness of the system and its need of support from external "casings"). The Salvation Army thus represents one value system in combat with others. Marie's system is fragmentary: she cares for the sick and the poor, but the major aspects of modern life—the professions, business, and politics—are excluded from her provinces. As convincing and as satisfying as the solution may be for Marie, and as convincing as it may sound to the unsuspecting reader (if indeed at this point in the novel one can still be unsuspecting), these attempts to stem the tide of disintegration are considered futile from an epistemological and historical point of view. In the "Disintegration of Values," the objective comment on the sects is by far less benign than the personal relationship that grows between Marie and Dr. Bertrand Müller. What is portrayed sympathetically on a personal level, must be rejected in the objective frame of a philosophy of history:

The numerous sects . . . have all developed in the same direction; they are all a rehash, a whittling away and levelling down of that old idea of a Protestant organon of values; they are all on the side of the "Counter-reformation:" for instance, . . . the Salvation Army not only resembles the Jesuit movement of the Counter-reformation in its military organization, but also exhibits very clearly the same tendency to centralize values, to draw everything into its nets, to show how popular art of every kind, down to the street song, may be reclaimed for religion and reinstated as "ecstatic aids." Pathetic and inadequate expense of the spirit. (SW, 527)

Nuchem and the Orthodox Jews oppose the subjective, ecstatic religiosity of Marie with self-obliterating obedience to a supra-personal body of laws devoid of any personal "ornamentation." They "have preserved the utmost rigour and severity of the Law as the last vestige of a bond with religious life on the earthly plane" (SW, 525). In an essay of 1934, "Theologie, Positivismus und Dichtung" ("Theology, Positivism, and Poetry") Broch provides additional historical background for his view that the Jews epitomize abstraction. He speaks of a "form of abstraction" which, by virtue of its development, "had to return to its Jewish basis: to the abstract mysticism of Judaism . . . and of Talmudism" (st. 375/1, p.202).

Dr. Bertrand Müller, a severely undernourished philosopher in the last few months of World War I, lives in a room next door to the Jews. Müller's curiosity is engaged by the "strange" life-style of the small group of Orthodox Jews and he comments on it with the naive prejudice of the outsider (SW, 541). Through Müller the young Nuchem meets Marie and in front of Müller's eyes their platonic relationship is acted out. Since both lovers are defined by their respective religious systems, the relationship can be viewed as the encounter of two mutually exclusive attitudes toward God. Common to both system, however, is the extreme degree of inwardness. Müller prods his two charges to make the following declarations:

I said to Nuchem: "You are a suspicious people, an angry people; you are jealous even of God and are constantly pulling Him up even in His own Book." He answered: "The law is imperishable. God is not until every jot and tittle of the Law has been deciphered." I said to Marie: "You are a brave but a thoughtless people! You believe that you need only be good and strike up music in order to draw God near." She answered: "Joy in God is God, His grace is inexhaustible." (SW, 559)

Broch had always seen abstraction as a symptiom of modernity. But his appraisal of this phenomenon changed over the years and was at first not connected with Judaism. As a young man and recent convert to Catholicism (1909), he had lamented the absence of ornamentation and seen the resultant abstraction as the demise of Western culture. About two decades later, the Jews in *The Sleepwalkers* became the symbol of abstract modernity. In the context of the novel they are one splinter group among many, rigorously escalating the consequences of positivistic thinking. Still later in life, Broch returned to Judaism, a move consonant with his view of history as progressive abstraction. Toward the end of his life, in *The Guiltless* of 1950, he finally judged a protagonist for his flight from accepting the modern, abstract predicament.

Almost two decades after the completion of *The Sleepwalkers*, Broch re-evaluated Marie and Nuchem in a letter to Daisy Brody. His changed interpretation of abstraction amounts to a personal confession:

I don't know from what point of view you consider today Salvation Marie . . . When I think back, I see on the first level an admonition to the Jew Nuchem: "Don't let yourself be seduced into any legends [*Legendenhaftigkeit*] no matter how sweet, but remain with your abstract book, remain a Jew, remain with your Thora." On the second plane however, I see an admonition to the poet: "Don't let yourself be seduced by any promise of salvation; *Dichtung* does not mediate grace; rather, the road to grace lies in cognition, and only when you have gone that road all the way it may perhaps be possible for you to return to *Dichtung*; but then you will not need it anymore." (*GW*, VIII, 318)

Marie, Nuchem, and Bertrand Müller represent three versions of the disintegration of values. All three are reacting to the Kantian "loneliness of the I"; Marie's and Nuchem's answers are at opposite ends of the disintegrative spectrum, while Bertrand Müller's is outside it. Marie and the Salvation Army represent the subjective, personal relation with a superior value system, into which they hope to fit as large a segment of the world as possible. The attempt is a conscious borrowing from the past, doomed to failure like all sectarian efforts. Nuchem and the Jews renounce the personal and ecstatic gratification of the past and open themselves without hesitation to the "horror of the absolute." Theirs is the extension of the Kantian concept of duty which renounces ecstatic and subjective fulfillment in order to obliterate the self in obedience to the law. Bertrand Müller is attempting the breakthrough into a state of being which would again realize the fullness of the Platonic Idea. The extremes of the irrational and the rational approach as exemplified by Marie and the Jews need to be reconciled again in order to restore the harmonic balance. Bertrand Müller, the professed Platonist, acknowledges the impossibility of restoring this balance and, with it, Platonism. In fact, it seems that the Platonic ideal can exist only as paradox, that is, as impossibility and negation rather than affirmation. "I said to myself: 'You are a fool, you are a Platonist, you believe that in comprehend-

ing the world, you can shape it and raise yourself in freedom to Godhood. Can you not see that you are bleeding yourself to death?' I answered myself: 'Yes, I am bleeding to death' " (SW, 559).
Berlin is the first locale of sleepwalking. In some concluding sections of the novel, again set in Berlin, a tentative answer to sleepwalking is sketched. Sleepwalking is a dreamlike departure from value systems; it fails to reach any "new lands" precisely because it is dreamlike, irrational, and temporary. Bertrand Müller in Berlin speculates that eventually a new integration and a new unity will come about. Although he has no concrete suggestions, he assumes that it will be a unity of smallest dimensions which must first be achieved in the individual before it can gather momentum to become an historical force. But even this integrative hypothesis is couched in wonderment and questioned: "Is it the suddenly awakening conviction that the unity of thought and being can be realized only within the most modest limits? Both thought and being reduced to their minimum!" (SW, 575). Müller here voices a hope that is not at odds with Broch's opinions. Broch places the burden of history, the contribution to a specific Zeitgeist, squarely on the shoulders of each individual. He demands what the sleepwalkers were incapable of fulfilling: conscious, deliberate efforts to establish a unity of the rational and irrational forces reflecting the Platonic totality. Like his protagonist, he cannot point out concrete approaches to this integration of values. He has to rely on his philosophical systematizations to provide an alternative to the leader-and-redeemer hopes which trace the road into bondage rather than integration. This alternative points in the direction of a cognitive, utopian holism.

It is the positivism that characterized Luther and the whole Renaissance, the same double affirmation of the given world and of the need for ascetic severity, a doctrine that is now fulfilling its essential implications and tending towards a new unity of Thought and Being, towards a new unity of ethical and material infinity. It is the unity which informs every system of theology and which must endure even if the attempt is made to deny the reality of Thought, but which takes on a new lease of life when the scientific point at which things are assumed as true coincides with the point at which things are believed to be true, so that the double truth once more becomes single and unambiguous. (SW, 639)

In subsequent years, Broch repeatedly mentioned the prophetic quality of The Sleepwalkers. This does not mean that he longed for the apocalyptic prophecies to be fulfilled, but that he felt he had correctly analyzed the conditions and dangers of the "vacuum of values." Barely two years before Hitler's advent to power he offered an analysis of the mechanisms and temptations to fall for leader figures. At the same time, he dispelled any hope that such outside intervention might bring release from individual responsibility. From this point of view, *The Sleepwalkers* documents the difficulty of living up to the metaphysical-cognitive responsibilities in the "loneliness of the I."

CHAPTER 4

The Road to the Anschluss

THE truncated Austria found itself battleground of divergent
political factions. During the early 1930s, the crises of the
previous decade intensified and led in early 1934 to civil war. The
demonstrations and the riots of July 15, 1927, in front of the Palace of
Justice had strengthened the position of the *Heimwehr*. This patri-
otic, reactionary, and paramilitary organization was financed by
Mussolini's Italy and small sections of the industry to the detriment of
the *Schutzbund*, the Social Democrats' military recruits from the
local *Arbeiterwehr* formations. In June, 1931, the closing of the
Creditanstalt, the leading Austrian banking institution, triggered a
major crisis and threatened Central Europe with economic chaos.
The Nazis profited from these turmoils; they infiltrated Austria from
Germany and intensified their organizational efforts.

Engelbert Dollfuss had become a member of the Austrian cabinet
in March, 1931, as minister of agriculture. Two months after Hitler's
ascent to power (on January 30, 1933), and exactly two years after he
had joined the cabinet, he initiated his own brand of dictatorial
government. The *Schutzbund* was disbanded, the Constitutional
Court was suspended, and press censorship was imposed. Following
the example of the *Heimwehr*, Dollfuss looked to Fascist Italy to
guarantee Austrian independence against Fascist Germany. When
"Mussolini pressed for decisive anti-parliamentary measures, especially the destruction of the Social Democratic Party," and the
"*Heimwehr* resorted to intimidation of the authorities in the federal
states," civil war erupted on February 12, 1934. It ended with the
total defeat of the *Schutzbund* and the Socialists: "The government
assert[ed] control, the Socialist leaders [were] arrested or driven into
exile, the Party and the trade unions [were] outlawed."[1] The Rome
Protocols of March, 1934, strengthened the ties between Italy,
Hungary, and Austria. After the turmoil of the civil war and the
ousting of the Social Democrats, the Nazis believed Austria ripe for

takeover. Their *Putsch* in Vienna on July 25, 1934, failed, although Dollfuss was assassinated. Schuschnigg became chancellor in a country that was at the mercy of foreign pressures and interest groups. In such a political climate, the publication of *The Sleepwalkers* went relatively unnoticed. Although the critical acclaim led to translations of the novel and its publication in England and the United States in 1932, the disastrous economic instability in Germany, where it was published in 1931–1932, prevented a financial success: "Publishing houses and writers . . . suffered from the depression; the number of books published was hardly affected, but their price had to be reduced, and the income of writers, including bestselling authors, fell steeply."[2] Broch's hopes for an income from the novel dwindled. As his financial situation worsened, he became haunted by the specter of the Musil Society, collecting contributions to support Robert Musil's work on *The Man Without Qualities* (*GW*, VIII, 97, 114).

An avalanche of essays followed the publication of the novel.[3] They appear to be of a totally apolitical nature. Broch's position in these essays (as in *The Sleepwalkers*) remains adamantly idealistic, in the sense that he takes the turbulence of the age to be due to a spiritual vacuum and metaphysical anguish, and not primarily to political or economic havoc. According to Broch, the demagogues and ideologues rising within Austria as much as outside its borders, exploited spiritual uprootedness; yet he considered fighting them tantamount to fighting effects rather than causes. He believed that demagogues would no longer present a challenge if the spiritual disorientation of the era could be rectified. Here Broch sees the contributions of the poet-novelist to be of extreme political significance. In essay after essay from the years 1933–1934, he stresses two major areas: the poet's cognitive task to present a Platonic totality where attainment of that totality through confrontation with the irrational-metaphysical realm is symbolized in the Orphic descent; and the distinction between the ethical act and the aesthetic realm.

In this context, the seemingly apolitical nature of the essays becomes charged with political relevance: Broch sees the poet's cognitive mission as the only justification of literature in catastrophic times. Without proper regard for this conversion of cognitive efforts into ethical achievements, and of ethical achievements into political statements, the entire political dimension of these essays is lost. Broch's insistence on *Dichtung* as the only means left to assuage man's metaphysical anxieties and thereby to become a political force was never again as pronounced as in the first half of the 1930s.

The second major area of these essays concentrates on the distinction between the ethical and the aesthetic realm. Again, Broch's particular use of commonly accepted terms bars easy access to an understanding of these categories. For Broch, aesthetics is an ethical category, relevant to any field of human endeavor. The sketchy definition of the "aesthete" (exemplified in Eduard von Bertrand in *The Sleepwalkers*) is here carefully elaborated. Fundamental to Broch's categories is his distinction between the open and the closed value system—the open system being able to accommodate cognitive advances, the closed system dogmatically excluding them. The open system, due to its cognitive activities, is ethical; the closed system, which feeds on the semblance of activities but is actually static, is aesthetic and "evil." Within the open system, Broch goes on to distinguish between the ethical act and its result, which he considers aesthetic (since as a product it has become static and closed) (*st* 247, 90). The concept "aesthetic" has, therefore, two meanings depending on the provenience of the static product or, as Broch says, on the "strange Janus-face of the concept 'value' " (*st* 247, 90). The aesthetic product of ethical-cognitive activities in an open system becomes superannuated as soon as the activities are concluded; nevertheless, it is part of the tradition and represents the conservative tendencies within the continuing development. The aesthetically "evil," on the other hand, is the product of an imitation system, that is, a system which is closed but pretends to be able to cope with new cognitive advances through dogmatic decrees. Broch condemns this category in the strongest terms possible and indicts the "aesthete" as the archcriminal, who deflects man's metaphysical anxieties and aspirations into easy accommodations in the here and now.

Yet the strongest word Broch can find for these aesthetically "evil" products, the result of man's abdication of the cognitive task, is *Kitsch* (trash). *Kitsch* and *Verkitschung* (the production of trash) are, hence, ethical-cognitive categories. When he applies them to literature, specifically to the novel, he sees *Kitsch* fabricated in all those works that aim at entertainment without regard for the cognitive task of literature, that is, *Trivialliteratur*. More significant than as literary classification, *Kitsch*, as a category of ethical-cognitive deprivation, becomes singularly important in politics. With Broch's definition of *Kitsch* in mind, one can accept that demagogues, dictators, and charismatic manipulators of masses are viewed as *Kitsch* phenomena.

A statement like "purple *kitsch* apocalypse" (*st* 209, 239), which Broch made four years after the end of World War II, then stands as the worst indictment of apocalyptic thinking and attests to how closely *Kitsch* is related to the "demonic" perversion of ethical standards. (These clusters of concepts will become significant ingredients of the *Mountain Novel, The Death of Virgil,* and *The Guiltless.*)

After the completion of *The Sleepwalkers* and while working on some of the seminal essays on the theory of value and on *Kitsch,* Broch also began work on a novel which was never completed. It is known as the "Filsmann" fragment. Mention of work on this book fills his correspondence for the next two years. The material deals with an industrial family in contemporary society and provided Broch with the basis for a play which he wrote during this time. The play had its première at the *Schauspielhaus* in Zurich on March 15, 1934, under the title *Denn sie wissen nicht, was sie tun* (*For They Know Not What They Do*), altered from the original title *Dirges* (*Totenklage*) (*BBB* 316, n.).

The play was read by Stefan Zweig, whose reaction Broch summarized in a letter to his publisher Daniel Brody, on October 20, 1932:

. . . the anonymous machine of male society and its vacuous perpetuum mobile must be more sharply contrasted with the mourning of the women and provide it with that justification which, as I mentioned to you, is not yet sufficiently motivated through the play itself. In order to bring the contrast out more clearly, Zweig suggests that I transpose the recovery of the Filsmann company totally into the anonymous, that is, to base the recovery of the support of the government.—This is Zweig's main objection, if it can be called an objection. And since it hits home, I am seriously considering changes. I cannot judge, however, whether these changes will realize the final, grand form, purged of all the dregs of a family drama, as Zweig would wish for. (*BBB,* 229)

The eradication of family traits in favor of anonymity may have struck a consonant chord in the author of a philosophy of history which predicts an ever-increasing manifestation of the abstract. At the same time, the suggestion must have mutilated against the author upholding the individual as the one and only bulwark against depersonalization and anonymity. Indeed, three days later Broch changed his mind when he wrote, again to his publisher: "What Zweig says about the absolute anonymity of the events sounds good, and yet I cannot accept it. I am somehow opposed to his suggestion to introduce the

government to salvage the Filsmann company and thereby to totally
eradicate the family aspects; my reaction is perhaps based on the fact
that this would again strengthen the political momentum . . ." (BBB,
230).
    In late 1932, The Sleepwalkers had been published in the United
States and Warner Brothers expressed an interest in filming it. At the
same time, Broch was being considered to write a movie treatment of
James Joyce's Ulysses on the basis of a lecture he had given on this
work in the early part of the year.[4] Although these plans never
materialized,[5] they show Broch's readiness to accept any job to
improve his financial situation.
    In February, 1933, Broch's publisher still hoped to publish the
"Filsmann" novel by the end of the year (BBB, 263). Instead of
completing this novel, however, Broch wrote and published several
short prose works.[6] The speed and seeming facility with which he
wrote these sensitive studies of the unconscious attest to his great
skills as a narrator—a fact which was clearly apparent in The Sleepwalkers. Despite the difficult times, Broch had publishers interested
in his work. Suhrkamp, editor of the Neue Rundschau, asked for more
essays, and the Fischer Verlag hoped to publish a novel to follow
Broch's critical success of The Sleepwalkers with a more accessible—
and hence saleable—work. Broch complied, putting aside the
"Filsmann" material. In July and August, 1933, he wrote Die unbekannte Grösse (The Unknown Quantity), a minor novel, which he
subsequently reworked into the screenplay for a film. Before publication, the novel was serialized in the Vossische Zeitung between
September 17 and October 7, 1933.
    The protagonist of The Unknown Quantity is the young mathe-
matician Richard Hieck who learns, through contact with irrational
forces (the death of his younger brother and falling in love with the lab
assistant Ilse), that the scientific, rational approach alone does not
come to terms with the "unknown quantity." In a comment on the
novel, Broch states: "[The novel] should depict that condition of the
soul in which the purely scientific, mathematical thinking in its
extreme rationality necessarily turns into its irrational mystic opposite, approximately into that condition which Kant expressed in the
phrase 'the starred skies above and the moral law within me,' and
which, as absurd as it might seem at first glance, is part of the
significant components of our times" (BBB, 283). At a slightly later
date, in a more detailed commentary on the novel, he reemphasizes
the poetic task:

Whatever raises the claim to be called poetry has to do with the simplest basic drives of the soul, with birth and death, with love and nature and social communion, with the primordial symbols of their expression, but not with scientific materials: the mathematician Richard Hieck hence has to be occupied with mathematics only to the point where mathematics becomes the point of crystallization of these primordial powers of the soul, in other words, to the extent . . . that the cognitive process of mathematics can serve as the exponent of a deeper dynamics of the soul. (*GW*, X, 169)

Two years later Broch saw the novel correctly in a more critical light:

. . . the Unknown Quantity was meant to uncover the irrational background of a life directed toward purely rational cognition and wanted to demonstrate how a breakthrough from the irrational (the death of the brother and beginning love) reconnects the consciousness which had become independent, how it reconnects it with its origins in the soul, so that that particular unity of cognition can emerge which must be viewed as the basis of all religiosity. . . . Now it is true, this small novel has not accomplished this task: I am not sure such a broad theme can be treated in 180 pages. I always had the feeling of experimenting while I wrote this book, daringly experimenting (which includes the period of six weeks in which it was written), but I know that this book is not completed, that I only achieved the semblance of unity through a rhetorical trick, but that actually everything remained open. (*GW*, VIII, 124)

The relatively large number of short prose works (*Novellen*) which Broch published in 1933 led him to think of his next project as a "novel in novella-form" (*Novellen-Roman*), which should combine the various novellas. He also referred to this project as the "Zodiac Stories." In 1932, through Jolande Jacoby, who organized several of Broch's lectures in the Vienna *Kulturbund*, Broch met C. G. Jung (*BBB*, 195, n.).[7] Although in the *Mountain Novel* and *The Death of Virgil* there exist various levels of "natural" affinity between Jung's theory of archetypes and Broch's cognitive use of mythology, the "Zodiac Stories" make an all too obvious use of this archetypology. In the "Remarks Concerning the 'Zodiac Stories,' " written toward the end of the rather prolific year 1933, and sent to Peter Suhrkamp, Broch explains: "The Zodiac Stories are an experiment. They attempt to create as 'living experience' primorial symbols of the soul, such as the lion, the bull, fishes, but also the triangle. This means they try to create an emotional aura in which it becomes understandable that these constructs have a metaphysical symbol content which endows the concrete and frequently trivial thing with the power to represent a large suprasensual realm" (st 209, 293). Daniel Brody, to whom Broch sent a copy of the "Remarks Concerning the 'Zodiac Stories,' " immediately criticized Broch's intent and pointed to the amateurish handling and misunderstanding of the "primordial symbols" (BBB, 298, n.). The plan of the "novel in novella form" was never carried out. Only after World War II, in 1949, when the Munich-based publisher Weismann was interested in reprinting works by Broch, did he return to these stories. He incorporated them, after considerable changes, into the novel The Guiltless.

Late in 1933, political pressure began to be applied to writers in Germany. Like their German colleagues, non-German authors wanting to publish in Germany had to register with the Reichsverband deutscher Schriftsteller (BBB, 304, n.). There was a chance that he would no longer be allowed to publish in Germany. In December, 1933, Broch thought the repression had abated (BBB, 304). His hopes were not justified. With exception of the Schönberg essay, "Gedanken zum Problem der Erkenntnis in der Musik" ("Thoughts Concerning the Problem of Cognition in Music") in the Fischer-Almanach of 1934, no further work by Broch was published in Hitler Germany after December, 1933. Similar to many other intellectuals, Broch had no resources to fight the approaching totalitarian regime. One only has to think of Broch's mentor, Karl Kraus, and his acerbic comment "I cannot think of anything more to say with regard to Hitler" ("Zu Hitler fällt mir nichts mehr ein"), to realize the complete helplessness and paralysis of the intellectual of nonactivist persuasion.

Instead of seeing that many of the personal problems experienced in these years were extensions of the political situation, Broch saw the political worries only as one aspect among many that caused personal stagnation and discomfort. In October, 1934, the same year that witnessed civil war and a Nazi-Putsch, he accounted for his dissatisfaction in this matter:

As is generally known, I have not done any work since the Unknown Quantity. Beginnings are evident in the projects for the novels, in the Kulturbund lecture and in the Schönberg essay. But nothing beyond that. Even the treatise on spirit and irrationality . . . so urgently requested by the Rundschau[8] was left lying for months and I am completing it only now. This was a year of sterility. Occupying it with the writing of plays was a pretense, even though one of the plays can be considered a success. Yet there are several external or quasi-external reasons for this sterility: (a) my constant financial worries, due to my various obligations, and increased through large repairs on our house in Vienna—one more reason which turned me so abruptly to write for the theater—financial worries consume a tremendous amount of time; (b) the extremely complicated situation in my personal life which—seen from the point of view of productivity—also is part of the external hindrances; (c) the political events in the world in general, those of February and July in particular, events which, after all, went under my skin; (d) the interruption through the première in Zurich, which came at an extremely inconvenient time. (*GW*, VIII, 101–2)

These problems, personal though they were, were still perceived as peripheral to the "true" problem, one of completely internal dimensions. Broch continues in the same letter:

But more important than all these external obstacles which, from this point of view, have only symptomatic significance, is the work-internal obstacle. This is the principal obstacle. It concerns the great problem of the place of cognition and of the poetic in and in relation to the present world: Joyce was the first who saw with perfect clarity that the time for the novel of trivial entertainment is over, that the cataclysms in the world necessitate a cataclysm in the poetic creativity—provided its existence is still justified—and that the problem bears on a radically different and radically new kind of totality—more so than ever before. (*GW*, VIII, 102)

In October, 1934, Broch left the city because, as he wrote in a letter of October 20, 1934, "my soul and my health no longer could take Vienna" (*GW*, X, 359; also VIII, 106). The flight from the city into the country became a trait of the narrator and main protagonist of a novel he seems to have begun writing at that time, the *Mountain Novel*.[9] Broch, however, saw the ambivalence of such a move more clearly than his character. Speaking in the same frame of mind that made him see the Jew as the epitome of abstraction, he wrote in a letter of March 18, 1935: "If one really wants to work, one must be able to see a tree or a mountain or the sea. The city is terrible. But this, too, is a symptom of the approaching end of art and spirit: for everything spiritual and artistic is actually a function of the city, and has always been" (*GW*, X, 361).

The pattern of frequent relocations, so characteristic of his years in exile, began during his last years in Austria. His daily existence became a constant battle between financial expediency and the search for optimal working conditions. He first moved to the Broch house in Baden near Vienna. Yet "since the maintenance of the Baden household was too expensive" (*GW*, X, 361), he temporarily accepted the invitation of friends to stay in Laxenburg, only to find: "I have peace, I don't spend any money, and everything would be splendid if only I could bear the flat country around me. However, I cannot look at it anymore and hence shall have to take flight again soon. Probably to somewhere in Tyrol, perhaps Orkney" (GW, X, 361). It was not Orkney, but Mösern near Seefeld in Tyrol, where Broch took up residence in September, 1935.[10] In June, 1936, he left Mösern, and after a series of temporary residences, including an early winter sojourn in the Styrian village of Alt-Aussee, he returned to Vienna. He stayed there until November, 1937, then returned to Alt-Aussee.[11] Here he was apprehended and jailed on the day of Austria's *Anschluss* on March 13, 1938.

I   *The Demagogue's Take–over*

Work on the *Mountain Novel* accompanied these meanderings. During the early stages of composition, Broch was strongly convinced of the importance of this work. He wrote to his friend and publisher, Daniel Brody, on July 5, 1935:

I am the last person to overestimate a novel and its completion (you know that this skeptical attitude is one of the most difficult problems of my life and of my work); nevertheless, I know that the only meaning of my life lies in this work, and that I have as much to give to the world as any of the best who still struggle with spiritual and ethical questions, even if the receptiveness of the world is quite impaired. . . . (BBB, 384)

Yet the novel never fulfilled its author's aspirations. Of the three extant versions only the earliest one is finished. Immediately after its completion in January, 1936, Broch began to rework it, but soon doubts about the legitimacy and function of *Dichtung* in view of the ever darkening political situation slowed down progress of the work. With specific reference to Hitler Germany and Mussolini's invasion of Ethiopia, he wrote to Daisy Brody, on February 26, 1936:

This is, above all, confirmation that in a world where such things are possible—it is the world, not merely Germany! the African War too is part of it—intellectual, or poetic, or other cognitive work has become superfluous and "pre-March" [*Vormärz*]. . . . If only I had already started the second volume, it would be simpler. Much of this self-consuming skepsis will be integrated into that part. The trick will be to justify its existence, neverthe-less, or at least to provide the semblance of such justification. For the time being, I have to encapsulate myself as much as possible in an ivory tower and create a kind of "pre-March"; it helps that it is already February. Hence I push on with a bad conscience, doggedly obstinate, trying to make a go of it, halfway successful; and I could be so much more successful, if there were no bad conscience, and if the world were constituted differently. (*BBB*, 405, n.)

During 1937, he abandoned the project completely. He resumed work on the novel only in the last years of his life, at the request of a publisher. This third version was only half finished when Broch died in 1951. Even the absence of the definite title points to the unfinished state of the novel. Since Broch himself had referred to the *opus* as the "mountain novel," this designation seems valid and more neutral than "The Wanderer," "The Tempter," or "Demeter or the Enchantment," which were also, on occasion, mentioned by him.

The events narrated in the first version of the novel concern the intrusion of an alien into a homogeneous village community. The "wanderer" and "tempter" Marius Ratti appears one day in a secluded mountain village and finds work with one of the local farmers. Gradually he incites the mountain population with his demagoguery; the villagers are swayed by his garbled promises of a new "golden age" based on male supremacy and a blood-and-soil ideology. (The literal-mindedness of Marius and a group of villagers let them look for the "golden age" in the reopening of collapsed gold mines in a mountain hovering above the village.) The desperate attempts to fabricate a new, cosmic unification of man and nature culminate in an outburst of mass hysteria in which Irmgard, a young woman from the village in love with Marius, is murdered in an ecstatic and quasi-ritual ceremony attended by the entire village population. After this climactic event, the villagers return to their ordinary lives, little changed by the blood-sacrifice; Marius is elected to the village council.

In this novel, Broch uses as a backdrop the panorama of an imposing alpine landscape with its seasonal changes. Similar to the three parts of *The Sleepwalkers*, the events span the period from early spring to incipient winter. Against this background Broch sets a plethora of villagers, each showing a different degree of susceptibility to the ideas and promises of Marius. The narrator is the country doctor who, not unlike Broch, has fled the city to live in closer contact with the "natural" life of the country. He learns that the rural mode of life offers neither refuge nor intact value systems. The major opponent of Marius, the demagogue, is Mutter Gisson (the name has been viewed as an anagram of *gnosis*). She is the grandmother of the murdered girl, Irmgard, and represents intuitive, archaic knowledge which both Marius and the doctor want to find. While the country doctor is eager to adjust his life to the harmonious rhythm of nature, as demonstrated in Mutter Gisson, Marius wants to appropriate her "knowledge" into his male cult as a quasi-mythical bond and a sign of dominance over the world of women.

The village microcosm reflects, on the scale of a model, the macrocosm of the world with its extreme anguish and lack of direction in the transitory phases of changing value systems. The *Mountain Novel* is an extremely political book in which Broch pursues the consequences of the leader-expectations expressed in the third part of *The Sleepwalkers*. The abdication of individual responsibility and personal judgment leads to subordination to the alluring promises of a demagogue and allows a rebarbarization by means of "magic," where blood cults and human sacrifice become acceptable practices. Direct reference to the historical reality of Hitler Germany, observed at close distance, can easily be detected in the novel. Marius, the hypnotic and self-hypnotized orator, who is obsessed with word associations, resembles Hitler, and the jesting dwarf Wenzel is a caricature of Goebbels. Wenzel is the willing instrument of Marius' promises of a new order and obediently organizes the paramilitary youth movement. The scapegoat role of the Jews falls on the Wetchy family—Calvinists, city people, outsiders.[12]

The Sleepwalkers showed the disintegration of values in three successive stages. The philosophical essays in the novel trace the process from the past, and the "Epilogue" extends hypothetically into the future. In the *Mountain Novel*, the layers of time are juxtaposed and compressed into the events of approximately nine months, except at the very center of the novel (*B*, I, 216–35), where the country doctor reminisces about his love for the pediatrician Barbara after World War I. The stacked time levels of the novel represent historical, legendary, and mythological time.[13] The juxtaposition of these time layers carries Broch's view of the progress of history from the archaic to the modern/abstract. Concepts which are basic to his ethics are again fully evident: his view of history as a series of "breakthroughs in knowledge" into ever greater abstraction intersects with the demand that the novel must be "religious" by upholding the Platonic totality which encompasses the irrational components released in disintegrative periods. The free-floating irrationality motivates hymnal-mystic remarks by the various protagonists. These remarks are "unnatural" and out of character when viewed from a psychological and realistic point of view. In distinction to his achievement in *The Sleepwalkers,* Broch did here not successfully integrate the many strata of the rational-irrational polarity. Yet criticism of the novel on account of its overburdening mysticism misses the point, since what we have is only a draft. Nevertheless, the structure of the novel is clearly evident. It is firmly rooted in Broch's concept of history and shows a striking congruence with the theory of value and the statements on systems, opposition systems, and imitation systems in his other novels as well as in the essays. Irrespective of the "tortuous" and "devious" distinctions between system and anti-system,"[14] one can gain a clear understanding of the novel through the "systems-approach," which shall be followed here.

Marius' ideology is the most easily recognized for its negative connotations. His promises to restore justice in the village by "conquering" the mountain and taking its gold, as well as his visions of establishing a male hegemony do not need explications to be recognized as hallucinatory, mad attempts to institute an atavistic order. His foreshortened vision of a new order, founded on violence and dogmatic fiat, and his desperate belief in the attainability of his earthly paradise relegate him to the imitation system of the aesthete. Yet if Marius represents the imitation system, he does so in opposition to the original system of Mutter Gisson.

Mutter Gisson's system represents knowledge and wisdom; it is built on her intimacy with nature and its cycles, and a close acquaintance with death. Mutter Gisson is the one person in the novel who is not afraid of death and who is therefore free of irrational fears and anxieties and immune to Marius' promises. In her person, the rational and irrational, life and death, reach such a degree of union that she has transcended the fear of dying. This state was not given to her by birth or magic but had to be worked for. When her husband, the hunter Gisson, was killed she underwent a spiritual death, from which only the awareness of life around her—her children— resurrected her. After she had conquered death, so to speak, and returned to life, she was able to bring both realms together, to live an ever more harmonious existence full of knowledge and wisdom gained through the experience of death. Yet this harmonic balance *sub specie temporis* of Mutter Gisson cannot be the ultimate goal of Broch's vision, tempting though it may be. This is made clear in many different ways: although Mutter Gisson is able to redeem herself from the fear of death and thereby lead a wise and knowledgeable life, she cannot transmit this knowledge to others—exactly because the knowledge has to be lived, and cannot be learned through transmitted words. She cannot teach her daughter, who leads a hard, closed, and unhappy family life, or her granddaughter, who falls victim to Marius. She cannot teach Marius (who thinks she withholds her knowledge out of avarice) or the country doctor, who understands that knowledge has to "grow"—in contrast to Marius, who simply wants to "gather" it up.

The harmony and balance of Mutter Gisson's existence—an earthly approximation of the Platonic harmony—has however a concomitant characteristic which *sub specie temporis* becomes a drawback. The abolition, or more precisely the spatialization of time, which was for Broch the by-product of the attainment of the Platonic harmony and equilibrium, is converted into stasis and passivity. And these are exactly the qualities Mutter Gisson has acquired after conquering spiritual death. Mutter Gisson's noninterference at the ritual murder of her granddaughter brings this out very clearly: redemption can only be self-redemption, never mass redemption as Marius proclaims. Her noninterference also marks the limits of her system, which is no longer capable of absorbing new challenges such as those posed by Marius. In harmony with nature and its great cycles of life and death, Mutter Gisson transcends the time levels into a state of panpsychic timelessness: she is the Mutter Gisson of the narrated present and symbolizes the Magna Mater of archaic myth.[15] When she says to the country doctor "my time is over," she not only predicts her personal death but also the end of her rule and authority, and speaks the verdict over the archetype she represents. The matriarchal society which she represents, and which is sure in its knowledge but passive and nonmilitant, is being subjugated by Marius into visions of male hegemony. That Mutter Gisson's end was inevitable is perhaps more clearly explained by reference to the system than by reliance on her words and deeds alone. Her self-contained wisdom and knowledge was possible in a static system, such as a secluded mountain village, sheltered from the influx of modern society and technology. Mutter Gisson can ignore the radio and the mechnical harvest equipment (typically enough, in the small upper village, where she lives, the harvest is still thrashed by hand, as opposed to the larger lower village) and the plight of the Wetchy family as belonging to an inconsequential opposition system; she can absorb the alien system presented by the country doctor, since he never questions her authority but, on the contrary, seeks refuge in the

wholeness she has to offer; but she is curiously impassive against
Marius' militant inveiglements.

While Mutter Gisson (passively) and Marius (aggressively) are both
ensconced in their respective systems, it is the country doctor who
represents the inconsistencies of transitory phases. In the wake of his
unhappy love for Barbara he leaves the city, abandons medical
research and the concomitant "abstract" scientific profession to seek a
life in contact with nature and its cycles. He leads a hybrid existence
with an amalgamation of flight into the past and advance toward the
future. His house is modern but incomplete (despite faucets and wash
basins, it has no running water). Ignorant of the healing properties of
herbs, a specialty of Mutter Gisson's, and unable to overcome the
farmers' distrust of "modern," manufactured prescriptions, he finds
himself preparing medications in his office. While he is repulsed by
the physical ugliness and intense anxieties of the Wetchy family, he
cannot simply ignore them, as does Mutter Gisson, nor can he side
with Marius, who fashions them into the village scapegoats. He
considers it his duty to help them and in this manner stands between
Mutter Gisson (nature and the past) and the Wetchys (the future in
the city). Yet when the Wetchys' return to the city indicates an
acceptance of the horrors of modern, abstract, anxiety-ridden existence, the country doctor upholds his flight into a past which, even
while he is looking on, loses its aspect as a refuge and develops into
the nightmare of terrestrial hell. But most of all, the country doctor's
unresolved in-between-times position is evident in his relation to
women. He idolizes a mother-child cult and while clearly aware that
it is historically passé (as symbolized by the plaster madonna of the
pilgrims' church), he concludes his account of the events by hoping
for a new piety, to be incarnated in the newborn male child of Agathe
(*B*, I, 439). The mother-child cult is a retreat into a historical past, but
since it supersedes matriarchy historically, it also indicates historical
progress.

A view of Mutter Gisson in relation to her three "sons" can provide
another key to the various systems simultaneously at work against
each other. Mutter Gisson has one natural son, the hunter Matthias.
Though he is in total agreement with her in almost every respect, he
has broken out of the agricultural orientation of archaic matriarchies
and chosen the nomadic life of the hunter. The ensuing independence from the matriarchal system is expressed in the fact that he is a
bachelor, not inclined to fulfill his mother's wish to marry and have
children. The country doctor is a kind of "adopted" son and easy to get

along with because he represents no challenge to Mutter Gisson's system. He and Agathe are present at Mutter Gisson's death as the only witnesses still in contact with the unity she represents. Marius is the "false" son; false because his entire conception of what she stands for is false; false because he wants to be initiated into her system for false (exploitative) reasons; and false because the imitation system with which he challenges Mutter Gisson and entices the village is premised on false assumptions. If Mutter Gisson represents an archaic matriarchal myth, Marius demonstrates its perversion into an imitation system in the guise of patriarchal hegemony. In his cultic, chauvinistic demagoguery, Marius rejects the development into ever greater abstraction and longs for a return to mythologized nature. Imitating Mutter Gisson's intimacy with the cycles of nature, he is yet unable to confront death; he drowns his fears in blood and violence and exorcises them "magically."

A characteristic common to all of Broch's novels is a tendency for geometrically arranged structural patterns. The *Mountain Novel* can be diagrammed as a quaternity of systems pinpointing the various protagonists. Mutter Gisson, though on intimate terms with death and the irrational and representing a harmonious system, is closed to historical progress. Opposed to her is the system of Marius, representing a deliberate repression of the fears inspired by the irrationality of death, and attempting to exorcise them by magical means. This is the imitation system propagating hate, terror, and death under the guise of redemption. The third cornerstone in this quaternity is the system of the country doctor, an uneasy and eclectic opposition system. When the doctor watches the slaying of Irmgard, mesmerized and unable to interfere, it is made explicit that no amount of good will and humane intentions alone suffice to stem the tide of anxieties erupting from the irrational. Despite the doctor's cogent comments on the events in the village and his humane personality, he is left singularly defenseless in the outburst of mass hysteria. In this character Broch has given a warning signal for rational and reasonable people who believe themselves immune against rebarbarization.

The fourth element of the quaternity is the Wetchy family. Calvinists and city people, they lead a dire existence in nature and a community to which they do not relate and where the only reason for staying is a meager financial income eked out by selling the products of technology: insurance policies, farm equipment, and radios. In terms of Broch's philosophy of history, the Wetchys are the most "abstract" people, uprooted and dislocated as only the Jews were in

The Sleepwalkers. In their alienation and "otherness" they become easy scapegoats of Marius' invectives. They alone of all the village inhabitants are not present at Irmgard's murder. For all their imperfections, their fears, their physical ugliness, and the dislike they inspire in everybody, these are the people of the future—a fact which is substantiated by their move back to the city, into the vanguard of technology and modernism and into the abstractness of existence.

If the four systems can be viewed as a spatial, geometrical pattern acted out in the confines of the mountain village, a similar quadruple structure can be identified on the temporal level. The novel presents in four of the protagonists four major stages of civilization. Mutter Gisson stands for primeval matriarchy; yet clearly, as she herself realizes, her time is over. Marius' imitation system represents the imposition of male hegemony over natural cycles. Marius comprises the various stages of "emerging man," from his desire to be son to Mutter Gisson, through the assumption of the role of husband and father (*B*, I, 248, 249), to exclusive male hegemony and the subjugation of woman. Historically, this change signals the development from matriarchy to patriarchy, from harmony with nature to domination of it. The doctor's idolization of the mother-child cult offers a sentimental version of patriarchal man's longing to annul his emancipation. Broch views this sentimentalizing negatively, as the dissolution of austere myth into the closed system of charming legend.[16] (The doctor's chiliastic expectations in the age of abstract secularization belong as much to the closed system and are, in Broch's terminology, as much *Kitsch* as the plaster madonna of the mountain chapel and the pilgrimage for the *Steinsegen,* the blessing on the mountain rock.) While the country doctor remains tied to the hopes for redemption proffered by the closed system, the Wetchy family epitomizes the trend toward a city-oriented and technology-dominated future. In that family, Broch has striven for a synthesis of the "matter-of-fact" qualities of Huguenau and the child Marguerite, and the ethical components manifest in obedience to the law of an unimaginably abstract god exemplified in the Orthodox Jews of *The Sleepwalkers.* The juxtaposition of these "modern" qualities in the Wetchy family provides at least a sketchy glimpse of man as he survives the "atomization of values."

The systems view can be further exemplified in a minor theme, the deaths of the three women, Mutter Gisson, Irmgard, and Barbara. Mutter Gisson, at the end of a long and full life, "lives into death." The metamorphoses, which in Broch's work always indicate the

opening up of a deeper awareness, dominate: song fuses with the
sounds and silences of nature; light dissolves firm contours and
becomes its own reality. Here, more than in any other of Broch's
literary writings, the description of a *participation mystique*
threatens to burst the frame of the narrative. In *The Death of Virgil*,
the strong emphasis on the visual and auditory elements of such
participation allows for concrete rendition even of the most abstract
states. But in the *Mountain Novel*, the concrete basis is abandoned
for an indulgent mystification.

This is particularly obvious in the example of Irmgard's violent and
"false" death, suffered within the imitation system. Her death cannot
redeem the village and establish the communal ties Marius had
hoped for in the form of magical blood bonds; it cannot even bring
peace to Irmgard herself though she embraces this death with
eagerness. In a last manifestation of her effusive oneness with nature,
Mutter Gisson searches, in the manner of shamans, for the soul of her
dead grandchild, who has been misled into a travesty of redemption,
and genuinely redeems her into harmony with the natural cycles.
Broch pursues in none of his other writings the consequences of a
death falsely died into such a purely speculative beyond. Not even in
The Death of Virgil, his monumental exploration of the boundaries
between life and death, would he allow himself again to be side-
tracked from mysticism into mystification.

The suicide of the pediatrician Barbara is the other example of a
death falsely died in this female triad. Barbara kills herself following
the failure of a Communist plot to assassinate a politician—a plot
which she had been instrumental in devising. In an extended
flashback, significantly located at the center of the novel, the country
doctor reminisces on how he had met Barbara in the children's ward
of a city hospital, how they had fallen in love, and how he had hoped
they would be married and have a child. Barbara is, up to a point, the
modern version of the ideal woman. Living in the city and practicing
medicine, she is in intimate contact with technological society as it
works for the good of mankind, combatting death with concrete
means. Being a pediatrician, she integrates the motherly role of
woman into her professional activities. Depite the physician's technical and scientific knowledge and skills in practicing the art of
medicine she bases her diagnoses on intuition. When Barbara, in one
instance, does not follow her diagnostic instincts but the suggestion of
a man—the country doctor—the child dies. This insecurity with
regard to her own abilities (an insecurity Mutter Gisson would never

have felt) shows in other respects too: she feels that her profession, a substitute motherhood, excludes the possibility of ever having children of her own. She cannot see how personal satisfaction through a fulfilling family life is compatible with a satisfying role in society. The country doctor subscribes to the same dualistic view. He opts for Barbara's abandoning her career to become the mother of their children, while she denies herself children as well as marriage in order to find them symbolically on a vaster scale: her children are the children of the hospital, her marriage is to Communism. Becoming pregnant is tantamount to forsaking the social and political role she had constructed for herself. Here Communism, in a strongly idiosyncratic interpretation, is viewed as incompatible with the aspirations and hopes of private life. Communism, in both Barbara's and the doctor's eyes, insists on the negation of the individual for the sake of the "cause," culminating, if need be, in the sacrifice of human life (in Barbara's instance, in assassination and suicide). Although her death occurs within an infinitely more conscious and more rational context than Irmgard's magic sacrifice, the death of each is required by a system which is antihuman. Despite Barbara's progressive value system and all her humanly engaging features, Broch shows that she, too, adheres to the wrong system, since it negates the value of life.

Yet the doctor's alternative is equally unacceptable. It denies personal as well as social progress for the sake of upholding traditional rules which are irrelevant in a new society. Barbara's need to join the Communist Party is closely related to her choice of profession: in both instances she satisfies the need to help, and to change existing practices and standards. The doctor's myopic view is reemphasized when he leaves the city after Barbara's death and takes refuge in the country of Mutter Gisson. As in *The Sleepwalkers,* Broch demonstrates all the negative options available to people during disintegrative phases of history. He shows the fallacies of their decisions at the same time that he demonstrates their need to belong to value systems, even if they are "wrong". Yet in none of his writings is Broch willing to portray a value system which sketches in concrete terms viable possibilities for the "new man." (Significantly, the Wetchy family disappears from the narrative context once it moves into the city.)

The *Mountain Novel* is a political book in the sense that it shows the psychology of demagoguery and mass psychosis. It contributes toward a critique of historical consciousness through an analysis of mythological thinking. As a farewell to previously held mythologies, it enacts the tenacity with which the human mind clings to and incarnates mythological patterns in an effort to structure reality. The most valuable insight here is that myths are subject to historical change, an observation that militates against any absolutist conception of sempiternal archetypes. At this point, Broch's protagonists in the *Mountain Novel* become symptomatic of a condition he has analyzed in its historical context: ". . . we experience everywhere today a euphoric and spasmodic revival of all forms of religion; and humanity is more than ever in constant readiness to follow whoever demands dedication to something, even if this something is recognized for the surrogate it is" (*GW*, VIII, 106).

The novel fails when the critical frame of historic relativism is absorbed into the panmystic effusions of Mutter Gisson and her anachronistic disciple, the country doctor. Too much detailed care is devoted to the scenes of transpersonal *participation mystique* as symptoms of "a euphoric and spasmodic revival" of religious forms. The doctor's mystic experiences offer only one variety among many, documented in the novel, to find refuge in a metaphysically oriented value system. Yet this exemplary quality is frequently buried under the impact of too many dominating visions of all-unity and harmony. When the *participation mystique* insinuates itself as an "absolute" answer, the basis for criticism of religious attitudes is destroyed. The novel then becomes one more propagator of one more religious experience, rather than a statement on religious phenomena as subject to historical change and as response to historical conditions.

II   *Search for alternatives—the League of Nations?*

Broch's ambivalence toward writing literature intensified drastically during the years in which he wrote the *Mountain Novel*. His letters of the second half of the decade were much more skeptical about the possibility that the novel can fulfill the role religion once played in containing man's fear of death and in keeping alive the Platonic Idea. While he was at work on the *Mountain Novel*, he increasingly felt that "the contemporary world in its disintegration of values no longer has a place for intellectual and artistic achievements" (*GW*, VIII, 148).[17] What was previously the highest ethical duty now became an unethical undertaking: "It is almost unethical to force something upon [the world] that it does not need, instead of giving it—if one really wants to be ethical—what it does need" (*GW*, VIII, 148). Yet even in the face of fascism he could not see that individual efforts would no longer make a difference in stemming a disastrous tide. The idealistic "constant" with its pronounced emphasis on the individual was ineradicably part of Broch's way of thinking and was evident in his suggestions for ameliorating the world situation: "What [the world] needs [is] the alleviation of its spasms; on the large scale this could be done politically; on the small scale by taking care of a group of people and by helping them as much as one's strength allows; this, of course, the egocentric poet is not in a position to do" (*GW*, VIII, 148).

Despairing over the poet's mission—and anything less than a mission was unacceptable—Broch repeatedly wondered whether he should not go back to the field of his strongest talent, mathematics (*GW*, VIII, 156), although he realized that the scientific development of the last few years (the period since he left the University of Vienna in 1930) must have overtaken him (*GW*, VIII, 156). Broch's situation in 1036, on his fiftieth birthday, was clouded. He was depressed over the political situation; fighting for reprieve from harrassing family obligations; torn over the decision between science and literature; doubtful of the cognitive-ethical efficacy of literature amid spreading fascisms; and haunted by the awareness that he was running out of time. This consideration weighed heavily on him, as is evident in the many references to aging in his correspondence; it also became an "objective" criterion in his essay on James Joyce, which was originally written in honor of Joyce's fiftieth birthday in 1932 but not published until 1936. He began to doubt that cognition was the high road toward the unattainable Platonic Idea and wondered "whether human simplicity and forthrightness is not *above* cognition. . . ." He mused: "the older I become and the more I look at my own life, the clearer it is to me that the actually positive side lies in this simplicity and in the simple human relations, let us dare say, of the heart . . ." (*GW*, VIII, 155).

While Broch was increasingly hemmed in by the Kantian categorical imperative, which was an inadequate instrument to deal with mass phenomena and mass hysteria, he was simultaneously engaged in a losing battle where his platonically oriented poetic mission was concerned. The discrepancy between the recognized political ineffectiveness of literature on the one hand, and the insistence on its Platonic-religious mission on the other, led to an ever widening polarization which, according to Broch, could only be overcome with ever more imposing literary creations—with myth:

Sub opooio aotornitatis our times certainly allow the creation of great works of poetry and not merely of detective stories; but the discrepancy between temporality and timelessness is so extremely great, and the skepsis about values has become so overwhelming, that only an overpowering work of art can withstand these times. This work would barely belong to these times any more, but already prepare the future integration of values; it would belong to the future, at least in its religious aspects—a work of art, which could only be created from the cataclysms of these times, hence a mythical work; vide Homer. (*GW*, VIII, 148–49)

The struggle to penetrate to those irrational levels, where the mythical imagination creates unselfconsciously, lies at the core of Broch's creative endeavors, in the *Mountain .Novel* as in all his subsequent literary works. Yet despite his "literary and intellectual qualifications which are good perhaps even very good," he did not have the talent for "the Homeric mythical work" (*GW*, VIII, 149). As Broch saw it, only Kafka, among all the writers he knew, had penetrated to those levels where the myth of the new age may take its shape. In the Hofmannsthal essay, written in the last years of his life, he speaks for himself when he states bluntly:

For the modern myth, which so many poets have the ambition to write, does not exist: there exists only something which could properly be called countermyth. For myth is cosmogony; it is description of the primordial forces threatening and destroying man, and myth opposes their symbolization by Promethean symbols, no less gigantic and heroic, demonstrating how man can overcome what is apparently unsurmountable and how he can live on this earth; nothing of this applies today. . . . [Ours is] the situation of extreme helplessness, and Kafka, not Joyce, has done it justice; in Kafka we find the beginnings of an adequate countermyth in whose repertory the heroic symbols, the father–and even the mother symbols' are of small importance or even superfluous because what really matters is the symbolization of helplessness per se, which means the symbolization of the child. (*GW*, VI, 164)

Since Kafka[18] is the only "true" poet of our age according to Broch's definition, Broch relegates himself to those authors who, in the manner of epigones, make use of traditional mythical patterns in order to comment on the present. He nevertheless traveled in the best company, as he jokingly admitted: "The professional writer can only long for these things [the creation of the new Homeric myth], be his name Joyce, Mann, or Broch (as you see, I am rather self-assured in selecting my companions) but he does not have them and will never be able to have them" (*GW*, VIII, 149). Or: "In this sense, 'artistic' writers like Joyce or Th. M. are simply atavisms, much more

Victorian leftovers [*Plüschsofa*] than one would expect, and unfortunately I too belong to them" (*GW*, VIII, 155).

Sometime during 1936–1937, Broch stopped work on the *Mountain Novel*. He turned to what seemed politically more relevant work and started to draft sketches for a "Resolution," to be submitted to the League of Nations, whose prestige was at a critical low while the international situation had reached new dimensions of political crisis. The League had hesitated far too long to take a firm stand as an instrument for the preservation of peace. In October, 1935, Mussolini had embarked on war with Ethiopia and, more ominously, in March, 1936, Hitler had occupied the demilitarized Saarland without causing much protest. This *coup* established Hitler as a dominant European power whom Mussolini did not want to antagonize. The days of Austrian independence, based on Italian protection, were numbered. When the Spanish Civil War erupted in the same year, the League's attitude of noninterference was equally unfortunate.

With the "Resolution" Broch resumed a practice he had abandoned in 1919, after his contribution to the post–World War I economic and social situation in the essay "Constitutional Dictatorship as Democratic Council System." In direct response to political events, he now again sought to chart a practical political solution inspired by maximum respect for individual man. His suggestions for the League of Nations were not unlike several other attempts of that time, such as the "International Peace Campaign," designed to reestablish the League as the prime instrument in preserving peace (*Re*, 9).

Broch had led a rather peripatetic life since leaving Vienna in the fall of 1934 in a state of exhaustion and panic. He may have returned for the larger part of 1937 because he needed to do research in the theory of law and philosophy of politics.[19] Work on the "Resolution" provided him with the impetus to develop a "theory of humanity" and set the guidelines for his studies in the theory of politics and democracy in the years of exile.[20] Although Broch had a philosophical system at his disposal and a methodology flexible enough to include a "theory of humanity" and its subdivisions of law, politics, and a theory of democracy, the fields of inquiry he staked out were enormous. Nothing in his background had prepared him for these disciplines. This complete change amounted to a beginning from scratch, not unlike the time when he opted for literature instead of mathematics. But now Broch was over fifty years old and the political situation allowed for even fewer chances of success than ten years earlier. Yet the "theory of humanity" became most important in his search for justification of intellectual endeavors. Broch's despair over the inefficacy of literature as a tool of ethical and political enlightenment lessened as he reaffirmed the conviction that ideas and the work of the intellectual are the factors ultimately shaping history. While this conviction was consistent with his theory of cognitive breakthroughs, the shift from a poetic to a philosophical-discursive presentation of these breakthroughs necessitated a painful reorientation in his thought. Broch's faith in the importance of intellectual work is sounded in his presentation of the "Völkerbundstudie" ("Study for the League of Nations"): ". . . intellectual work and the intellectual are often reproached as being ignorant of the ways of the world; and this reproach has intimidated many an intellectual to withdraw into the 'ivory tower'; yet this ignorance of the world has, over and over, changed the course of history . . ." (GW, IX, 47).[21]

The "Resolution" consists of seven "Principles," additional "Desiderata," and an appendix. In them, Broch proposed to anchor the conditions for peace in the recognition of human dignity and human rights, not as abstract entities but concretely incarnated in every human being. (This conception foreshadows his later formulation of the "earthly absolute" in which every abstract pronouncement must become infused with the content "man.") To safeguard against nationalistic interpretations of human rights and human dignity, their recognition should not be left to the discretion of individual governments but be the concern of an internationally composed body charged with law enforcement. Though no government was mentioned by name, Broch clearly referred to events in Germany and the treatment of the German Jews by the Nazis. He stressed this point further in his opposition to legislation through which "wrongs can be intensified to legalized injustices" (Re, 38), and in his polemics against "forced emigration and expatriation" (Re, 41). Against the background of the Italian invasion of Ethiopia and the Spanish Civil War, he remained an adamant pacifist, suggesting not only that wars should be avoided, but that those attitudes which lead to dehumanization and make wars acceptable, should be punished (Re, 37). At the same time, the League of Nations should engage in active propaganda for its principles, using all available means of modern advertising to create a countercounsciouness to the prevailing terroristic strategies of the Fascists.

A series of letters dating from November, 1937, attest to the fact that Broch considered the "Resolution" completed. He contacted prominent persons, such as Albert Einstein, Thomas Mann, Jacques Maritain, Stefan Zweig, and the publisher of his first philosophical essays, Ludwig von Ficker, hoping to submit the "Resolution" to the League of Nations with their backing. The correspondence is interesting insofar as it reveals Broch's basically conservative or antirevolutionary attitude, expressed in strict adherence to parliamentary procedures and his acceptance of "necessary" compromise.[22] The author of "Die Strasse" (1918) and of the view (1931) that "revolutions are insurrections of evil against evil, insurrections of the irrational against the rational, insurrections of the irrational masquerading as extreme logical reasoning . . ." (*SW*, 636–37) was not likely to advocate drastic, let alone radical, measures to advance a case premised on the respect for and dignity of every individual human being. In answer to Maritain's suggestion to control the war industry, in particular the production of crude oil, by placing it under the supervision of the League of Nations, Broch finds this proposal too provocative. He answers Maritain on November 14, 1937: "I am not of this opinion. One must not provide the adversary—and here one must count on those who are addressed as being adversaries—in advance with the opportunity to refuse; in my view, the maximum of what can be attained at the present is a discussion on the full floor of the League of Nations; even the initiation of such a discussion would be hampered if one burdened it with too many material concerns, which would be refused anyway" (*Re*, 85–86).

Undoubtedly, Broch's propositions were intended to provide the League with a new ethical basis after the luster of its initial statutes had been so pitifully tarnished. With his insistence that the dignity of every human being become the cornerstone of any constitution and be placed under the jurisdiction of an international court, Broch may well have found the Archimedean point from which to move the societies of the world into an approximation of global peace and harmony. Yet considered in the context of political practice, one cannot help but be amazed at his naiveté, despite his appreciation that ". . . no ethical goal can be pursued without a 'realistically' oriented political [*realpolitischer*] background" (*Re*, 16). Not only was he naive when he opposed Maritain's action-oriented suggestions with those stressing further discussions, he was also singularly myopic when he interpreted political events. On Italy's invasion of Ethiopia he said: "The key to the situation was Italy, which would have liked to make ideological concessions if her justified claims for a

collective policy of mandates in the colonies would have been
satisfied even to some degree; only with great hesitation and, again,
with ideological concessions did she then turn to an alliance with
Germany" (Re, 16).[23] Broch's criticism of the League of Nations was
in agreement with general sentiment; similarly, his view of Italy was
conditioned by prevalent pro-Italian propaganda.

In his suggestions for a more durable League he ignored the very
problem which caused its crisis and eventual demise: laws and statutes
are always dependent on the power of the executive to enforce them.
The impotence of the League was not due to faulty statutes but to the
vacillating attitude of its members who in turn reflected specific
national interests.

The "Resolution" was not published as originally intended. As
Broch later saw it, this was fortunate. As late as January, 1938, he still
hoped to have it printed, albeit in a limited number of copies. The
Anschluss on March 13, 1938, abolished these plans. A local zealot of
Alt-Aussee, the mailman, who wanted to ingratiate himself with the
new regime, provided information on Broch's correspondence. As a
result, Broch was immediately thrown into jail. His publications
played no role in his arrest. As he noted in a letter from a much later
date, this incarceration forced him to confront the possibility of death
and provided the visionary and mystic impetus for the cognitive quest
of death soon to be embodied in The Death of Virgil. On March 31,
Broch was released from jail to go to Vienna. The next few months
were taken up with hectic activities to obtain a visa while living under
the constant threat of being apprehended and sent to a concentration
camp (Broch's mother died in Theresienstadt). Various friends and
acquaintances, among them Franz Werfel, Robert Neumann, and
indirectly James Joyce[24] helped to obtain an English visa, and Broch
was able to leave Vienna for London on July 29. After a brief sojourn
there, he followed a long-standing invitation of Willa and Edwin
Muir, the English translators of The Sleepwalkers, and spent two
months with them in Scotland. On the basis of affidavits and recommendations of Albert Einstein and Thomas Mann, he subsequently
obtained an American visa valid for four months. Despite the Munich
Agreement of September 30, 1938, he was convinced that war was
inevitable and "two days after Munich" (GW, VIII, 169) he left by
ship for the United States.

CHAPTER 5

The Descent ad inferos

IN the early 1930s, after the completion of *The Sleepwalkers*, Broch established a pattern which proved a tremendous handicap to his creative output. He would begin work on some project only to find its "ethical relevance" overtaken by political events. In the six years between the completion of *The Sleepwalkers* and his emigration, the frequency of beginning, interrupting, resuming, and finally abandoning a project is particularly obvious. If the political situation caused the intellectual disorientation and the fragmented approach, the years in exile should have provided a unifying focus. But the pattern persisted, though apparently for different reasons.

The sources of Broch's income and his living conditions in exile from late 1938 until 1951 are interesting, since they reflect his aspirations, frustrations, and accomplishments. Broch arrived in New York on board the Dutch steamship "Statendam" on October 9, 1938. For the next few months he took up residence in various inexpensive boardinghouses in the vicinity of Columbia University and established contact with the Writers in Exile—PEN Center (American Branch). The American Guild for German Cultural Freedom paid him a stipend for a few months. He immediately became active in rescue activities, in securing affidavits for prospective emigrants, in setting up funds, and inadvertently built up a correspondence of tremendous proportions. On the basis of his continued preoccupation with the "Resolution", he submitted in mid-1939 a "Proposal for the Foundation of a Research Institute in Political Psychology and the Study of Phenomena of Mass Hysteria" to three institutions: to the Institute of Advanced Studies in Princeton (c/o Albert Einstein); to the New School for Social Research; and to the Rockefeller Foundation. In consequence, Einstein was instrumental in Broch's being awarded a small stipend from the Oberlander Trust.

In March and April, 1939, Broch was invited to the home of the influential critic Henry Seidel Canby in Killingworth, Connecticut, then spent a brief period in Davenport College at Yale University. Through Canby's support, Broch was awarded a Guggenheim fellowship for a period of eighteen months. The fellowship was granted for work on *The Death of Virgil*. This meant that Broch had to discontinue his studies in mass psychology and political theory in order to write a novel. From June through the middle of August of the same year he stayed at the writers' colony at Yaddo, where he reimmersed himself in work on the novel and where he met Jean Starr Untermeyer, the future translator of *The Death of Virgil*. For the next month, while Einstein was away, Broch lived at Einstein's house in Princeton. After Einstein's return in mid-September, Broch took lodgings of his own in Princeton, where he remained until the spring of 1940. After the German occupation of France, Broch returned to New York in order to work more efficiently for those refugees who had escaped to France and were now desperate to enter the United States, Mexico, and the South American countries. The Guggenheim fellowship expired in 1941 with the novel far from complete; the major part of Broch's time had been spent working on behalf of refugees.

In 1941, Broch contributed to a collective statement, *The City of Man: A Declaration on World Democracy*, issued by a number of concerned American and refugee intellectuals. The participants consisted, among others, of Thomas Mann; his son-in-law G. A. Borgese; Alvin Johnson, director of the New School for Social Research in New York; and Christian Gauss, dean at Princeton University.[1] A few months later, when Broch needed recommendations to back up an application for a grant submitted to the Rockefeller Foundation, these scholars and friends proved helpful. In May, 1942, a one-year Rockefeller grant was awarded for research in the theory of politics and mass psychology.

The contacts in Princeton continued to bring Broch good luck and friendship. In June of the same year, he was invited to the home of Erich Kahler in Princeton, where he stayed as a guest for the next six years in close and cordial relationship with his host. Compared with the desperate situation of many other emigrants, Broch was fairly comfortably off. In April, 1943, the Rockefeller grant was extended for another twenty months, providing Broch with a meager, though secure income. Yet when the grant expired, at the end of 1944, Broch had no "book" to show for the two and a half years of financial support.

Instead he had completed *The Death of Virgil*, which appeared in English and German as World War II drew to its end. He had decided to finish the novel in order to justify the continued trust and help of many friends. Although he realized that this esoteric and difficult work did not live up to his own critical standards in 1945, he had finally "delivered" on the Guggenheim fellowship. To spend even more time refining a novel that pointed toward noncommunication and the ivory tower, Broch felt, would have been immoral, considering his doubts about the efficacy of *Dichtung* (*GW*, VIII, 280–81). These very problems are reflected in the novel itself, where Virgil, in an extreme gesture of humility, allows the incomplete work to exist not as a document to art but to friendship.

In January, 1946, Broch received yet another fellowship for a period of eighteen months, awarded by the Old Dominion Foundation which later became the Bolingen Foundation. The stipend was granted for continued work in mass psychology. Yet this was the period following World War II, and as in 1940, most of his time, energy, and money went into helping refugees. He invested his resources in sending CARE packages,[2] was involved in the activities of the American Committee for Refugee Scholars, Writers and Artists,[3] and became entangled in an avalanche of correspondence which, as he frequently pointed out, drained his time and energy more than any other activity.

An example is the extensive correspondence Broch carried on with Thomas Mann and the Nobel prize-winning physicist James F. Franck. Franck's group sought support for a petition to the United States government to send food and to desist from taking revenge on Germany at the conclusion of the war.[4] Instead of a unilateral support of Germany, Broch suggested preferred treatment of those persecuted by the Nazi regime. He sought to add legislative proposals designed to democratize Germany and thus to avoid a resurgence of Nazi ideology. All these efforts proved superfluous since the appeal was never submitted. In November, 1945, President Truman had sent a special envoy, Byron Pierce, to investigate the situation in Germany. Pierce's report, and strong pressure from the Quakers, led to decisions by President Truman which made the appeal unnecessary. It seems ironic that so many of Broch's practical suggestions for more humane politics and a firmer establishment of democracy through appropriate legislation and education were either made obsolete by events or ignored by institutions, where they ended in archives.

After the expiration of the fellowship from the Old Dominion Foundation in June, 1947, Broch had still not produced a book on

mass psychology. He was then sixty years old and without financial
support. Although *The Death of Virgil* was a major literary achievement, he found himself in a more precarious situation than when he
first arrived in the United States. From Princeton he wrote on July
17, 1947, to his friend Brody of his thwarted hopes and aspirations:

To tell you right away of myself and the mass psychology: it has not been
completed and this has brought me—for the first time in nine years—into a
truly catastrophic situation. Had it been completed, I would have been
assured of a position here at the Institute and for the rest of my life I would
have been taken care of well, indeed more than well. This I had been
firmly promised. However, I am not finished, cannot even predict when I
will be. Hence it is a basically embarrassing situation, for *if* anything should
still happen, it will happen due to their good graces and I will have to accept
whatever is being offered to me. Even when I have finished the book, in one
or two years, I can no longer make the same demands that I could make
today. And most idiotic of all is the fact that this delay is to a large extent
due to the correspondence; since Europe has been reopened, it has taken at
least half of my time. (*BBB*, 483)

Broch had found it impossible to complete the political studies
when the fellowships paid him to do so. Now, without any source of
income, he was forced to bow to the plans of publishers. He reluc-
tantly accepted to write an introduction to the collected works of
Hugo von Hofmannsthal, which the Bollingen Foundation planned
to publish (*BBB*, 489). As could be expected from Broch's manner of
work, even a project which at first did not interest him and which was
supposed to be quite short, soon engendered his interest. The
introduction grew into the lengthy study "Hofmannsthal und seine
Zeit" ("Hofmannsthal and his Times"). It is an impressive analysis of
the social and cultural background of *fin-de-siècle* Vienna, the period
which Broch came to call "the gay apocalypse." In the meantime, the
publisher became impatient. Under his pressure Broch finally produced a short introductory piece, while the bulk of his study remained unpublished until after his death.

Not only were his prospects for a professional position darkening,
but in June, 1948, on the day he was scheduled to make a presentation at the United Nations, he fell and broke his hip.[5] For ten months,
he stayed in Princeton Hospital. After his release in April, 1949, he
could no longer occupy his old room in the Kahler house: he had
become incapable of climbing stairs (*BBB*, 496). During the summer
months, Saybrook College at Yale university offered him room and

board. In the fall, when the students returned, he took a room of his own near the college and retained his residence in New Haven until his death in 1951.

All along, the fragmented work pattern continued. During the postwar period, German publishers again demanded his work. He answered with *The Guiltless* in 1950 and continued his work on mass hysteria and the psychology of politics. His essay of 1950 "Trotzdem: Humane Politik Verwirklichung einer Utopie" ("Nevertheless: Humane Politics. The Realization of a Utopia") is the last political document published during his lifetime. At another publisher's urging and under financial duress, he began to rework the *Mountain Novel*. On the eve of his first trip back to Europe and following earlier heart troubles, he died of a heart attack in New Haven on May 31, 1951. He is buried in Killingsworth, Connecticut.

I *Virgil's quest*

Broch started work on *The Death of Virgil* in spring, 1937. According to his later reminiscences, the Austrian radio network had asked him to read from his work. [6] Broch had recently (in December, 1936) published his "Erwägungen zum Problem des Kulturtodes" ("Reflections Concerning the Problem of the Death of Culture") as a response to the darkening political skies and the outbreak of the Civil War in Spain. In a similar spirit, he now wrote "Die Heimkehr des Vergil" ("Virgil's Homecoming"), because

. . . it did not need much reflection to remember the parallels between the first pre-Chrisitan century and ours—civil war, dictatorship, a dying off of old religious forms; indeed, even the phenomenon of emigration offered significant parallels, namely, in Tomi, the fishing village on the Black Sea. In addition, I knew of a legend in which Virgil had wanted to burn the Aeneid and—accepting the legend—I could assume that a mind such as Virgil's could not have been driven to such an act of despair by petty reasons but rather that the entire historical and metaphysical content of the epoch had had its share in the decision. (*GW*, VIII, 243)

Soon after completion of the brief story Broch began to expand the text, dividing his time between it and the "Resolution." The text accompanied him to the prison in Alt-Aussee, where he began a totally new section, the "elegies on fate." [7] He continued work on the novel during his stay with the Muirs in Scotland in August and September, 1938, while waiting for the American visa. Encouraged by the Guggenheim fellowship, he resumed work sporadically in the

United States soon after his arrival and completed the novel as World
War II drew to its end.

The novel describes the last twenty-four hours of Virgil's life. It is
divided into four sections, with each of the first three sections
increasing by a basic unit and the last one returning to the length of
the first section, that is, 1x, 2x, 3x, and x. Each section bears a double
title: Water—the Arrival; Fire—the Descent; Earth—the Expectation; and Air—the Homecoming. The four sections indicate way
stations on Virgil's journey into death. At the same time, Virgil
experiences within the cycle of one day the cycle of his entire life,
which opens into a cosmic cycle of becoming and dying and is part of a
metamythological structure of Broch's own device. [8]

A mythological deity presides over each of the first three sections of
the novel. However, the limits are fluid and all of the mythological
figures and references keep appearing to the very end of Virgil's
consciousness, which coincides with the end of the novel. The
pervasive use of classical mythology in the novel serves several
functions. Above all, it substantiates the historical portrayal of Virgil
and creates the specific narrative limiting factor. It draws on contemporary psychology, notably Jung's theory of archetypes, where the
mythological figures are understood as forces of the collective unconscious; Virgil's "process of individuation"[9] is completed when he has
achieved recognition and integration of these forces within himself.
As carriers of cognition, these myths serve as significant epistemological tools, accompanying Virgil on his cognitive journey into death.

Coming from Athens, the dying Virgil arrives in the train of Caesar
Augustus in the late afternoon at the harbor of Brundisium in
Southern Italy. The arrival by ship occurs under the auspices of
Poseidon, god of the oceans, shaker of the earth, creator and tamer of
horses. (The attributes of this god are used "realistically" when, for
example, Virgil's fever hallucinations make him feel the earth shake
underneath him or transform the stability of the room into the rolling
waves of the ocean.) The masses, assembled to greet the arriving
Caesar, jam the harbor and prevent an orderly disembarking. The
slave-boy and musician Lysanias guide Virgil's ascent to Caesar's
castle which in the falling night appears infernally lit by torches; and
he accompanies Virgil to his room in the tower. The tower evokes the
ivory tower, appropriate for the artist Virgil, but the southwest
exposure of his room also has mythological significance as the direction which the dead must face when buried. The detour to the castle
under Lysanias' guidance, designed to avoid Virgil's embroilment

with the mob, is of no avail. In the ascent through the Misery Alley (*Elendsgasse*), Virgil experiences the obscene jokes, the brutality and the filth of the plebs. As artist and aesthete, he cannot bear this confrontation and veils his head. This exposure is, on the epistemological level, an encounter with those who have no aspirations and are cognitively unredeemed. On the psychological level, it is a first confrontation with the frightening realm of the mothers who, significantly, call Virgil a "baby." In the course of the night, Virgil will run the gauntlet from the obscene, primordial mothers via a blunt Aphrodite-whore in the second part of the novel to the sophisticated, alluring temptress Plotia, seducing the adult Virgil into staying with her in her "love nest" in the third part of the novel. In all these instances and their numerous variations in the novel, the female is viewed in the conventional archetypal interpretation as the unconscious and as the agent opposed to deliberate conscious development.

Virgil's arrival by water also reenacts a primordial birth issuing forth from the realm of the mothers. Within the cycle of twenty-four hours, Virgil will recapitulate his life from birth to death, integrating his childhood into adult life. His success is reflected in the transformation of the female figure, when the chthonic powers are overcome through acceptance, and Plotia is "redeemed" into the "eternal feminine" who, in the fourth part, with a beatific smile and with Lysanias (as the redeemed child-aspect) in her arms, points Virgil's way into death.

The second part of the novel describes the descent to the fires below—to the realm of the god Vulcan, brother of Poseidon. This ugly and limping god, cuckolded husband of the love-goddess Aphrodite and exquisite craftsman and artist, presides over that part of Virgil's journey in which Virgil is forced to accept in himself a part of human nature he had hitherto ignored: the chthonic, brutal, obscene, emanating from this realm as merciless laughter and cruel beauty. At the beginning of the second part, Virgil lies in a foetal position in his bed. Yet the foetal position is also the position in which many cultures bury their dead, and the bed in which Virgil lies metamorphosizes into a ship—remembrance of his recent voyage but also foreshadowing the ship of death. Appropriate to the foetal position, Virgil reminisces about his childhood, then about cognition and poetry. From an epistemological point of view, all these thoughts are childish. Virgil fancies himself knowledgable when the events of the night will tell him he is not. Under the impact of "the distressing fever that wavered up to the skin from unknown, red-glowing depths" (DV, 77)—an indication that the fever rises from the Vulcanic realm—Virgil abandons his foetal position, at first to sit up; then, a violent attack of his illness, tuberculosis, drives him out of bed and he struggles to reach the window and some breath of air (DV, 94–95). The physical change of posture (from lying prone to standing erect) reflects an epistemological condition which succintly summarizes Virgil's journey:

. . . when she [the soul] has stretched out, abandoned to sleep, to love, to death, when she herself has become an outstretched landscape, then her task is no longer the merging of opposites, for in sleeping, loving, dying, the soul is no longer either good or evil, she has become only an unbroken endless hearkening: spread out to infinity, infinitely held in the orbit of time, infinite in her repose, she is absolved from growth. . . . (DV, 79)

This horizontal position is overcome when: " . . . the human soul reaches out from the dark abyss, where her roots are entwined in the humus of existence, and strives upward even unto the sun-drenched dome of the stars, bearing upward her cloudy sources from the regions of Poseidon and Vulcan, bringing downward the clarity of her Apollonian goal . . ." (DV, 79).

Standing at the window and looking out into the night, Virgil becomes confident: he hopes to finish the Aeneid and thinks—still in the early part of his journey into individuation—that he has almost arrived: "One needed no guide on such an easy path, and also no stern awakener; for the incandescent, shimmering sleep of the world endured without interruption; one needed only to stride forth, to wander out into the realm of the unrecallable; all boundaries were opened and nothing was able to halt the wanderer . . ." (DV, 108). The extent of Virgil's misapprehension is evident in the painful and lengthy subsequent confrontation with the horror figures emanating from the Vulcanic realm. These nightmare fantasies, though frequently related to "realistic" events, find an explanation on the physiological level in Virgil's fever. Psychologically, they are those aspects of his personality which haunt him because they have not yet been integrated. On the epistemological level they trace Virgil's cognitive growth, the pitfalls and temptations to which he succumbs and his ultimate self-redemption in the "knowledge of death."

In accordance with Broch's theory of the "I", in which he posits the biological and psychological layers surrounding an epistemological "I"-core,[10] the "epistemological sphere of the unconscious" (GW,

VIII, 166)[11] transcends the psychological level in cognitive content. For this reason, Virgil is the vehicle rather than the conscious originator of thoughts which emerge in extended lyricisms from this sphere of the unconscious. The extended hymnal sections of the novel provide the cognitive reference system which measures Virgil's erring journey. Broch chooses the lyrical and hymnal tone to convey Virgil's cognitive ruminations because the lyrical is the most subjective mode of expression; barely structured by consciousness, it is most closely in touch with the irrational, that is, with the inarticulated fear of death. The lyrical allows the least "processed" access to the vast reservoir of the unconscious. According to this theory, Virgil's totally internalized and subjectivized visions *must* be rendered through the lyrical medium, for it is the only vehicle capable of expressing the cognitive approach to death.[12]

The epistemological sphere of the unconscious also manifests itself every time Virgil experiences passively that he is being held, that he is *preisgegeben* (offered up), that knowledge is, literally, occurring in him. For example: "It was not he speaking, it was the dream that spoke; it was not he thinking, it was the dream that thought; it was not he dreaming, it was the dome of destiny, radiating into the dream which dreamed" (*DV*, 203). The wider frame of the epistemological sphere frequently penetrates into Virgil's consciousness in the form of questions he is unable to answer. Thus, for example, he stands at the window and witnesses the drunken arguments of two men and one woman down below in the street and wonders: "Who had the three been? Had they been sent out from Hades, sent out from those miserable slums into the window of which he had looked, pitilessly impelled by fate? What else must he witness? What else must he encounter? Was it not yet enough?" (*DV*, 115). These questions are comments on Virgil's previous ignorance when he had thought the end of his journey was at hand; now he knows that further confrontations are in store for him, even if he is still ignorant of their nature.

Driven to the window by an attack of coughing, Virgil sees the shadows of the drunken triad cast by the fires of the night guards on the walls opposite the nocturnal castle. This scene is an allusion to Plato's cave as much as to the Vulcanic realm. The two drunken men, one of them tall, skinny and limping, the other one smaller, obese, and crowing in a tenor voice, and the woman, vile, harrassing, and arguing with the men, subsequently appear at significant moments in Virgil's cognitive journey: either at the end of an insight into the Vulcanic, infernal nature of laughter, art, and beauty, or as impetus to

a renewed effort on Virgil's part to understand the realm they
represent.[13] Thus, after the triad has disappeared into the night,
there follows the hymn to beauty, which is the "aesthetic" reaction to
the slovenliness of, and the obscenities uttered by, the three. But on
a deeper level beauty properly belongs to the realm of the three
drunkards, for lack of commitment to cognitive growth characterizes
both. In three successive waves Virgil is overwhelmed by lyrical
outpourings which reveal the tie between beauty and its inherent
cruelty (since it is indifferent to ethical criteria) as well as the stasis of
beauty striving after permanent equilibrium and effecting a spatialization of time which eliminates growth and development. Beauty
reduces all activities to games where drunkenness and irresponsibility rule supreme. It feasts on the elimination of the criteria for good
and evil and of an ethical ordering of chaos into cosmos.

In *The Sleepwalkers,* the aesthete and the aesthetic had already
been condemned; in *The Death of Virgil,* the verdict is still more
forceful. Beauty is defined by a closed system, by an "enduring now."
In the context of the mythological references in *The Death of Virgil,*
this stagnant, growth-stunting state is "the unchanged and unchangeable Saturnian realm through the whole of time, persisting
from the golden age to the age of brass, aye, even beyond it to the
return of the golden age . . ." (*DV,* 79). In the first cosmogonic sketch
of the novel (*DV,* 117–124), the interconnection of beauty with the
Saturnian realm and their participation in a precreative condition (the
inchoate realm of the mothers) seems arbitrary and difficult to
comprehend. Only with Virgil's growing insights will these cosmogonic bits of information, contained in the lyrical hymns and
elegies, gain a coherent structure; they will be revealed as a mytholo-
gization of the cognitive process, transposed into cosmos-creating
dimensions. The vertical, cognitive growth pattern, symbolized
in the ascent from the Vulcanic to the Apollonian realm, is inter-
sected by the horizontal, static line of the Saturnian sphere. This
intersection charts Virgil's cognitive difficulties. The temptation to
remain attached to the Saturnian realm stands against the duty to
ascend toward Apollonian clarity. Here, as in all other instances,
the Vulcanic realm and its emissaries serve a double function. On the
one hand, they represent the infernal fires, the rejection of the
cognitive drive, the curious amalgamation of beauty with obscenity.
On the other hand, they provide the impetus for cognitive labor,
whether physiologically through fever hallucinations and attacks of

coughing, or cognitively through challenging Virgil's self-complacent aestheticism.

The reading of the novel is rendered difficult because the epistemological sphere of the unconscious does not offer its reservoir of knowledge as an objective measuring device for evaluating Virgil's progress or mistakes. Insights from this sphere become available to the reader only as they penetrate to Virgil's consciousness. Virgil frequently thinks he understands when, in fact, he has much more to learn. The insights he gradually gains are not cumulative in the sense that new realizations can simply be added, but each new insight demands a qualitative change of the entire preceding stage. Hence, Virgil's slow cognitive growth is one of the reasons for the many metamorphoses which occur in the novel and which force constant reinterpretations of the previous material.[14]

Virgil had been driven to the window and to the erect, adult position by a violent cough and fever. Standing by the window, he had witnessed the triad, though at first unable to make any sense of their appearance. The hymn to beauty, which then literally occurred to him, provided a new frame in which he could judge their meaning: he now begins to see a connection between beauty, the triad, and himself: "Then he understood: the three staggering below . . . had become witnesses against him. That was why it had been necessary for them to come. That was why he had had to await their coming. They had appeared as witnesses and complainants, to accuse him of sharing in their guilt, alleging that he was one of them, an accomplice, a perjurer and guilty even as they . . ." (*DV*, 131). Though Virgil attempts to integrate this insight into his life as poet and artist, he is not yet ready for a reevaluation. Instead, he projects into the myth of the poet Orpheus all the negative connotations he suddenly realizes are associated with the artist: " . . . he was an artist, a poet, an enchanter of those who hearken, singer and hearer shrouded in the same twilight, he, like they, demonically caught in the spell of beauty, demonic in spite of his divine gifts, an enchanter, but not the savior of man . . ." (*DV*, 136).

In seven successive waves, each one initiated with "he knew" or "and he also knew" (*DV*, 138–42), Virgil comes to understand the futility of his art and of his conception of the artist. Slowly and painfully, he starts to personalize this understanding: he too had failed because he had created beauty rather than truth and had forsaken the duty to cognition which alone justified art. These pages

contain Broch's theory of the function of art and his demand that
ethics abolish aesthetics. Projected into the dying Virgil, this is
Broch's farewell to the artist's insistence on the autonomy of art. At
the end of this series of overwhelming insights, Virgil again connects
them with the drunken triad (DV, 143).

The impact of these realizations is so strong that Virgil cannot
physically sustain it: ". . . he hung brokenly over the window ledge
. . ." (DV, 144); and he becomes part of the peculiarly dead antiworld
of the drunken triad: "He heard the stifled laughter in the stone-
heated, form-fixed silence of the surrounding night, he heard the
taciturnity of consummate perjury, the obdurate hush of a guilty
conscience, robbed of speed, of knowledge, of memory . . ." (DV,
144). While he is bent over the window sill, the next round of insights
sweeps over him (DV, 144–46). In anguish he appeals seven times to
Plotia (DV, 147–52), the woman whose love he once rejected for the
sake of his art. The circle of his insights widens: it now includes the
realizations that he has led a false life and never loved rightly, that
"people meant nothing to him," that he had only "considered human
beings as lifeless building blocks with whom to erect and create a
death-fixed beauty . . ." (DV, 152), that he had failed them and
himself by ignoring their common humanity. Again, reference to the
triad concludes the Plotia invocations (DV, 153).

A five-times repeated litany of woe, reminiscent of the lamenta-
tions of Thomas Mann's Dr. Faustus, initiates the descent into hell.
Still hanging over the window sill, Virgil physically experiences the
terror of emptiness as a horror of petrification and suffocation. His
readiness for contrition and self-extinction crumbles under the impact of this hell from which he desperately wants to escape: ". . . the
stone was dead, dead without an echo to the unasked question, dead
the stony labyrinth of the universe, dead the shaft on the very bottom
of which the naked ego, abased to extinction, divested of both
question and answer, barely existed. Oh, back! back into darkness,
into dream, into sleep, into death! Oh, back, just to be back once
more, fleeing and fleeing backward once again into the sphere of
being! Oh, flight . . ." (DV, 161).[15] A physical reaction immediately
follows this desire to retreat into the Saturnian realm (dream, sleep,
death are all associated with horizontal positions), and the next phase
of Virgil's journey begins:

. . . he felt himself flung to his knees, and bowing deeply under the immense
burden of the blind-unmoving, invisibly-transparent universal emptiness,

flight-benumbed, flight-paralyzed, the laden shoulders bent down, he sought with dry and lifeless hands blind-fingered for the wall of the room, . . . with hanging head he crept like an animal through the benumbed aridity toward the most animal of all goals, toward water, so that bent over in the sheerest animal necessity he might lap at the silver-trickling moisture. (*DV*, 161–62)

When Virgil crawls to the water fountain like an animal, he enacts an animal aspect of his nature. After he was confronted with the crowds in the harbor, the women in the Misery Alley, the drunken triad, and after these encounters pushed him to the recognition of failed duties, failed art, failed love, failed help, failed humanness, he must now confront the horror visions of sheer animality. A five-times repeated litany of woe preceded Virgil's topsy-turvy fall into the universe of hell, which he experienced as dry, stony, heavy, yet empty and infused with a light deprived of "shining" quality. It made him recoil in terror from his readiness for contrition and pushed him into animality. A five-times repeated litany of woe follows these events and thus surrounds Virgil's breakdown. Yet the second litany also serves as an epistemological reference system for the stages ahead. It sends him on a journey through all the negative presences of unredemption, on "a journey of ceaseless beginnings and ceaseless endings, a journey across the un-space of memory, across the un-space of stagnated straying, across the un-space of unrecallable trance-life; it proceeded without movement, a whizzing journey through all the transformations of un-space, inevitably accompanied and encompassed by them, dimensionless in their trance-stagnation, dimensionless in their trance-movement, always however within the undimension of horror" (*DV*, 164).

Virgil's physical posture during this journey remains that of an animal which "creeps trembling under some dark shrubbery" (*DV*, 163), after he had "suddenly and without deliberation . . . reached the bed and was crouching in it pitifully, his throat constricted, a dry coldness in his limbs" (*DV*, 163). Virgil now experiences the Vulcanic realm proper, no longer its emissaries. This journey signals a renewed confrontation, albeit on a greatly abstracted level, with the negative versions of all that Virgil had hoped to accomplish. In these passages, the apparent redundancy of Broch's language may seem onerous, yet it is motivated by the zeal to coin words for states of negativity normally considered beyond words. No combination of horrors should remain unsaid, but must reveal the negatives of a fullness and totality which Virgil will only attain in the last stages of his journey. Nightmare visions reminiscent of Hieronymus Bosch's paintings lead Virgil to the nadir of this infernal geography. Exemplifying the animal level of Virgil's condition, frightful hybrid creatures beset Virgil's journey: "half-birds were perching on the roof-top, terrible grave-birds with fishy eyes in a crowded row, owl-headed, goose-beaked, pig-bellied, gray-feathered with feet that were merely human hands webbed for swimming, brooding birds flown from no countryside, whose flight was unfit for any land" (DV, 170). They settle in a region that epitomizes the Vulcanic landscape in its mixture of the "mountain deserts of Tartarus" (DV, 156) and the "volcano of nothingness . . . from which the fire flooded out in a flowing un-element and stood still" (DV, 172). Death (more correctly nonlife), the infernal fires, and a grotesque animality are the proper realm for the denial of humanity and its perversion into drunken irresponsibility.

The masses also belong to this realm because, in Broch's cognitive scheme, the mass is composed of individuals who have abdicated their cognitive quest. In the context of the mythological reference system, this means they are part of the eruptive and perjurious Vulcanic realm. Masses, too, want to be redeemed; not, however, on the basis of their own cognitive efforts, but rather by being led and guided. The political relevance of this view is particularly evident when one considers that this novel, with its strong indictment of the masses and of those tendencies which make masses out of individuals, was written during World War II. In the "Resolution", Broch had made it clear that it was not war he considered the primary evil to be combatted, but the dehumanizing tendencies which relieve the individual from personal responsibility and make war and any other atrocities acceptable.[16] The appropriate landscape for such deliberate destruction of humaneness is the infernally lit netherworld; at the same time it is a most graphic description of Germany during this period. " . . . on every side the tomb-streets and tomb-cities of the death-inhabited world were ablaze, on every side the stony aimlessness of human fury glared forth, as did the jubilation, the sacrificial madness of men; on every side the cold flames of human passion stood stiffly erect, and humanity was being discreated . . ." (DV, 173).[17]

Virgil reaches the nadir of his journey when he begins to realize that contrition, indeed self-extinction, for which he is prepared, must be accompanied by corresponding acts. The painful search for the proper acts finally culminates in his outcry "Burn the Aeneid!" (DV,

178). Here again, it is the epistemological sphere which induces the *metanoia*, when Virgil experiences the insight as stemming not from his own conscious self, but from deeper levels within him. ". . . that which he had long known, long suffered, long understood was wrung from him, escaping him in a tiny, inadequate expression of the inexpressible . . ." (*DV*, 178).

This insight marks a decisive turn in Virgil's night of anguish. Yet his body posture, although no longer a panic-stricken crouching, indicates a renewed Saturnian pose: "he lay there with closed eyes and he did not stir" (*DV*, 178). In this pose he is subjected to temptations testing the strength of his newly gained convictions. Virgil recognizes and rejects the charming attempts by the slave-boy Lysanias to lure him from the way he now sees before him (*DV*, 178–82). But he succumbs, when Lysanias addresses him as father, "which was like a gift, like a reward for his self-abnegation, a dispensation for his vigilance . . ." (*DV*, 185), and he accepts the wine Lysanias offers him to drink. Wine, best grown on "vulcanic soil," with its association of intoxication, is a growth-stunting and extremely negative offering. The consequences of drinking are immediately apparent: "that much he just managed to remember, and then everything became dim; dimmer and dimmer, and he no longer remembered the name, nor any name . . ." (*DV*, 186). Lysanias' "childish" offering sends Virgil into the realm of the nameless, the province of the mothers. It reduces him to the state of a child, when he had aspired to the role of father as the one who gives names and institutes laws. Yet the realization that he had failed to raise the names of things in his poetry jolts Virgil back into renewed awareness that the *Aeneid* must be burned.

As in previous instances, a strong argument against the autonomy of the work of art and the romantic myth of the poet as *creator mundi* is made in these passages. Virgil despairs because he has not lived up to the myth; later he will come to reject the aspiration itself as aesthetic, hence false. The subjective presentation of his gradual realization emphasizes again the tortuous process in which this conviction is gained, rather than simply the result. In response to Virgil's reflections on poetry, Lysanias once more tempts him, this time by quoting from the *Aeneid*. But now Virgil is not distracted. Sensing that he is caught in the web of "Vulcanic" entanglements, realizing that he is still imprisoned in dreams, he patiently awaits the next phase. And again, the epistemological sphere surfaces, in the lyrical "elegies to fate." These hymns to fate and dream, to form, and to creation are the antipodes to those that had initiated the descent, the hymns to beauty, form, and laughter. While the earlier cluster concentrated on the ethical crime of perjury which denies creation and growth, and on the closed systems in all their aesthetic nondifferentiations, the later cluster sketches a cosmogony of the cognitive and creative processes. This is the core of Broch's mythologized epistemology.

Brochian mythologizing mixes the Jungian archetypal myth of consciousness with the Judeo-Christian covenant, and presents them in the antithetical relation between ethics and aesthetics. In the hymns to fate, the Jungian principle of the unconscious is present in the "womb of the primeval, darkness-enshrouded mother" (DV, 200), out of which "the god delivered himself/From his inexistence and became Father,/Calling the name of light out of muteness" (DV, 200). The dualism of mother-father, unconscious-conscious, is not only an archetypical, but also a stereotypical manner of representing cognitive processes, and Broch merely repeats prevalent intellectual concepts. As his own contribution, he inquires into the forces motivating god/Father into action and consciousness and locates them in Fate. Fate is present in the primordial, precreative mists and precedes any differentiation into creation and creator. Preceding differentiation, it lacks ethical criteria. Since only creation and the succession of creative acts creates time, primordial Fate is a static entity; this stasis, too, relegates Fate and its timelessness into the aesthetic sphere. Since Fate shares in the primordial union of nondifferentiation, it also contains the one prerequisite in which alone creation can occur, namely, form. The hymn opens with this dense statement: "Fate, thou camest before all the gods,/Thou wast prepared in the mists long before any creation,/Nakedness thou of the clouded beginning, and true/to self alone, the cold, all-penetrating form" (DV, 200). The admission that creation can occur only by assuming form immediately leads to the crux of Broch's ethics-aesthetics antithesis. Since Fate can manifest itself only in created form, it remains, as created product, in the aesthetic and static realm. Broch applied the consequence of this insight rigorously to all his writing. It involves the recognition that everything created, hence the world as it exists, always and inextricably belongs to the aesthetic realm. Virgil's disregard for the created state, evident in the long conversation with Caesar Augustus, stems from this realization. Nothing less than continuous creation qualifies as ethical, and no regard for form (and tradition) must lure into the realm of the aesthetic. The difficulty of maintaining a "permanent revolution" of creativity, that is, of constant cognitive breakthroughs, is here much more obvious than it was in *The Sleepwalkers.*

Although Fate is an entity before and after the act of creation, it does not explain the origin of the dynamic quality of the creative, that is, cognitive act. One must accept the possibility of self-generation, in which "the god delivered himself/From his inexistence," in order to account for any creation at all. Creation is an ethical commitment, for which there is no self-evident or necessary reason. It is solely based on the pledge and carried out in obedience to duty. This pledge is the mythologized covenant between "man and the gods" in which they commit themselves to existence and cognitive striving. Broch also uses the conventional myth of the titan Prometheus to authenticate the cognitive urge. The "divine spark" is the image which connects Prometheus' titanic efforts with the Vulcanic realm from which the sparks burst forth; it can either ignite the world in universal conflagration or stimulate the individual to attain the highest cognitive states.

Creation is an extremely fragile process and constantly endangered. The most obvious temptation is to work for the aesthetic effect, thus creating a false timelessness (represented in the novel by the aesthete Lucius and by Caesar Augustus' aspirations for "eternal" fame and glory). There is also the trap of reverting to the simplicity and irresponsibility of precreation, that is, to the nondifferentiated state (expressed in the novel as the lure to *return* to childhood, under the tutelage of the nameless and shapeless realm of the mothers). In addition, an even stronger threat to creation emanates from the Vulcanic realm: the deliberate denial and destruction of the creative processes. This is expressed as the "breaking of the pledge" or as "perjury," when creation is indiscriminately confounded with precreation. From this point of view, seemingly divergent realms are variations of the same basic tenets: the drunken triad with its most salient characteristics of laughter and perjury; the primordial mothers; the slave-boy Lysanias and the temptress Plotia; and the Saturnian landscape spread out horizontally. In view of the constant dangers and temptations, commitment to this "titanic nevertheless" becomes an almost absurdist gesture of assertion. Yet this commitment is man's one human and humane faculty. It assures liberation from the irrational imprisonment in the "eternal now" and mandates the progressive, linear movement of the open system. Man becomes an individual (as opposed to a being submerged in the masses) only if he commits himself to the continued and arduous task of cognitive striving. The difficulty of this path is amply demonstrated in the many pitfalls, temptations, and dead ends which mark Virgil's journey.

Virgil responds to the hymns and to his newly gained realization of the confining roles of fate and dream by attempting to break out of them. This response demonstrates a cognitive breakthrough on his part, which he must follow through if he is to liberate himself from entrapment in the static: " . . . he lifted himself in the enormous, god-like effort required of him and with a final piercing through of the dream's border, with a final shattering of every sort of image and every sort of revelation, with a last shattering of memory, the dream grew beyond itself, he growing with it: his thinking had become greater than any form of thinking . . ." (DV, 270). Yet this shattering is only relative growth, it is progress, not attainment. Virgil reaches "a second memory, the memory of aeons and universal experience" (DV, 207), but he still has a long journey to travel. After he has seen himself as part of closed and static systems, after he has physically experienced their horror, and after he has exerted himself to the utmost of his capacities to burst these confinements, he rests in profound expectation. A twelve-times chanted homecoming litany prefigures the homecoming of the last part of the novel and presents Virgil's reorientation. The litany initiates a state of profound anticipation and of total emptiness of self as the precondition for deepest insight: "He stood at the boundary, he stood at the edge of destiny, at the border of chance, he stood at the boundary with blank expectation, with blank listening, with blank looking, with blank wisdom, yet drained as he was and in this blankness he knew that the borderline would be opened" (DV, 219).[18]

The realization that he must destroy the Aeneid was wrought from Virgil when he felt engulfed by the flames of the underworld where burning the work of art would be a most appropriate gesture. At the end of this journey through hell, and balancing the order to destroy, now stands a constructive command: "Open your eyes to Love!" (DV, 221). This love is the redeemed aspect of duty. Virgil will learn to fulfill his duties during the day ahead in preparation for the ultimate vision of Love. After these two insights, for which an entire horror- and fever-ridden night was necessary, Virgil recapitulates the events of the night. He falls asleep in the early hours of the morning, strengthening himself to translate insight into practice (DV, 221–30).

The third section of the novel, "Earth—the Expectation," contains Virgil's dialogues with his friends in which he attempts to implement the insights gained during the grueling battles of the night. Apollo rules this section, although the Vulcanic realm is never completely abandoned. The influence of the netherworld continues through Virgil's feverish hallucinations, where eclipses of the sun, earthquakes, and rolling seas metamorphose his sickroom into cosmic turmoil. Apollo's complex mythological associations are omnipresent. As god of measure and ratio, he presides over the great dialogues. Together with his son Asclepius he is revered as the chief god of healing. (Kos, birthplace of the physician Hippocrates, was the center of worship of Asclepius. This fact is obliquely referred to when the court physician Charondas mentions Kos as his birthplace. Healing can mean healing for life as well as proper preparation for death. Charondas' name alludes to this; "Charon" is the name of the old man who ferries the souls of the dead across the river Styx to the lower world.) As god of light, Apollo "became a god of mortal and moral purity, and therefore of order, justice, and legality in human life."[19] Under his auspices, Virgil will make his last arrangements, dictate a new testament, and dispose "justly" of the unfinished *Aeneid*. After the contrition of the preceding night, these acts can be seen as atonement, and again, it is Apollo who grants purification. Yet Apollo also presides over Virgil's cognitive quest. As the "shining Archer armed with his bow" (*DV*, 266)[20] he grants highest insight at the ultimate moment of consciousness as it crosses the threshold into death: " . . . he alone struck by the arrow, he alone pierced by the light, may see the dark veils tear asunder, so that with failing eye, still peering, already in blindess, he may see in a single glance the primal dome of oneness, the dome from which he sprang, as he fathoms beginning and ending, this being of night and of light" (*DV*, 264). Broch will pursue Virgil's dying to exactly this moment.

The "Earth" part of the novel is divided into seven sections of uneven length. In the first section, Virgil's friends, the country squire Plotius and the poet Lucius, try to dissuade him from burning the *Aeneid*. Art, the nature of reality, love, and honesty are explored contrapuntally. While his friends argue for the "Saturnian" and aesthetic position, Virgil insists adamantly that he failed as an artist and a human being exactly because he had not transcended these boundaries. Virgil does not yet realize that despite the most committed "titanic" efforts, the cognitive boundaries can only be expanded, never broken open in the here and now. Neither the creation of art nor any other cognitive act can break through temporal confinement; this ultimate possibility can occur only in a rightly "lived" death, as will be apparent in Virgil's last stages of dying. In the conversation with his friends, Virgil still believes that "genuine art bursts through boundaries, bursts through and treads new and hitherto unknown realms of the soul, of conception, of expression, bursting through into the original, into the immediate, into the real . . ." (DV, 255). While Plotius and Lucius are full of love and admiration for their friend, they do not understand him.

In the second section, Virgil's desire to implement his new convictions in the outside world combats renewed temptation from within. Lysanias reads to Virgil the passage of Aeneas' return from the netherworld through the gates of ivory. The choice is characteristic. The gates of ivory release false dreams. Throughout the novel, ivory is associated with falseness, with beauty and illusion, that is, with the aesthetic realm.[21] Lysanias projects into Virgil a leadership role, tantalizing him with the illusion of worldly attainment. A house-slave, assigned to Virgil's services, conjures up in Virgil's mind the figure of a Golem. This Golem begins to assert a counterposition to the temptations of the slave-boy Lysanias. He represents stern duty, unredeemed by purposive cognition. (Clay [Lehm] is here the denominator that connects the unredeemed aspect of the Golem-slave with the unredeemed realm of the mothers.) Now that Virgil has admitted the ethical force of duty, the house-slave, as a projection of Virgil's mind, will help him ward off renewed temptations, and pressure him to comply with the last duties on earth.

Duty is one of the key concepts of the entire third part and appears in various guises. In the mythological context of the novel, it is an austere variiation on the freely contracted pledge. Together with time and death it forms one cluster of associations. In the mythological terms of the novel, Zeus' primordial killing of his father Kronos instituted a succession of rulers and thereby a succession of time, leading to death. Duty assures the responsible structuring of time and an orderly sequence of events. Apollo, as the son of Zeus, is equally subject to duty, riding "the fire-wagon . . . on through the heavenly pavillion, day after day in the zenith . . ." (DV, 266).

The unstated assumption in this use of classical mythology is the myth of the fall as it pertains to the Judeo-Christian tradition. The primordial crime creates consciousness and with it a dualism of self and the world. Broch projects into the classical frame of reference of Virgil's mind the thought that time and history, man's creation, are the result of a criminal act. History is reduced to metaphysics when an initial evil (murder) gives rise to all subsequent acts. In Broch's system, evil is then defined as acts which ignore the implications of the primordial crime and which set up a scheme that simulates prelapsarian conditions. In terms of the novel, this is the Saturnian realm. Good acts are those that dutifully acknowledge the legacy of the crime by honoring the forces it set in motion, that is, consciousness and with it discrimination, time, and the cognitive process.

The mythological succession Kronos-Jupiter-Apollo presents time sequences in a manner familiar from earlier novels. Historical periods follow in close succession or are juxtaposed, and the emphasis is on the last, disintegrative era. In *The Death of Virgil*, the sense of an ending with its disintegrating values is invested in the reign of Caesar Augustus who duplicates on earth occurrences in the heavenly spheres; the rule of the Olympian gods, notably Caesar Augustus's patron god Apollo, is drawing near its end. The projection into the future centers on the house-slave who reveres a most unknown and abstract god. As in *The Sleepwalkers* and in the *Mountain Novel*, the tendency toward abstraction indicates the future. In the case of the house-slave, and in order not to violate historical accuracy, the advent of this abstract deity is embedded in circumstances resembling those of the advent of Jesus Christ.

The arrival of the court physician Charondas in the third section calls Virgil back from these cosmogonical projections. Under Charondas' supervision, his assistants ready Virgil for the imminent visit of Caesar Augustus. Virgil conceives of these activities as part of ceremonies in which he is prepared as a sacrificial offering In this section, the art of the physician is explored according to the polarity of ethics and aesthetics. Charondas is vain and settles for the aesthetic reward of worldly renown. Yet he is not simply the "pure" aesthete. He is thoroughly knowledgeable in his field and genuine concern motivates his medical decisions. The ambivalence associated with the physician, a recurrent theme in all of Broch's novels, appears here in a new version. Comparing himself to Charondas and to his friends, Virgil falls short in his own opinion. He had been the "pure" artist, while Charondas the physician and Plotius the country squire had carried on with their duties in the services of mankind, motivated by concern and love. Bearing in mind the last command of the fever night, Virgil realizes how much his work lacked reality because it lacked these qualities.

In response to this insight, the fourth section of this third part deals with love. Since Virgil does not know which path to follow consciously, he battles with his own projections as they emerge from the unconscious and integrates them into his self. In his hallucinations about having neglected love, Plotia comes to seduce him into the timelessness of their sexuality. In the preceding confrontations, Virgil's ethical commitment had carried the victory over the aesthetic temptations to opt for sempiternity. Now he succumbs to Plotia's enticements, following her to bed in the dense thicket of elm trees. (Elms serve a function similar to ivory—they dispense illusion and false dreams.) Twice emissaries from the realm of duty interrupt their attempts to make love, first the Golem-slave, Virgil's own projection, then Caesar Augustus, the worldly representative of the realm of duty.

The preceding parts of the third section, indeed the entire novel, build up the confrontation between Caesar Augustus and Virgil in the fifth section. One of the reasons for the excruciating second part now becomes obvious. The reader has accompanied Virgil through his horrors and pains and witnessed the process in which he acquired the convictions which he now upholds against Caesar's arguments. Not to know the origin of these convictions would make them appear arbitrary statements easily refuted by Ceasar's cogent attacks. Art and architecture, statesmanship, peace, governance of the masses, knowledge, and death are explored in the contrapuntal manner of the previous conversations. (The counterpoint technique of presenting the ethical and aesthetic positions on various topics in a series of intricate responsories conveys Broch's system-oriented, geometrical approach, intended to exhaust "systematically" the variations on a theme.)

Yet Caesar Augustus is not an aesthete out of firm belief and conviction (such as Lucius) but rather out of skepticism and fatigue. Tired gestures are his frequent attributes (indicating that he and his era are coming to an end), and his features become hard, stern, and sharp as he insists on the fulfillment of duty. He bears a physical resemblance to Lysanias, which underscores his "boyish" and illusory convictions that he can institute lasting peace and permanent prosperity. He is ruler of the Saturnian realm (transposed to the political plane as *Pax Augustana*), and heir to the legacy of the Titanic crimes as well as to their humanizing consequences. Jupiter/Zeus is the god to whom he traces his ancestry, and Apollo is his special patron god.

The dialogue between Caesar Augustus and Virgil culminates in Virgil's insight that human activity must be directed toward cognition of death (*DV*, 321), while Caesar Augustus contents himself pragmatically with the cognition of life. Virgil's intransigence forces him to reject poetry, the expression of "impatience for cognition," since it is unable to *be* cognition (*DV*, 321).[22] Caesar Augustus, on the other hand, demands Virgil's *Aeneid* as the spiritual bond to seal his worldly achievements. Virgil sees the failure of his art (as of all activity, including Caesar's political achievements) related to its symbolic quality, which can never render, but only mirror, an unobtainable reality. (*DV*, 327). Virgil's insistence on the absolute barriers against cognition of ultimate reality echoes Broch's early acknowledgement of the Kantian "boundaries of reason" and the impossibility of ever perceiving the Platonic Idea. Virgil goes so far as to postulate that the entire phenomenal world must be comprehended as symbol—and symbol only—of an ulterior reality which becomes accessible only at the moment of death.[23] Caesar Augustus sees in Virgil's contentions a denial of his own worldly achievements. Virgil's and Caesar Augustus's sides are argued with equal conviction; there can be no reconciliation between the radically metaphysical orientation of Virgil and Caesar Augustus's deliberate confinement within the material world.

Caesar's goals seem thoroughly respectable in contrast to the demagogueries of Marius in the *Mountain Novel;* yet they, too, must be rejected by Virgil because earthly achievements can never allay man's true source of anxiety, the fear of death. Virgil insists on the duty toward cognition of death, a metaphysical quest, which alone guarantees a stable foundation for ruling, since under these conditions ruling never becomes an end in itself. Augustus is bound by duty toward pragmatic goals. Internal peace, pacification of the empire's borders, education and the preservation of learning, satisfaction of physical needs (including entertainment), and well-functioning laws are to him the highest goals in statesmanship. The inconclusive, grating arguments veer from philosophical discussions to personal animosity. Augustus finally screeches, very much in the manner of the screaming triad, and accuses Virgil of jealousy and hate. His fierce shouting abolishes all pretense at abstract considerations and introduces a personal, indeed intimate, relation, possible only among friends. Now he is not Caesar Augustus, the Roman emperor, but Octavian, Virgil's seemingly betrayed friend. To pacify the raging Octavian, Virgil dedicates the *Aeneid* to him. With this offering of friendship and love, Virgil sacrifices the *Aeneid* not to destruction but to continued existence. In a gesture of extreme humility, he overcomes the last vestiges of the aesthete's impulse not to allow imperfection to exist. Momentarily relieved of the official roles of ruler and poet, the two friends affectionately reminisce and

banter about a disagreement in their youth. Their reconciliation is
the most moving scene in a novel that abounds in cerebral brilliance.
The sixth part is exceedingly short (five pages). Augustus, again the
emperor surrounded by his court, gives a brief speech thanking Virgil
officially for the *Aeneid*. He holds forth inveterately as the skilled
statesman while the *Aeneid*, his booty, is taken away. Yet as the
personal friend Octavian, he leaves to the dying Virgil the most
appropriate gift: Apollo's laurel, the golden bough, needed to gain
access to the netherworld.

In the last section of this third part, Plotius and Lucius help Virgil
to fulfill his final duties. Virgil makes last changes in his testament.
Plotius proffers help on the physical level, Lucius on the intellectual.
Virgil is again besieged by Lysanis, Plotia, and the house-slave. But
as he is able to overcome Lysanias' and Plotia's distracting temptations, they lose their negative aspects. Only the slave remains as the
stern task-master, since Virgil has not finished his tasks. In a movement which closes the circle of Virgil's journey, he returns in his
hallucinations to the harbor to embark in his last voyage. On his
descent through the Misery Alley, he passes all the figures, real and
imaginary, whom he had confronted before. He loses the slave-boy
Lysanias, who remains in the chthonic realm of the mothers, the very
realm to which he had wanted to seduce Virgil. Similarly, Augustus is
now vegetating on a heap of rags, inviting Virgil to join him in his
ill-conceived search: ". . . we must keep on going back, we must
reach beyond the first forefathers; we must return into the mass that
sustained us, we must go back into the humus of the beginning . . ."
(*DV*, 420). Twice, the approach of Virgil's physical death seems to put
a premature and unredeemed end to his search; twice the stern slave
recalls him. As his last commitment to the earthly sphere, Virgil
bequeathes his seal ring to Lysanias.

The last part of the novel stands under the heading "Air—the
Homecoming." The German original for "Air" is *Äther* and points to
the Greek conception of *aither* which "was widely regarded as divine
and as a place of souls."[24] This is the realm into which Virgil's ultimate
journey will take him. In this part, Virgil divests himself of all earthly
contingencies and penetrates to the beginning of creation. In reverse
order, he traverses the seven days of creation, participating physically and sensually in the process of unbecoming. Receding through
creation, he shares in the animal, vegetable, and mineral forms of life.
He recapitulates physically stations he had passed cognitively before.
The night spent in the tower room of Caesar Augustus's castle,

attended by the Golem–slave, he reexperiences for instance as an "unwieldy shapeless tower, a spar of clay, destitute of all limbs, a shapelessly-powerful, shapelessly-towering stone giant" (*DV*, 476). He retains consciousness of all these metamorphoses until at last he arrives at "the word of discrimination, the word of the pledge, the pure word" (*DV*, 481). The novel ends as Virgil's consciousness advances into the state beyond the word.

II   *The Ring and the Symbol*

As Virgil retraces the seven days of creation, he closes the "ring of the earthly." The ring is one of the most important and most pervasive images in the novel.[25] It occurs as a concrete object, as a structural device, and as a philosophical principle. As a concrete object, it is, for example, Virgil's seal ring with "the winged figure of a genius . . . engraved into the polished carnelian" (*DV*, 71). It was given to him by Plotia and accompanies him on his voyage. At the conclusion of the third part, as he approaches the threshold of time and the earthly, and labors to fulfill his last obligations, he bequeathes it to Lysanias. Coming from Plotia and given to Lysanias, the ring symbolizes the closed realm of illusion and imprisonment in false timelessness. Virgil's bequest frees him to proceed beyond. His nearly completed individuation shows in the last part of the novel, in the transformation of "the winged figure of the genius" into "the fleeing figure of the boy, naked in its transparency although still that of Lysanias" (*DV*, 454). On the continued road toward unification of complementary aspects, this figure is then absorbed into Plotia: " . . . the same face though with a new name, the nameless, transported boyish face became that of Plotia Hieria, the boy inseparable from her, she inseparable from the boy, identical in the blurred and fading gesture she had taken over from him, pointing, the ring on her finger, to the east" (*DV*, 455).

This transformation occurs early in the last part, as Virgil crosses the threshold into paradise on the journey back through creation. At the end of that journey, and as Virgil is about to experience the primordial word, the final transformation takes place. Plotia and Lysanias are no longer identified with the ring, since Virgil has left behind the realm which is circumscribed by it. He has entered the penultimate reality of the *Bilder*; accordingly, only the image on the ring remains. Lysanias and Plotia become "the image of the boy in the arms of the mother, united to her in a sorrowful smiling love" (*DV*,

480). This smile contains the meaning of creation, "the whole *significance* of the interminable occurrence" (*DV*, 480). In the sorrowful smile love has superseded duty. At the end of the second part, Virgil was commanded to open his eyes to love. Now he has arrived at the vision of love which symbolizes redeemed man, and that state of "peace without conflict" (*DV*, 480), for which creation occurs forever anew.

As a structural device, the ring outlines Virgil's geographical journey from the harbor up to the castle and back to the harbor. Virgil's inner journey takes him on a circular voyage in the opposite direction: first down to the Vulcanic realm, then up to the Apollonian clarity. The circular pattern is also evident in the many correspondences of themes and concepts which are first introduced in a negative context, undergo a series of transformations, and are finally redeemed.[26] The progress of the novel also follows a circular pattern, insofar as it is completed at the juncture of end with beginning. The Ouroboros, the "serpent of time"[27] (*DV*, 186), is a powerful ring device to measure the time structure of the novel as it relates to Virgil's cognitive journey. In addition to this mythological time ring, which symbolizes man's relation to his own consciousness, there are historical time rings, equally couched in mythology. Most obvious, there is the the Saturnian ring of sempiternal repetition. Then there are the rings of "classical time," indicated in the Kronos-Zeus-Apollo succession. These classical time rings are, in turn, embedded in the Judeo-Christian ring of time. The slave points forward to the advent of the kingdom of the son, the New Testament, at the same time that Virgil breaks the ring of classical time and recedes through Paradise, the realm of the father, and of the Old Testament, to the creation of time itself.

As a philosophical principle, the ring indicates the closed system. However, closed systems are multifaceted structures and carry different connotations. The closed system can be an imitation system. Lysanias and Plotia in their most pernicious aspects, when they tempt Virgil into the imitation of eternity, the false timelessness, belong to the imitation system. Then there are closed systems which are constantly discarded and superseded in cognitive revolutions. Such closed systems do not pretend at aesthetic completion and stasis, but serve as stepping stones for further cognitive advances. Unlike the aesthetic products of the imitation systems, they are not created for their own ends. Virgil exhausts and discards several of these systems in the harrowing night.

The Death of Virgil contains Broch's most radical statements about open and closed systems. He maintains that there are no open systems at all, only open goals. Only the closedness or openness of the goal determines whether a system is aesthetically evil or ethically committed. If systems progress toward an unattainable goal, they cannot take themselves as end products. They avoid the belief in their own timelessness or in the Saturnian suspension of time. What seems a tautology becomes for Broch the basis of his theory of symbols. In time, in life, man is inevitably bound or chained[28] to time and life, is caught in the "ring of the earthly" and trapped in the closed system of existence. Transcendence of time and the earthly in the here and now is impossible.

This seemingly realistic world view becomes the core of Broch's Platonic idealism. While the world is accepted as material and nontranscendent, it is denied "true" reality. Its reality is that of symbols only. When the idealistic vision is declared the true reality, the material world becomes image, mirror, echo, appearance—concepts in which the novel abounds. And even here, the two possibilities are retained: appearances are false in the case of imitation systems, true in the ethically motivated ones. This explains Virgil's repeated and desperate failure to reach reality. His journey can be viewed as a series of cognitive advances until he comes to understand the nature of reality. When Augustus accuses Virgil of jealousy because he denies reality to the emperor's achievements, Virgil wants to explain to his friend just that: the emperor's achievements are real as symbols, but not as achievements in themselves. Insofar as Augustus rejects this interpretation, he belongs to the aesthetic realm.

Virgil's search for the "cognition of death" is a search to break the boundaries imposed by the ring of earthly existence. Augustus, by contrast, contents himself with the "cognition of life." Although "cognition of life" includes an awareness of the phenomenon of death, this death is unredeemed because it lacks the vision of ultimate reality. For Augustus " 'Death is part of life, he who understands life understands death as well' " (*DV*, 321), and " 'life means as little as death; life leads to death and both amount to nothing' " (*DV*, 322).[29] As so often, a concept, in this instance death, does not convey an unambiguously positive or negative connotation, but depends for a clear definition on the system in which it occurs. Augustus remains entrapped in the ring of the earthly which includes death as a return to clay and to the humus without cognitive redemption.

Only when the frame of reference is the radical denial of reality *as* reality does it make sense that Virgil begins his journey, just before he meets the Vulcanic triad, "in the fore-court of reality" (*DV*, 104). But reality, even though sham reality, is not a monolithic entity. For the initiate, it consists of many layers, all of which must be penetrated before ultimate vision is attained:

> Reality towering behind reality; here the reality of friends and their language, behind this an unquenchably lovely memory of a boy at play, further back, that of the caves of misery where Augustus was obliged to live, and beyond these the threatening, brittle and linear entanglement spread out over all existence, over world upon world, behind which was the reality of the flowering groves, oh, and behind this, oh, undiscernible, so undiscernible, the genuine reality, the reality of the never heard, though ever forgotten, ever promised word, the reality of the creation rising anew in the rays of the unbeholdable eye, the reality of the homeland—and the goblet in the hand of Plotius was of ivory. (*DV*, 425)

With absolute consistency, Broch connects the reality, which Virgil conceives as "genuine reality," with ivory. Virgil's cognitive impatience, even at this late stage, would like to abbreviate the cognitive process. Although reality has become increasingly transparent, the ring of the earthly has not been broken. In a meticulously detailed and agonizingly slow process, Virgil approaches the cognitive boundaries. Divested of any physical attributes and "a seeing eye, divine and discriminating, and for all that a human eye" (*DV*, 476), he experiences the union of *Abbild* and *Urbild* (*GW*, III, 527)[30]—but he is still in the realm of the *Bilder*. After he finally perceives the "Urbild aller Bilder" (*GW*, III, 532), the image disappears. Only an enormous *Rauschen* (rumbling) remains, in which, however, the *Urbild* of all *Bilder* is invisibly preserved. In analogy to the *Bilder*, which were reabsorbed into the *Urbild*, the *Rauschen* returns to primordial sound. As "pure word," it is word without image, beyond language. The ring of the earthly has finally been completed.

III   *A Monument to Paradox: Affirmation Through Negation*

In the thirteen years which lie between the publication of *The Sleepwalkers* and that of *The Death of Virgil*, Europe underwent the most cataclysmic events of this century. While large parts of the world were going up in flames, Broch pursued in his hero with singular dedication the road to the interior. Concentration upon the experience of death was, as Broch saw it, a necessity and his most personal answer to the political situation. He expressed this opinion in a letter to Egon Vietta on September 14, 1947:

> . . . you mention the "validity" of the book. Well, the book *was* valid so long as I had not thought about publication, which means before my emigration and the year afterwards. The menace Hitler made death very real—some of the passages were written in jail. I was not only certain that I could no longer publish anything, but I also wanted to familiarize myself with the experience of death, so long as that was still possible. The experience is a necessity for everyone who can no longer find the traditional consolation in religious tradition. I concentrated most exclusively upon the experience of death, worked myself completely into dreamlike states of trance, and wrote everything down almost automatically. (*GW*, VIII, 271–2)

In no other document is Broch's metaphysical orientation and the concomitant passivity as obvious as here where his reaction to the "menace Hitler" is a preparation for death in the most dignified and consummate manner his philosophy admits. In view of the atrocities which accompanied death in most instances during the period *The Death of Virgil* was written, such preparation seems a luxury which was granted to few. Broch, who fought for the dignity of human life, did not take into consideration the obstacles impeding the dignity of death as cognitive consummation. The death upon which Broch concentrated was, under the circumstances, a privilege and not one of the "human rights."

But even if circumstances allowed for the experience of death Broch hoped for and described in *The Death of Virgil*, Virgil's road is not easy to follow. The suggested self-redemption and implicit redemption of the masses into responsible individuals is extremely difficult to pursue. *The Sleepwalkers* and the *Mountain Novel* had shown the impossibility of finding viable alternatives to despair and leader–or redeemer fixations despite the best intentions and willingness on the part of the protagonists (Esch, Pasenow, the country doctor). And Virgil, a trained intellectual and desperate to make the breakthrough, frequently strays into the Saturnian realm and succumbs to distracting temptations.

The Death of Virgil is a monument to paradoxes. It highlights the *vita contemplativa* at a time when the inefficiency of this ideal was most painfully obvious. For once, Broch portrayed a hero whose death might provide an answer to the accusation leveled against the sleepwalkers, namely, that they do not know why they die (*SW*, 646). Yet Virgil's self-criticism contains Broch's criticism of Virgil's ivory-

tower existence and culminates in Virgil's sorrow over having es-
chewed active participation in life. As in his other novels, Broch offers
again a negative example, that is, he shows how *not* to lead a life.
Virgil's case is different from that of other Broch protagonists only
insofar as Virgil realizes, in his dying hours, that he has failed and has
a chance to repent. His death avoids the need to show how, precisely,
he should have lived.

Strictly speaking, the very existence of the novel is a paradox. It is
written by an author who had abjured literature and chosen the *vita
activa* even while he created one of the most inaccessible novels our
century has to offer, second perhaps only to James Joyce's *Finnegans
Wake*. The questions raised in the novel as to the ethically right way
of life are answered only outside the novel, in Broch's involvement
with refugee committees, work on petitions, rescue activities. Broch
spent years creating one of the most breathtaking and overwhelming
novels, but found it acceptable only where it ceased to be literature
and became help. Only then it stood no longer in opposition, but
became a companion to his other commitments.

The particular kind of help that Broch expected from *The Death of
Virgil* was associated with the cognitive-religious-political complex.
In this respect, the novel became the religious novel Broch had
wanted to write in the *Mountain Novel*. It is Broch's religious novel
offered in a completely secular context. It is religious because it
should help to face the experience of death; it is secular, because it
would do so without reliance on religious tradition. At precisely this
point, Broch's political and metaphysical aspirations converged so
that he saw no inconsistency between his mass psychology and the
novel. He wrote to Aldous Huxley, soon after the publication of the
novel, on May 10, 1945: "For in my mass psychology I am ultimately
working on the same problems as in the Virgil: here, too, I am
concerned with the processes which lead the human being to the loss
and regaining of his *vérités fondamentales,* in short, his religious
attitudes" (*GW*, VIII, 216).

The religious-political intent of the book aims at a wide readership.
Yet *The Death of Virgil* is an esoteric and difficult novel and precludes
a large audience.

As an aspiring secular bible, it purports to help man die by offering
a mythologized epistemology instead of religious dogma. Yet these
tools of self-redemption few will want to or be able to use.

Furthermore, *The Death of Virgil* is a paradox where its existence
as a work of art is concerned. Broch's skepticism about art is projected

into the dying Virgil. The process which led to Virgil's agonized outcry "burn the Aeneid!" and which was translated into Broch's life as a turn away from literature, is depicted in great detail. This farewell to literature can be viewed as a logical conclusion to a paradoxical situation which Broch had formulated in the early 1930s. The inherent logic of the work of art, its autonomy, was seen at odds with its purported need to communicate. The *Eigengesetzlichkeit* (inherent logic) of the work of art expressed cognitive gains, but did this in the spirit of positivism, that is, in pursuit of its own internal system and without regard to a common value center. As the work of art became more perfected according to its own demands, it also became more incomprehensible. In order to assure communicability and comprehensibility, the work had to contain known elements and thereby violate the cognitive breakthrough mission. *The Death of Virgil* hovers precariously on the threshold of a positivism which is condemned by its author. It makes few concessions to easy comprehension and veers, on occasion, close to incommunicability. There is no compromise solution between the rigors of the work of art for its own sake and the demands imposed by the need to communicate. Broch made the radical choice to turn away from literature.

This turn from literature was not only occasioned by the danger of positivism beguiling the artist. It was also connected with the insurmountable problem which centered on the cognitive limitations of literature and its metaphysical political inefficacy. Pursuit of the work of art for art's sake is immoral; the metaphysical impact as secular religion is impossible. At the very time that the novel, according to Broch, has taken over the task from religion to reflect Platonic totality, the conclusion is reached that it cannot carry out these expectations. Broch sees this double bind as a particular, modern predicament. It did not exist as long as a dominating value center informed all activities, including literature and the arts. Starting with Goethe, it fell to the novel to keep alive the reflection of Platonic totality, thereby offering spiritual solace in a fragmented world. *The Death of Virgil* declares it impossible to comply with this task, at the same time that the novel strains most intensely to be such solace. Caesar Augustus sees in the *Aeneid* the spiritual bond needed for his empire, but the dying Virgil finds consolation only after he has rejected literature. That Broch chose one of the major works of world literature to exemplify this point stresses the uncompromising conviction of his insight.

Despite the extreme inwardness of *The Death of Virgil*, the

skepticism, the paradoxes, and the denials expressed in it, the novel
ends on a positive note. This achievement is quite significant, as
evident when contrasted with the only other monumental document
of Germany's descent into hell, Thomas Mann's *Dr. Faustus*. Mann's
novel concludes with the hero's descent and the narrator's passive
submission to events. Serenus Zeitblom, the narrator, hopes against
hope for forgiveness and grace from an authority above. In Broch's
novel, Virgil engages in his own redemption. He crosses the nadir of
hell and traces, tenuously and with many mistakes, a precarious path
to self-redemption through cognition.

CHAPTER 6

The Guilt of the Guiltless

WEISMANN, the Munich based publishing house, approached Broch in 1948 with the suggestion to reprint the novellas of 1933 (the "Zodiac Stories"). When Broch saw the galley proofs of the stories after a hiatus of over fifteen years, which had seen the rise and fall of the *Tausendjährige Reich*, he wrote that he was "so profoundly embarrassed that in order to save what could be saved and to give coherence to the pieces, I had no other choice but to set them retrospectively in a good frame . . ." (*GW*, VIII, 373). Recuperated from a broken hip and a hernia operation, Broch spent the summer of 1949 at Saybrook College at Yale University, where he added six additional stories, a "Parabel von der Stimme" ("Parable of the Voice") and three poems to the original five novellas (one written in 1918, four in 1933).[1]

The eleven stories are divided into three parts, each part preceded by the "Stimmen" ("Voices") which introduce the three respective historical periods: 1913, 1923, and 1933. These "Voices" Broch had originally wanted to call "Cantos." He desisted, to avoid allusions to Ezra Pound. The "Voices" provided a level of critical commentary on the events depicted in the stories proper. The tripartite division and the specific historic dating recall *The Sleepwalkers*, where a similar arrangement had been used to show progressive disintegration. In *The Guiltless*, two stories (those of 1913) serve as an exposition; the major events occur in 1923, in the seven stories of the middle part, and the last two stories, set in 1933, provide a coda and point to the political horrors ahead. The novel opens with the "Parable of the Voice" which envelops the historical perspectives of the "Voices" in a metaphysical dimension.

The eleven stories span a period of twenty years, beginning on the eve of World War I and ending with Hitler's rise to power. They are loosely interconnected, as the various characters meet each other over a twenty-year period. The palette of characters ranges from the petit bourgeois high-school teacher Zacharias, his wife Philippine, the laundress Melitta, and the servant Zerline on the bottom rung of the social ladder to the impoverished but quite aristocratic Baroness v. W. and her daughter Hildegard. Through the various protagonists Broch investigates the political and social attitudes which allowed the rise of fascism. All the characters are guilty of the advent of Naziism because their indifference allowed Hitler's takeover to occur. Broch attacked indifference as the primary factor allowing destruction, barbarism, and fascism. In this sense, *The Guiltless* is his most outspokenly political novel. As on previous occasions, he does not focus on the historical events per se (although they are alluded to in conversations), but concentrates on the individuals who contribute to the coming events through inactivity or inertia.

The one protagonist who comes in contact with all the others is A., a Dutch diamond dealer who made his fortune through clever speculations in the South African diamond fields. He is the nameless young observer of the first story. His fixation on the floor pattern of a coffeehouse, where the tiles form the design of the St. Andrew's cross, hints at his name. Broch makes A.'s desires and predispositions obvious in his—imaginary—participation in a conversation at the next table. He reveals a fairly common Oedipal involvement in which the son wants to usurp the father's position through "buying" the mother and killing the father with economic superiority. A. arrives ten years later as the "Prodigal Son" in an unspecified German town[2] and finds lodgings with the Baroness v. W. who will become the "Bought Mother." (The capitalized expressions in quotation marks are titles of some of the stories.) As a Dutch citizen and hence "neutral" (*GL*, 139), A. benefits from the economic chaos of the Weimar Republic. He buys up real estate and speculates in the fluctuating currency market. On one of his evening outings, he accidentally stumbles into a meeting of the Socialist Party, which discusses the then controversial Einsteinian theory of relativity. At the end of the meeting he makes the acquaintance of Studienrat Zacharias and invites him to a glass of wine. Together these two drinking companions embody the attitudes "from A to Z" (*GL*, 147) that allowed for the rise of fascism: from A.'s indifference and amused disgust to Zacharias' impassioned speeches on the destiny of the German nation.[3] "Studienrat Zacharias' Four Speeches" are steeped in real drunkenness which, in the years ahead, will be replaced by ideological intoxication. The seemingly drunken verbiage abides by the same logic of the closed system as the inflammatory speeches of the tempter Marius in the *Mountain Novel* and the charming and childish temptations of Lysanias in *The Death of Virgil*. Broch shows with scathing irony the absurdity, indeed criminality, of the closed-system thinking and its ultimate basis in the fear of death. As Zacharias says:

But that is our destiny and we can't evade it; time and again we must pass through injustice to achieve justice, world justice; time and again we must sink into evil in order to raise ourselves and the rest of the world to a state of higher perfection, and time and again in our hands injustice has been transformed into justice, to our own surprise. Because we are the nation of the infinite and hence of death, while the other peoples are bogged down in the finite, in shopkeeping and money-grubbing, confined to the measurable world because they know only life and not death and consequently, though they may seem to rise so easily and so far above themselves, they are unable to break through the finite. It is incumbent on us, for their own salvation, to subject them to the punishment of death-pregnant infinity. A hard, a colossal course of instruction, forsooth! (*GL*, 143)

Broch establishes a close correlation between ideological affiliations and sexual practices which is consistent with the accepted Nazi stereotype but seems too facile in the context of the novel. Zacharias' ideological self-inflation, his obsession with obedience and death, transfer into sadomasochism. A.'s neutrality and indifference turn into sexual impotence and withdrawal into filial devotion.

Intertwined with the stories of A., his attachment to the Baroness v. W., and his fleeting contact with Zacharias are the stories of the laundress Melitta and her grandfather. A. meets Melitta in "A Slight Disappointment," the Broch story of 1933 which pays homage to Kafka's impact. Out of sheer curiosity, A. enters a house and loses himself in the labyrinths of backyards and stairways until he meets, high up in the attics, the laundress Melitta. A.'s dreamlike estrangement from reality during these scenes recalls Kafka's traumatic world, but with a difference: Broch always distinguishes between the character's experience of the world as enigmatic, and the presentation of this experience as exemplary for an historical condition.

Under the direction of Zerline, Baroness v. W.'s chambermaid (in the "Ballad of the Procuress"), A. and Melitta have a brief affair. Yet Hildegard, the baroness' daughter, finds the affair inconvenient. When she informs Melitta that A. would marry her (Hildegard) anytime she said so, Melitta, in despair, throws herself out of the attic window. In one of the most gruesome scenes of seduction and lovemaking, comparable to K. rolling in a puddle of beer with Frieda in Kafka's *The Castle*, Hildegard reduces A. to impotence (in "The Bought Mother"). Subsequently, A. withdraws with the "mother," the Baroness v. W., and Zerline to the hunting lodge he has purchased from a Herr von Juna, in which he will pass the next decade in seclusion with the two women.

After ten years, which A. spends putting on weight while Hitler has come to power, Melitta's grandfather, the old beekeeper and "The Commendatore," comes to A. to confront him with his failure as a responsible adult. A. has been nameless throughout the prior events (and only referred to by his initial), but the grandfather now calls him by name, thus investing him with full maturity. In expiation of his failures Andreas commits suicide, forming on the floor the St. Andrew's cross as he falls.

This novel is interesting because it documents different stages of Broch's creative development. "Methodically Constructed," written in 1918, is the earliest story, and at the same time the most detached and experimental. The encounter between Zacharias and his future wife Philippine, and the events leading to their marriage, are viewed as plausible and probable, but are hypothetically "constructed." Two different endings indicate that Broch was more interested in exploring the range of actions possible within a given set of circumstances than in providing fully drawn character portraits. This experimental attitude vis-à-vis the protagonists is typical for the earlier Broch. It is still prominent in *The Sleepwalkers*, where the author dispenses altogether with descriptions and merely states: "Besides, after the material for character construction already provided, the reader can imagine [how this came about] for himself" (*SW*, 158).

"The Prodigal Son" (1933) points in the direction the stories of 1949 were to explore, a direction already evident in the *Mountain Novel* and *The Death of Virgil*. The metaphysical symbolism becomes more prominent, and the constant attempts to break from the timebound into the Platonic realm, to break from the fictional time scheme into a transcendant realm, frequently block the narrative. These Platonizing effects become particularly pronounced in "The Bought Mother" and "The Commendatore." Premised on Broch's theory that the deepest epistemological level of the "I" can only find expression in the most subjective lyricisms, lyrical eruptions occur whenever the experience of reality as a stable system of relations becomes questionable. They culminate in A.'s hymnal self-accusations when he comes to realize his guilt for having led a sheltered and secluded life. This is not Broch at his best. Lyricisms in the service of metaphysics had been explored more profoundly in *The Death of Virgil*. A.'s self-indictment and expiation within a matter of minutes belittle a quest of whose difficulty the dying Virgil had given a more convincing example.

I   The "*purple kitsch apocalypse*"

The Guiltless continues the exploration of the rise of fascism at the point where *The Sleepwalkers* had left off. Again, Broch concentrates on the psychological and metaphysical anxieties of the individuals to explain the desire for guidance by leader–or redeemer figures. At the conclusion of *The Sleepwalkers*, the nadir of the "atomization of the value systems" seemed to have been reached. *The Guiltless*, however, demonstrates that there are deeper and more sinister levels yet to be explored. As in Broch's previous novels, references to apocalyptic events provide a consistent level of interpretation. In *The Guiltless*, in distinction to the other novels, Broch embeds the apocalyptic in what appeared to him at the time as the most denigrating reference system: opera. [4]

For about a year before the composition of the late stories of *The Guiltless*, Broch had been working on the Hofmannsthal essay. In this study, he came to the conclusion that opera and the operatic were the most appropriate embodiment of the "vacuum of values," and he saw Richard Wagner as the most gigantic genius of nonart, representing with uncanny artistry the bourgeois vacuum of values:

He knew that the times into which he was born would choose the operatic as its most representative form of all-inclusive expression; he saw how the new bourgeois capitals were in search of a new communal center as substitute for cathedrals and how they worked to raise the Place de l'Opéra to such dignity; and all this velvet-red and guilded, gas-lit solemnity corresponded to his own concepts of the tasks of modern art. (st 246, 141)

Art and a certain kind of politics are for Broch never very far apart. Speaking of Germany with its "hectic historical development, alienated from politics," he states that "instead of a concretely concerned [*konkret besorgt*] mood, there ruled a mood with eschatological overtones, so that metapolitics had to develop into meta-metapolitics without concrete content—briefly, into redeemer expectations" (st 246, 262). For this mood, Wagner with his "primitive-mysticizing redeemer allures" (st 246, 262) becomes the most representative spokesman.

Yet the messianic-apocalyptic expectations degenerate still further, into infatuation with the demonic and magic. This infatuation replaces the cognitive task and provides "decorative" (that is, insincere) excuses for ethical and political inactivity. Broch chose Mozart's most "demonic" opera, *Don Giovanni*, and Wagner's version of ecstatic death, *Tristan und Isolde*, to drive this point home. The epistemological level of the novel revolves around clusters of concepts associated with these two operas: infatuation with the infinity of death, and expectations of the apocalypse, of hell, and of the demonic. Since opera presents an aesthetic rather than ethical reference system, it is relegated to *Kitsch*. With Broch's ethics and his definition of *Kitsch* in mind, it should be obvious that he is here establishing the strongest categories of critical indictments which his philosophical system allows. *Kitsch* is the deliberate denial of the ethical dimensions of human endeavor, for which Virgil had so assiduously labored.

Opera, *Kitsch*, and infatuation with death, infinity, and the demonic are value categories. As such they belong to a specific historic era, the bourgeois age, and are hankered after by a specific type of person: the philistine. The epistemological frame of the "Voices: 1933" enunciates the intimate relation between the demonic, the philistine, and opera as magic quite clearly: "Oh, the philistine is the demonic pure and simple; his dream is an ultramodern, highly developed technique, unremittingly brought to bear on yesterday's aims; his dream is technically perfected *kitsch;* his dream is the professional demonism of the virtuoso who fiddles for him; his dream is the shiny, shining opera magic; his dream is shabby brilliance" (*GL*, 231). With these associations, the characters of *The Guiltless* are defined.

The *Don Giovanni* allusions in the novel are recognizable in the names of the Baroness Elvire v. W., in her maid servant Zerline, in Herr v. Juna at the hunting lodge, and in the "Commendatore." The *Tristan und Isolde* allusions are evoked when Zacharias speaks of the *Liebestod* he and Philippine had experienced during their courtship. (The opera is not mentioned by name since Zacharias is too uninformed to know more than the mere catchword *Liebestod.*)

Although these operatic references are clear and distinct, Broch feels in no way bound to follow the operas faithfully. Indeed, the freedom he takes with these apocalyptic "love-and-death" operas, whose content he literally perverts, provides a parodistic and devastating level of commentary. The principal figure of the Don Juan myth appears only in the recollections of the maid Zerline who, in a reversal of roles, seduced him. A. assumes the role of financially supporting the v. W. household. He moves with the two operatic leftovers, the Baroness Elvire v. W. and Zerline, to Herr von Juna's deserted hunting lodge, buying it as he buys the "mother" Elvire. With this move he does not succeed Herr von Juna in his role as lover but chooses to remain son and child. Yet the "Commendatore" comes to A., not to Herr von Juna, in March of 1933, to settle the account of a life spent in idleness and moral indifference. In contrast to Don Giovanni's unrepentant audacity, A. atones by shooting himself.

Melitta's grandfather, the "guest of stone" of the "Commendatore" story, is introduced more explicitly than any other character from *Don Giovanni* in an operatic context. Before he appears to A. (who significantly wonders whether he is not "a ghost, a tax ghost, an examiner ghost," *GL*, 249–50), he makes his approach known through a "powerful singing voice" (*GL*, 247). And even more specifically, "the song became a kind of aria" (*GL*, 246). When he enters A.'s room, he is viewed as an actor in his role: "In stepped a very old imposing-looking man, with a white mane and a white beard *hanging* around his head."[5] This specific appearance had been prepared in the historical and epistemological frame of the "Voices 1933," where it is stated: "We laughed no longer, now we saw / the mask of terror, the funeral kitsch / tied to the executioner's philistine face . . ." (*GL*, 232).[6]

A., too, is identified within the operatic reference system. He thinks in terms of "dress rehearsals" (*GL*, 210), and when the purchase of the hunting lodge has been completed, he realizes: "Final scene of an opera, thought A., a tragic opera, in fact— or at least tragicomic" (*GL*, 223). He also sees himself participate in an operatic scene: "And he, a naked man, with many bones and many joints, but nevertheless an operatic marionette under clothing consisting of many parts, moved toward the group" (*GL*, 224). As in the case of the grandfather, the "Voices 1933" provide the verdict (recalling a technique used in *The Sleepwalkers* when narrative and commentary were related through identical key words to indicate the "narrator as idea"): ". . . intent on slogans and marionette-like moved by them (including now and then the slogans of progress), but always a cowardly murderer and sanctimonious to the marrow—that is the philistine: Woe! Woe!" (*GL*, 231.)

Zacharias, too, is viewed as an operatic figure, though his *Liebestod* is the mock-parodistic exploration of the unity of the two lovers beyond the ecstacy of their common death into the realm below. The theme of the netherworld is introduced when Zacharias and A. emerge in a state of drunken stupor from the wine restaurant and pass a group of workers mending streetcar tracks in the middle of the night, wearing "great black masks" and communicating "in raucous shouts." In the noise of the "restless hammering as of scythe blades being pounded on an anvil" (*GL*, 156), the death symbol of the scythe blades fuses with that of the Vulcanic hammering on an anvil. In *The Death of Virgil*, the Vulcanic netherworld had been investigated. This night episode is an abbreviated replica complete with the gales of laughter, so demonically emanating from the workers. At the same time, properties of Zacharias and A. are emphasized which recall the drunken triad of *The Death of Virgil*. A. looks up to the "tall and gaunt" Zacharias, who is "limping a little" (*GL*, 156) and tries to show "his loyalty and friendship and devotion" (*GL*, 157). The third member of the party, the plump and screeching woman, joins the men as they arrive at Zacharias' home. She is Zacharias' wife Philippine, partner in the Wagnerian *Liebestod*. She wields, in modification of the sadistic whip, but for the same purpose and with equal efficiency, a bourgeois featherduster and explains to the stunned A. where they have lived ever since their ecstatic union ten years ago: in hell. And she predicts: "When a house is hell, it can only get worse and worse. And believe me, it will get worse. We haven't reached our last hell; far from it . . ." (*GL*, 163). The scathing indictment of the petit-bourgeois mentality widens into an attack on the ecstatic *Untergangsstimmung* (anticipation of doom), epitomized and glorified in Wagner's mythologizing.

The apocalyptic level is stressed in the biblical connotations of Zacharias' name. Zacharias was the eleventh of the twelve minor prophets of the Old Testament, famous for his strongly ethical exhortations. Like his prophetic predecessor, Studienrat Zacharias proclaims the advent of the new *Reich* with messianic zeal inspired by apocalyptic visions. His irrational, garbled mythologizing of the German nation and German destiny correlates with foreboding political events of the same period: Hitler's political activities culminated in the unsuccessful *Putsch* of November 8–9, 1923—a year which is still the time of "minor" events and minor prophets. (Zacharias' insignificance also shows in the lack of success of his statements on Einstein's theory of relativity.) A drunken *Studienrat* (high school professor), typical enough of the philistine mentality (replete with felt slippers and linoleum floors), may be a perfect vehicle for "the banality of evil." The interpretation of Hitler as a petit-bourgeois phenomenon, however, is incapable of rendering the enormity of the crimes. *Kitsch* and the demonism of opera magic are here made to carry critical implications far in excess of the ordinary use of these words and hamper the impact of Broch's criticism.

Hildegard's name also provides a key to her position in the demonic world of the apocalypse. She, like the other protagonists, presents a negative version of a positive example. Her description as "nunlike" (GL, 64) establishes the connection with the historical nun Hildegard von Bingen, "the first of the great German Mystics, a poet and a prophet, a physician and a political moralist, who rebuked popes and princes, bishops and layfolk, with complete fearlessness and unerring justice."[7] Hildegard v. W. in her outspoken, straightforward manners provides in the last of the eleven stories, "Passing Cloud," the demonic, modern counterpart of the medieval nun when, on the way to church, she has visions of the devil's imminent kingdom. Like Zacharias and Philippine, she is an inhabitant of the world below. She is at home in the hierarchy and geography of hell long before physical death ever occurs. The anti-world of the living dead seems to be the only province that Broch can visualize for the virulent negativity of these characters.

Several layers of hell—and netherworld images—converge in Hildegard. The most obvious and consistently repeated identification is with a blood sucking vampire. In A.'s shortsighted vision, this characteristic is modified into: "a bloodthirsty blue-stocking" (GL, 213). After Hildegard has provoked and witnessed Melitta's suicidal fall to death, she seduces A. who is ignorant of Melitta's death at the time he succumbs to Hildegard; but Hildegard plays her sinister act in full cognizance of the murder she has just "guiltlessly" committed. As behooves a vampire, she lives on killing, whether it is Melitta, her own desires, love, or A. (by reducing him to sexual impotence). Her vampire attributes become salient when she forces A. into a mock imitation of Christ's martyrdom before she takes him down to the realm of hell. When she digs her long fingernails into A.'s scalp, he feels: "The pain did not come gradually; suddenly it was there, sharp and inescapable because her hands followed all his movements. 'Crown of thorns,' she said with a laugh, 'crown of thorns.' And she did not relax the pressure until drops of blood trickled down over his cheeks; almost tenderly, licking a little, she kissed away the rivulets of blood, and when the drops ceased to flow, she signed with a tender regret: 'There isn't any more' " (GL, 214).

After they have entered hell under Hildegard's guidance and before she entices A. to rape her, they are briefly "caught up in nonspace, and just as in nonspace the souls of the dead, removed from any common bond, hover side by side without ever touching, so did they" (*GL*, 215). The climax of the seduction scene occurs when A. must admit that he cannot perform sexually. As a sign of triumphant victory, Hildegard "held him in an iron grip and her teeth bit into his shoulder until the blood came" (*GL*, 218). Her beautiful and strong teeth had been Hildegard's most outstanding physical feature long before she used them to stigmatize A., relegating him into the nonworld of impotence. Typical of the vampires that satiate themselves with the blood of their victims, Hildegard falls asleep immediately after she has drawn the blood from A.'s shoulder: "In sleep her jaws relaxed . . . she slept like a block of wood, no, like a stone, no, like a corpse; it was as though she were breathing through her skin, not with her lungs; his feeling, whether loving desire or desirous love, was subdued by the frivolous thought that he would be desecrating a corpse . . . he in turn fell asleep like a block of wood, a stone, a corpse" (*GL*, 218). This macabre battle of the sexes emphasizes the negativity of the scene as a pseudo-Manichean battle between indolence and indecision on one side, murderous blood thirst and keen destructiveness on the other.

Yet Hildegard's association with death and hell exceed her attributes as vampire. When she entices A. to rape her, she does so in a mixture evoking the temptations of the snake in paradise (only now the reward would not be knowledge, but pleasure) and Persephone's rape by Hades, who carried her off to the realm of the dead. Hildegard says to A.: "Don't you see that you're expected to rape me?" (*GL*, 216). Images and gestures from previous novels occur in a startlingly new context. At the end of the second part of *The Sleepwalkers* trilogy, Esch and his wife, Mutter Hentjen, "went hand in hand and loved each other" (*SW*, 340). Now, Hildegard tantalizes A.: " 'Hand in hand with you to the realm of the dead,' she laughed. 'And when we return to the world, our desires will never cease . . . is it a pact? Is it a promise?' " (*GL*, 213). The orphic passage through the netherworld for the sake of love had already been rejected in *The Death of Virgil*. And when Hildegard muses: "A guide to the realm of the dead, a guide into nonbeing, in the hope of attaining being . . ." (*GL*, 213), she repeats Marius' convoluted redeemer–and leader speculations, but also recalls Lysanias, the "little guide," who tempted the dying Virgil. Besides, the "pact" evokes the pact with the devil.

The negative connotations of the apocalypse-turned-hell find one more representation in the "Commendatore," the operatic visitation from death. Melitta's semimythical grandfather is by profession a beekeeper who called the adopted little girl Melitta, that is, "little bee". When he comes to see A., he speaks of him as a "drone" (*GL*, 257). (In another context, A. is identified with wasps, in each instance a non-productive variety of bee.) Here the poet of *The Death of Virgil* renders homage to another of Virgil's works, the *Georgics*, which concludes with the myth of the beekeeper Aristaeus.[8] Aristaeus, "guiltlessly" guilty of Eurydice's death, loses his swarm of bees. After various trials (the descent to his mother's underwater kingdom, the chaining of Proteus and forcing information from him, and the appropriate sacrifices to the offended parties) he finds a new swarm of bees, emerging from the decaying belly of one of the sacrificed animals. Embedded in the Aristaeus myth is the myth of Orpheus and Eurydice and the myth of the Thracian women, tearing Orpheus to pieces.

Although the Commendatore/beekeeper appears to A. in the role of judge, he offers by no means an "absolute" reference system. His introduction as an operatic figure is a first indication; his association with the Aristaeus–and Orpheus myths a second. He resembles the country doctor of the *Mountain Novel*, when he returns to the country after living in the city, and he resembles Mutter Gisson in her anachronistic harmony with nature. He raises an adopted girl, and, like Mutter Gisson, is unable to protect the young woman from her catastrophic encounter with first love. His view of nature is idealistic and precivilizational, so that his occupation as an itinerant apiculturist seems tinged with insincerity: ". . . his love for the bees was now tempered by a certain melancholy contempt of these models of bourgeois caution, discipline and savings-bank mentality, in short, of the bourgeois striving for security. He came to regard the life of the bees, and of all domesticated animals for that matter, as an intrusion of the unnatural into nature" (*GL*, 81). After having lived through World War I, suffered through the inflation, worked in a factory, he withdraws into the county and into a remoteness, which "enfolded him like a holy cloak" (*GL*, 87). But while "he strode singing through the countryside, a giant with a white beard and a white mane" (*GL*, 87), fascism and Nazism grow without meeting substantial resistance,

He becomes "guiltless" like the other protagonists. (In this respect, too, he is like Mutter Gisson, who witnesses the rise of Marius and the sacrificial slaughter of her granddaughter without any attempt to interfere.)

Consonant with his view of nature, he subscribes to a cyclical-catastrophic view of time and history, in which death and rebirth are suffered fatalistically: "Every two thousand years the cosmic cycle is completed, and the power of completion shakes not only the cosmos, but also and perhaps still more the human self—how could it be otherwise? The time of the end is the time of birth, and the unchangeable undergoes a change, the catastrophe of growth. Blessed and cursed is the generation that lives in the period of change. It has a task" (*GL*, 260). Broch employs here the same method of limiting perspectives as in his other novels. A. views the grandfather / beekeeper as judge and under his gentle probings prepares for atonement. But the beekeeper is himself a relativized character, with his assets and shortcomings. The cyclical view of time suits his character.

II   *Guiltlessness: a geometry of mind*

The operatic images of a *kitsch* apocalypse and mock descents into various hells alive with an assortment of philistine marionettes provide a scathing commentary on the characters and their actions. The presence of geometrical designs and Einstein's theory of relativity open another level of critical insight. In *The Guiltless*, the thesis of history as a movement propelled by cognitive and "revolutionary" advances in knowledge is focused in Einstein's theory of relativity. It serves as a frame of reference within which the actions of individual protagonists are evaluated. The extent to which they hide from the insecurity and instability accompanying the revolution of knowledge also becomes the measure of their guilt.

The dissolution of three-dimensionality into multidimensionality becomes one of the *leitmotivs* for the progressive disintegration of reality. This dissolution is subjectively experienced by A. and objectively correlated to the scientific advances represented by Einstein's theory of relativity. The implications of that theory are discussed in a meeting in 1923, attended by Studienrat Zacharias and A. The theory is the unstated symbolic reference point whenever hitherto stable contours begin to dissolve into dynamic movement. A. experiences this dynamization and simultaneous dissolution into multidimensionality with fear and anxiety, combatting it with the return to the

mother, "island of three-dimensionality amid the infinite" (*GL*, 261).
Going beyond *The Sleepwalkers*, where the development into increasing abstraction was hypothetically projected, *The Guiltless* con-
cretizes this abstraction in Einstein's theory and sets it up as an
inevitable development against which the protagonist's "romantic"
and conservative attitudes must be measured. Advance to the
abstract universe as indicated in Einstein's theory offers the only
possibility for an eventual reintegration of value systems. This
hypothesis finds a prefiguration in the introductory "Parable of the
Voice" and a striking affirmation in the "Voices: 1933," where Broch
connects his theses of an historically conditioned image of god and of an
infinitely unattainable value center. The acceptance of this dynamic,
abstract universe constitutes his final conversion to a frame of reference which he had rejected as a young man (in the lament over Adolf
Loos' "Ornament and Crime" in 1913, and in the diatribes against the
absence of ornamentation in *The Sleepwalkers* of 1931–1932).

Less radical than Einstein's theory of relativity as a critical frame of
reference but equally expressive of Broch's attempt at abstraction, is
the prevalence of geometrical designs in *The Guiltless*. Geometrical
shapes identify some of the characters. The triangle is A.'s particular
mode of perceiving the world and personal relationships. It domi-
nates the narrative from the moment he leaves the railroad station
upon arrival in the town where he will take residence in the house of
Baroness v. W., until he shoots himself. The triangle, and by
modification the three-dimensional, serve A. as a reference system in
which he formulates his reflections. A.'s often unconscious arrangement of surrounding phenomena into triadic constellations shows his
particular cognitive mechanisms and boundaries. Broch here repeats
a technique he had already perfected in *The Sleepwalkers* and again
used in *The Death of Virgil*.

A. experiences the arrival in town in the following terms: "Behind
him lay the station, forming the base of an elongated isosceles
triangle, the Bahnhofsplatz, whose apex pointed into the city
proper—a sort of funnel" (*GL*, 43). On the occasion of his first dinner
in the v. W. household, he notices the portrait of the dead judge v.
W. looking sternly down on them from above the sideboard. (Even in
such details, the juxtaposition of the bourgeois—the sideboard in the
dining room—with the dead and the apocalyptic—the baroness' dead
husband as stern ruler and judge—is most striking.) A. now perceives
the relationship of the judge to the women present in similar geometrical terms: "Hildegard had also raised her eyes to the picture; like

two converging streets her gaze and Zerline's culminated in the
father's eyes, whereas the baroness, who after all had been closest to
the man up there on the wall, looked almost guiltily at her plate" (*GL,*
65–66). This image is repeated in a variation when A. returns to the
railroad station to pick up his luggage. The third person narrative is
charged with the emotional ballast of A.'s perceptions, indicating the
"narrator as idea": "Here at the base of the triangle, the bustle and
dirt of a world without peace; outside, the coolness and measure of
the square. And menacing, at the apex of the pyramid, he whose
measured severity towers above the turmoil of humanity and dirt,
soars over man, the guardian of justice!" (*GL,* 71). Another variation
occurs in the topographical juxtaposition of triangles upon one
another. "Between the triangle of the park, whose outlines were no
longer clearly perceptible, and the triangle of houses something new
had injected itself: the triangle of street lamps in the middle of the
three streets" (*GL,* 74).

The female triad of *The Guiltless* is a variation on the female triads
found in *The Sleepwalkers* and in the *Mountain Novel.* Yet in *The
Guiltless,* the female triad undergoes dynamic changes. At one point,
the constellation shows a mother with two nunlike companions: "If
the baroness was the maternal element in this triangle, the childless
faces of Zerline and Hildegard were strangely united in their nun-
likeness, the one old and rustic, the other refined and young . . ."
(*GL,* 64). Then again, they are adultress (Baroness v. W.), procuress
(Zerline), and vampire (Hildegard).

Once the triangle is firmly established as basic form, it allows of
certain "ornamentations." The geometrical arrangement of the *Bahnhofsplatz* becomes quite complex: "Two symmetrical S-shaped
paths crossed the triangular park. At their intersection stood a kiosk,
surmounted by a large clock with three faces . . ." (*GL,* 44). And this
intersection, "where the two main paths crossed," was "the center of
the park, the center of the inscribed circle" (*GL,* 70–71).[9] Two
symmetrical S-shapes combine to form the mathematical sign for
infinity. The tension between triangle and infinity, between three-
and multidimensionality is one of the sources of A.'s personal fears
and anxieties, but also of the era at large, as concretized in the debate
over Einstein's theory of relativity. A.'s entire guilt of omission and of
human failure, of indifference and of indolence, can be captured
within this mathematical design. This is evident in his experience of
the world just before he shoots himself: ". . . a consoling triangle

bounded by tender-gray lines covered the whole northern half of the heavenly dome, and out of its center, profoundly clear and wakeful, colorless and unfathomable, timeless with age, the eye of the cosmos looked down with awe-inspiring familiarity, . . . the dissolution of the three-dimensional, flowed round the edges of the triangle, and borne by the blind eye of the center, . . . it flowed downward . . . in infinitely many dimensions" (*GL*, 268). After A. has shot himself, he falls in that position which designates the intersection of the two symmetrical S-shapes: the St. Andrew's cross.

This design seems to state that man is the center of the universe, of the three-dimensional, tangible world; that the infinite resides in the finite; and that the moment of death alone can bring the mystic fusion and vision of totality. But these geometrical figures indicate A.'s particular reference system alone. A. dies with a vision of the universe consistent with his cognitive frame, but this frame does not apply to all characters in the novel, much less can it be used as a general interpretation of Broch's mystic vision. This is obvious when one considers Hildegard's reference system, equally expressed in geometrical terms, but of a different nature. A. is the conservative, romantic individual; physically this is expressed in his Biedermeier beard, psychologically in his attachment to the Mother, and geometrically in the triangle.

Hildegard, in her "cool" demonism, is the person of the future. For her, the two sides of the triangle no longer converge into an apex, symbol of a hierarchic and closed order, but open up into parallels. Where A. disguises his face behind the old-fashioned Biedermeier beard, Hildegard's features are straight, even "beautiful in their straightness," and when she sits, "her feet were set down parallel to one another" (*GL*, 75).

In the last story, "A Passing Cloud," taking place in the summer of 1933, the "old maid" is on her way to church. On the way she encounters an individual whom the reader recognizes as Zacharias. As she walks up the incline to the *Schlosskirche* (ducal church), the third-person narrative serves to indicate her particular reference system: "When one has mounted the street to the gentle summit, the oblique line of house bases ends, the base line and and the rows of windows become reassuringly parallel, and not too far off one sees the Schlossplatz into which the street opens" (*GL*, 273–74). Yet, the parallels do not continue unchecked into infinity. At the end of the oval *Schlossplatz* (square in front of the church), into which the parallel lines of the street open, stands the *Schloss*, the grand ducal castle, and "catches the eye like a fine baroque backdrop" (*GL*, 273–74). The "backdrop" (*Kulisse*) immediately recalls the stage world of the opera, while the transformation of the parallels into the closed system of the ellipse (the oval of the *Schlossplatz*) hints at the peculiarity of parallels in the macroscopic spaces of Einsteins' general theory of relativity: they intersect in infinity. Here, however, the intersection has been projected back into finite dimensions, providing a most graphic representation of Broch's theory of imitation systems, which foreshorten the infinite into the finite. At the same time, mention of the Baroque (for which the oval was the preferred architectural design and the triangle the spiritual symbol) adds an historical reference system, fulfilling a similar function as the Middle Ages did more explicitly in *The Sleepwalkers.*

Hildegard, ascending to the *Schlossplatz*, after having passed Zacharias as he descends from there, feels his glance on her neck. Too well bred to turn around,[10] she decides to trace a big arch (in a *straight line* across the oval to the church steps, through the church and out a side entrance to an "austere double arcade") (*GL*, 279), and is now in a position to look from behind, without turning her head, at what is forbidden. As she "leans against the pillar between the two arches" (*GL*, 280), she stands at the temporal and spatial intersection of forbidden territory. On the psychological level she fancies her "pursuer" to be the devil. She sees herself, consonant with the perverted sexuality she had shown toward A., as the devil's "victim and bedfellow, she, prepared for witchhood" (*GL*, 283). Her excitement about seduction and rape is visualized in the appropriate geometrical terms. "The straight walks of the park intertwine, forming circles, they twine into an obscene knot in which all things are alike, and twining they devour one another, engendering each other forever anew" (*GL*, 282–83). Her sexual excitement culminates in the vision: "Inexorable the rape! in the glaring sun the jumble of devils strike up the round dance, the shadowless limping dance, to which in a moment the pursuer with his servile limp and servile bow would lead her away, inexorable his seduction and rape" (*GL*, 283).

When the old maid finally surveys the *Schlossplatz* from her vantage point between the double arches, she finds it empty of devils. The Nazi flag, implanted on the *Schlossplatz*, hangs limp, perhaps an indication of the still relatively quiet position of the new regime in its first few months of power, but also symbol of her thwarted sexual fantasies.

The flag hung limp on its pole, and the rape had been called off again [an oblique reference to A.], perhaps only postponed, but in any case called off for today. A malicious pleasure mingled with regret arose in the old maid's soul. Once again, perhaps for the last time, the cool beauty of the past and its work had defeated the limping plebeian demons and their superlatively stupid ugliness. (GL, 284)

Despite her straightforward manner Hildegard cheats. She perverts the open system into a closed one. In the guise of a pious old maid she fantasizes about the devil and rape. She is titillated by her visions of obscenity, yet clings to an old system in which she finds momentary protection and regretful relief. More of a coward and more of a hypocrite than the other protagonists, she, too, will join the *danse macabre* of the "guiltless."

The Guiltless presents Broch's strongest political indictments. Published five years after *The Death of Virgil*, it counteracts that novel's emphasis on the internalized, lyrical journey into the metaphysical realm of the cognition of death and attests to Broch's concern with political situations as the result of psychological phenomena.

The Guiltless draws on Broch's essays and on the research he had conducted intermittently since his arrival in the United States. The novel deals, partly as a result of that research—which in turn was motivated by concrete political events—with more concrete historical data than any of the preceding novels. In the light of more recent theories on mass phenomena, one may disagree with Broch when he maintains that the key to an understanding of mass-hysteria lies in the understanding of the individual. Yet his interpretation of Germany as a country gone to hell, inhabited by devils, vampires, and impotents in the guise of philistines, relies on a powerful vision embedded in a coherent system. The Germany of 1933 fulfills the prophecy of the advent of the Anti-Christ expressed in *The Sleepwalkers*. The atomization of the value systems has led to integration into an infernally closed imitation system. Hitler as Anti-Christ concludes the interpretation of German history as *Heilsgeschichte* or rather *Unheilsgeschichte*. [11]

CHAPTER 7

The Grand Defiance: Nevertheless!

B ROCH'S productive years as an intellectual extended from the
publication of *The Sleepwalkers* in 1931–32 to his death in 1951.
Twelve of these twenty years he spent in exile. However, life in exile
only reinforced interests and concerns he had brought with him from
Austria. Two of his major novels (*The Death of Virgil*, 1945 and *The
Guiltless*, 1950) draw on material outlined before he fled his native
country. The unfinished *Mountain Novel* was based on a draft he had
abandoned in Vienna during 1937. The major concepts of the mass
psychology and the theory of democracy originated in the "Resolution to the League of Nations" from the pre-*Anschluss* days. Even
Broch's working habits remained essentially the same. When he took
a stand on a contemporary issue in the United States in the Cold War
period, he would expand the topic on hand and provide an entire
theoretical structure into which it could fit.

Asked to evaluate the American influence upon his work, Broch
considered it to be zero in his literary writings, "since the irrational
structure, which is the basis of the poetic craft, is built in earliest
youth" (*GW*, VIII, 404). In the political writings, the situation is
somewhat different "since we are here dealing with rational
influences. Those have been considerable." And Broch specified
further: "Above all, I learned the effectiveness of democracy, learned
it in a thorough manner, not just *en passant*, and since I have now
been engaged for a number of years in studies of mass psychology and
therefore politics . . . this participation in the American democracy,
the direct observation of its advantages and deficiencies, was and is
for me extremely important" (*GW*, VIII, 405).[1]

Broch's first contribution published in exile was part of the collective statement *The City of Man: A Declaration on World Democracy*,
of 1941.[2] The slim volume attempted to set up criteria for a democracy capable of defeating fascism and totalitarianism, and identified the United States as the country to carry out this task. In his

142

"Autobiography as Work-Program," written soon afterward, Broch remembers: "it offered me great satisfaction to participate with these views in the *City of Man*, cooperating with a group which made it its goal to investigate the conditions for a new stabilization of the democratic ideal and to analyze it from all sides. As far as the extraphilosophical, concrete aspects are concerned, my first contribution at the conference consisted in delineating the economic problems; their exploration has been planned as a major point of the common work program" (*GW*, IX, 59). Broch's exposition of these problems in the "Autobiography as Work Program" is considerably longer (*GW*, IX, 59–77) than the joint statement which appears in *The City of Man*.

The City of Man shows unmistakably Brochian influence where the interpretation of Marxism is concerned. From the years immediately after World War I, Broch still adhered to the idealistic-ethical basis of Austro-Marxism: "Marxism would hardly have gripped the masses if its economic motivation had not been implemented with the resources of a moral will to justice."[3] Similarly Brochian terminology is used in the definition of democracy. "Universal and total democracy is the principle of liberty and life which the dignity of man opposes to the principle of slavery and spiritual death represented by totalitarian autocracy."[4]

The entry of the United States into World War II on December 7, 1941, channeled Broch's attention away from work on the *Death of Virgil* and toward his studies of mass psychology. In May, 1942, he received a grant from the Rockefeller Foundation. He became an independent assistant to Hadley Cantril, head of the Office of Public Opinion Research at Princeton University, which had sponsored the application.

I *"Total Democracy"*

The "Rockefeller Outline," submitted in English in early 1942 as part of the application for the grant, shows that Broch proposed a three-volume work in mass psychology (*GW*, VII, 257–82) and that he had done enough work to visualize the entire complex. During the nine remaining years of his life, he completed larger sections of this opus than one is led to believe on the basis of the incomplete edition, published by the Rhein-Verlag. Here, Broch takes the step from an analysis of conditions that lead to mass hysteria, to prescriptions about how to combat them; and he suggests a countersystem, effective enough to overcome the prevalent fascisms: total democracy.

The term "total democracy" had already appeared in *The City of Man*. The prescriptive measures to protect the "dignity of man" stem from the "Resolution." Broch found, that even the Unites States, stronghold of democracy, was not sufficiently immune to the dangers of fascism, spreading rapidly over Europe, and celebrating its latest official triumph in the collaboration of the Pétain government of France with Germany. He saw democracy as an "endangered species"[5] and felt that it could not afford to be indifferent to its own survival, but must take steps to protect itself. He stated in the "Rockefeller Outline": "Total democracy distinguishes itself from democracy as practised up to now by an inclusion of the regulating fundamentals into the norms regulating the mutual relations between individuals. Similar to the punitive practice of the Bolshevik or the National-Socialist State toward an 'antirevolutionary' or 'antinational' attitude respectively, total democracy would have to punish anti-humane behavior as such" (*GW*, VII, 279).

The "Rockefeller Outline" falls into three parts. The first part consists of the theory of mass psychology. Masses are formed when the individual seeks oblivion and protection from metaphysical anguish and spiritual helplessness by abdicating his personal responsibility in order to fuse with an entity larger than himself. For this condition, Broch introduced the term "twilight state of mind." It is not unlike Emile Durkheim's "rabaissement du niveau mental" in the sense that the individual forgoes an already attained level of awareness. When he gives up his individuality and fuses with the masses, he becomes an easy prey for demagogues. As Broch describes it: "Man loses the capacity of his specially human consciousness. He loses his individual mental physiognomy. The twilight state makes men to mass. The mass is the product of the individual twilight state of mind" (*GW*, VII, 259). As always, the specifically Brochian connection between individual ethical duty and cognitive advances based on consciousness is most prominent.

Yet this view opens a Pandora's box of inconsistencies, if not outright miscalculations, because it suggests an extremely idiosyncratic interpretation of history: if history is premised on development, and development on advances of knowledge, then the twilight state of mind is an antihistorical, even nonhistorical, condition. Masses would then have to be considered as historically nonexistent magnitudes. Broch had already intimated this much in *The Sleepwalkers*, when he insisted that only those acts which are in agreement with the autonomy of the "I" and hence manifestations of the cognitive search, can create values and, through values, history.[6] In *The Death of Virgil* he subsequently explored the antipodal forces by opposing Virgil's cognitive-ascending quest with the ahistorical, sempiternal realm of the mothers.

In the second part of the "Rockefeller Outline," Broch proposed to investigate the relationship between the masses and the leader figures. He distinguished between two basic types of leadership: "religious ecstasy on one side, the megalomania of the conqueror on the other" (*GW*, VII, 269). The elements of ecstasy (or "ego expansion") and panic (or "ego diminution") are seen as the two poles within which the masses swerve back and forth, manipulated by the leader who promises to convert panic into ecstasy. He fulfills this promise by singling out scapegoats as the cause for the "ego diminution." The novels provide a demonstration of the mechanisms Broch saw in operation. The *Mountain Novel* depicted the machinations of the demagogue Marius and his exploitation of the twilight state of mind in the villagers. The discussions between Augustus and Virgil in *The Death of Virgil* concentrated on the leader-father Augustus and his tired and skeptical assessment of the masses. *The Guiltless* showed how the progressive "rabaissement du niveau mental" prepares for the takeover of any demagogue.

Included in this part of the "Rockefeller Outline" is Broch's introduction to the theory of "psychical cycles in history." It is discussed in greater detail in the third part of the "Rockefeller Outline" and in the large fragment "Autobiography as Work Program" written at approximately the same time (*GW*, IX, 77–236). The theory postulates four psychical phases and interprets their ever-renewed sequence as dialectical progression. The four phases are: "(a) prevalence of a central value—fairly correspondent with reality until the completion of a closed system; (b) breakup of this closed system through hypertrophy of the deductive process; (c) institution of reality—without a central value system; (d) hypertrophy of various detached systems" (*GW*, VII, 271). The dialectical progression occurs since "in the course of the development the normal and abnormal phases relate dialectically like thesis and antithesis; each of the following phases therefore ought to be considered the synthesis of the two preceding ones" (*GW*, IX, 95). When Broch demonstrates the mechanics of this theory by referring to past history (*GW*, IX, 95–96), he simultaneously provides background information on *The Sleepwalkers* and on the soon-to-be-written *The Guiltless*. *The Sleepwalkers* focuses on the antipodal relation of the Middle Ages to the late

nineteenth and early twentieth centuries as exemplifications of phases
1 and 4, *The Guiltless* dwells on the Baroque and the first third of the
twentieth century as exemplification of phases 3 and 4.

Broch attached great importance to the scientific character of this
theory since he hoped that it would compete with the Marxist view of
history. In agreement with the Marxists' claim that history progresses
according to scientific laws, he demanded that a scientific theory of
history should allow to predict and influence the course of the future
(*GW*, IX, 99). He believed that his model had the same scientific
irrefutability as did Marxist economic theory. He hoped that his
theory was superior to the Marxist one, since it did not limit itself to a
view of man as defined by economics.

The possibility of influencing and predicting the future became
intimately connected with Broch's theory of democracy, which is
sketched in the third part of the "Rockefeller Outline." According to
Broch's antimaterialistic philosophy, the forces that can be called
upon to shape history are not material or political factors. Instead,
Broch would rely on the rational process of education to free man
from mass hysteria and the twilight state. Due to enlightened education, the two abnormal phases of the psychical cycles ("hypertrophy
of the deductive process" and "hypertrophy of various detached
systems") would diminish while the integrative periods would expand. Broch included chapters on a general "Theory of Conversion"
and on "Political Conversion" in the "Rockefeller Outline," in which
he defined conversion as a shift "from a closed to an open or more
open system" and insisted that "changing a closed into an open
system is the goal of the fight against mass aberrations" (*GW*, VII,
272). In contrast to religious conversion, which "makes use of irrational and rational instruments, nonreligious, that is, secularized,
conversion emphasizes rational understanding" (*GW*, VII, 273).[7]

The main tool in this secular, political conversion is propaganda.
Yet propaganda, in Broch's system, is not an irrational enticement by
demagogues, but "as an instrument of the fight against mass aberra-
tion must follow the line of rational persuasion and education" (*GW*,
VII, 274). "Rational persuasion and education" become the topics of
detailed proposals in the post–World War II era, culminating in
suggestions for an international university where the theory of humanity and of democracy would be taught, and where peace research
could be conducted. The goal of education would be to "demass" the
masses, thus making the individual impervious to demagogic ap-

peals. It would mean "to form a community out of a multitude of individuals living in a twilight state of mind" (GW, VII, 274). Broch realized the need for a power mechanism to protect this fragile democratic structure. The last section of this third part is concerned with questions on how best to enforce the ideals of this democracy and how to equip democracy with the legal means to protect itself against irrational infringements. The juridical measures to implement and enforce the statutes of a "Bill of Rights" and a "Bill of Duties" were the subject of later and more detailed treatises, but the foundations for their inclusion in Broch's system were laid in the "Rockefeller Outline."

In "Autobiography as Work Program," Broch elucidated the theory of psychical cycles. In doing so, he engaged in a bit of speculative geometry, which is interesting since it reveals Broch's manner of visualizing historical processes. As a series of designs, this speculation is clear and consistent, but as a theory of history it may be misleading, as Broch acknowledged: ". . . spatial images are part of the most frequent sources of mistakes in all so-called logical speculations, and the image of the circle is no exception . . ." (GW, IX, 97). Psychical cycles suggest, as Broch admits, a circular movement. Yet in a "relatively useless mental game" one can visualize that "the circle becomes an increasingly narrower structure until it is finally compressed into a line" (GW, IX, 97). The psychical cycles then occur along the line of the pendulum swing. Movement along the trajectory of a pendulum seems as inescapable as that within the circle, but it offers Broch a visual advantage to further expound on his theory: "It is precisely the movement of the pendulum which demonstrates that one can shorten the span or lengthen the middle stretch: provided mankind has a free will in the use of its reason, it should be in a position to avoid, or at least diminish, the plunges into mass hysteria once it has recognized the laws by which they operate" (GW, IX, 97). This middle stretch, no matter how long, is still a basically static representation of history as a continually repeated movement between two extreme positions. Broch did not see that it was thus in opposition to his conceptualization of history as a dynamic forward movement into ever increasing abstraction implying essential, qualitative changes.[8]

There is little documented evidence that Broch was more than superficially acquainted with the prevalent theories of mass psychology.[9] Whatever the extent of his background knowledge, his ap proach was both determined and limited by the Kantian "loneliness of the I" and the concomitant ethical directives.[10] Emphasis on the individual and the importance of his cognitive efforts barred any possible consideration of the mass as an entity *sui generis*, as proposed, for example, by Emile Durkheim. Yet this emphasis did not contradict his view that archetypal substrata operate in each character. Broch was in agreement with C. G. Jung, who similarly saw no conflict between positing, on the one hand, a collective unconscious, and insisting, on the other hand, on a process of individuation and self-realization. For both men, the overriding concept of "totality" implied an ideal state of completeness and conscious integration of irrational forces.

II *Dispersed Efforts*

The worst racial riots in the United States during World War II erupted in June, 1943. As Broch was prone to do, he reacted to these events by suggesting further improvements to his theoretical systems. He "amended" the regulative principles of the "Bill of Rights" with the "Bill of Duties" which focused on a "Law for the Protection of Human Dignity." The enjoyment of democracy, which grants rights to each citizen, would be coupled with the responsibility on the part of each citizen to protect the same rights in others. The five major points of the "Bill of Duties"[11] bear on (a) protection of the "Bill of Rights;" (b) protection against legislative discrimination; (c) protection against economic discrimination; (d) protection against civil discrimination; and (e) protection against hate campaigns. Each of these categories was accompanied by appropriate punitive measures to be enforced in case of violation. Although occasioned by the race riots in Detroit, and framed to protect all minorities, the "Bill of Duties" clearly refers to the situation of the Jews in Hitler Germany.

Broch realized that enforcement of these statutes could not be left to the discretion of individual governments. Hence, forever widening the range of his concerns, he proposed an International Court of Justice. In a similar manner, Broch explained the "Bill of Duties" at the conclusion of World War II in his "Remarks concerning the Utopia of an 'International Bill of Rights and Responsibilities,'" and circulated the document among his friends. He submitted the proposal to the newly established United Nations, in 1946, addressing it to the commission of Human Rights, which was headed by Eleanor Roosevelt. It remained unanswered.[12]

The same lack of response occurred in reaction to Broch's suggestions for an "International University" which would specialize in peace research and teach the theory of humanity.[13] Broch had worked on the manuscript in 1944 and again in 1946. Encouraged by his friends and sponsors, he submitted it in 1948, through the New School for Social Research and the office of its director, Bryn J. Hovde, to UNESCO in Paris (*GW*, VIII, 357). Yet beginning with the "Resolution to the League of Nations" of 1937, all of Broch's political proposals shared a similar fate: obsoleteness or oblivion in archives. Nevertheless, Broch persevered in constructing his "concrete utopia"[14] because he believed in the role of the intellectual, in the efficacy of rational propositions, and in the ultimate superiority of cognitive advances over material forces.

Despite the discouraging lack of response, Broch did not lack publishers interested in his work. This was particularly the case in Europe after 1945, but American publishers also asked for his manuscripts, particularly after the critical success of *The Death of Virgil*. Ironically, Broch had very little to offer. His major manuscripts—the study of mass psychology and the theory of democracy—were in a state of incompletion. From January, 1946, until June, 1947, he was once more offered a fellowship, by the Bollingen Foundation, for work on mass psychology. Yet his old work patterns persisted in the post–World War II period. In the immediate postwar period, and after publication of *The Death of Virgil* in the spring of 1945, he had turned again from intellectual pursuits to immediate action. He had cooperated with the American Committee for Refugee Scholars, Writers, and Artists, which tried to find positions for exiles upon their return to Europe, and he had spent his limited funds on CARE packages. At the same time, a new avalanche of correspondence in the wake of the European liberation threatened to bury him. After the fellowship expired in June, 1947, he was forced, for the first time since his arrival in the United States, to accept commissioned work in order to meet his expenses.

The Bollingen Foundation now asked him to write an introduction to their proposed edition of Hugo von Hofmannsthal's collected work. Broch argued for an edition of Karl Kraus's work instead, since his old admiration for Karl Kraus made him a natural choice. But the Bollingen Foundation insisted on the Hofmannsthal edition, and Broch immersed himself in research. Broch's initial reluctance was due to his view of Hofmannsthal as a *fin-de-siècle* poet, hence as an aesthete. In the early phases of the study, on September 30, 1947, he wrote to Erich Kahler: "The Hofmannsthal starts to take shape. Just as a homosexual relationship develops slowly between the chamber maid and the lady, so I feel toward H.: with a sense of slight perversity I overcome my repulsion" (*GW*, VIII, 273). Yet with continued research, the project grew into an analysis of the late Austrian empire in which Broch discovered not only Hofmannsthal's religious and cultural heritage, but his own as well. The brief introduction grew to booklength and exemplified Broch's theory of the vacuum of values at the turn of the century. Once Hofmannsthal assumed exemplary character against a vaster historical background, Broch could make his peace with the project. Exactly one year after the letter to Kahler he wrote to Brody: "Actually, it is not a book about Hofmannsthal, but shows how a highly talented person becomes a bad poet because, out of weakness, he subjects himself to the conditions of his times" (*BBB*, 498). As Broch became ever more absorbed in the study, the deadline for the completion of the introduction could not be met. When the Bollingen Foundation finally insisted on the manuscript, he dashed off a brief essay, while the major part of the research was only posthumously published. It is recognized today as one of the significant contributions to the scholarship on Hugo von Hofmannsthal.[15]

The Bollingen Foundation also commissioned an introduction to Rachel Bespaloff's *Iliad*, and for once Broch complied without delay. "The Style of the Mythical Age" (written in English) has very little bearing on the subject at hand. It is rather an exploration of what Broch termed "the increasingly abstract style of old age" and is a trial transposition of his law of "psychical cycles" into antiquity. It was published by Pantheon in 1947. Yet Broch could not content himself with such a singular statement. His plans immediately assumed vaster proportions. He had written an essay for a special edition of the *Neue Rundschau*, honoring Thomas Mann's seventieth birthday, "Die mythische Erbschaft der Dichtung" ("The Mythical Legacy of Literature") in 1945. Now he proposed a book, containing these two essays on myth and a third one on the same subject, still to be written. The project never materialized. In a letter to Günter Anders, written one year before his death, on March 15, 1950, Broch analyzed his tendency to write voluminously on any subject that came into his view:

I am so thoroughly lazy that I shall die of overwork. Your suggestion of a diary does not apply in my case. In my untamed and untamable laziness, I could never wring one line for a diary out of myself. The act of writing is such a horrible effort for me, that I can carry it out only under the severest "business pressure." Hence every small idea turns immediately into a book. . . . (*GW*, VIII, 388)

Although there may have been some truth to this admission, it could also be that Broch's holistic vision provided constant distractions from projects at hand. His philosophical framework was flexible enough to accommodate any contemporary problem, from race riots to modern physics, from abstract art to the Cold War. The all-inclusiveness of his vision forced a fragmentation of his time and interests and created a situation which did not allow for the completion of many projects.

He felt fortunate that ten months at Princeton Hospital (June, 1948, to April, 1949) afforded him uninterrupted working time. While in the hospital, he abandoned the Hofmannsthal study against better judgment and concentrated on the theory of knowledge which was to be incorporated into the mass psychology. On August 5, 1948, he wrote: "The basic reason for this terrible situation is the theory of knowledge, which I introduced like an island into the island of the Hofmannsthal study . . ." (*BBB*, 495). (The Hofmannsthal study was an "island" in the mass psychology.)

Why did he work in such an erratic manner? Under the stress of the operations, he might have felt that he should leave to posterity what he considered his true contribution. In a number of letters from this period (for example *GW*, VIII, 288, 319, 337), he mentions that this theory of knowledge has occupied him for more than twenty years, and he admitted to Daniel Brody on September 19, 1948: "Inner compulsion drives me to the theory of knowledge; I have spent half a year working on it and within the next six months it could be finished, provided I have peace and tranquillity. I have spoken with Weyl and other mathematicians and I have the impression that I really made a few discoveries. Otherwise it would really be too terrible; more than twenty years' thoughts are invested in it" (*BBB*, 496).

The theory of knowledge also remained unfinished. Not only did the Bollingen Foundation insist on the Hofmannsthal study, and the German publisher Weismann expressed interest in republishing Broch's novellas from the preemigration period, but the New York publisher Alfred Knopf asked Broch for a novel. In the same letter of September 19, 1948, to Brody Broch mentions: "Now Knopf came, sent his editor already twice to the hospital and absolutely wants a novel. I gave him the *Mountain Novel* and he is quite enthusiastic. I, of course, much less so" (*BBB*, 496). *The Death of Virgil* was Broch's great testament to the superfluity of literature. No wonder that he wanted to convince Knopf that instead of a novel they should publish his theoretical work. The study of mass psychology already belonged to the Bollingen Foundation, since they had paid him an advance and a stipend on it. So now, after two years of silence on the subject (that is, after submission of the highly technical proposal to the United Nations), he came back to the "political book," which consisted of his theory of democracy, including a treatise on natural versus human rights and the legislative structure of the democratic system. Broch stated, hopefully, in a letter of September 28, 1948: "I would feel much better if I could induce Knopf to publish the political book; this book I deem a necessity, while the novel is surely not necessary for today's world" (*BBB*, 498). Yet five weeks later, on November 2, 1948, he realized: "Knopf will not take the political book unless I also offer him the *Mountain Novel*" (*GW*, VIII, 305). Knopf was willing to look at the political manuscript, but now Broch had nothing appropriate available. In typical fashion (while he should be completing the Hofmannsthal study and was actually at work on the theory of knowledge) he rewrote the political material. Broch described this process drily:

In December the Under-Knopf was here and asked for an "outline" of the political book. . . . Whereupon I started the outline. Whereupon it grew to 100 pages. Whereupon I decided it would be better to write immediately the first part of the book. Whereupon I did just that, another 100 pages, even more. Whereupon he was here a week ago and took it along. Whereupon he called yesterday, expressed his enthusiasm and submitted it to the board of directors. Whereupon, in another two weeks, they will reject it. But I am glad I wrote it. I am now in a position to write the entire book in a jiffy and I still won't have to worry about a publisher since Princeton Press. . . . (*BBB*, 504)

Broch did not feel quite as cheerful about the proposal submitted to Knopf as one might surmise from this letter. Correspondence with Hannah Arendt shows less confidence. A few days before the Brody letter, on February 14, 1949, he wrote to her: ". . . about this book I am in despair. I wanted 500,000 readers for this book, first because it contains a 'message,' and therefore really should be read; secondly, because I finally deserve a little money; and thirdly, because I promised Knopf something of the sort. Hence, it ought to be written in an easy style and not have more than 240 pages. Yet I am confronted with an impossible task . . ." (*GW*, VIII, 323).

This "political book"[16] draws on the "Resolution to the League of Nations" of 1937–1938 and the legal studies prior to it, as well as on his formulations of the "Bill of Duties." It deals, as he wrote to Hannah Arendt, with "the new foundations of the natural rights which now, for good reason, I rename human rights. As far as I know the literature on the subject—as a matter of fact I know it only up to approximately 1936[17]—nothing similar has ever been constructed. The political philosopher Schiffer, whom I asked, thinks—I hope with justification—that even after that period nothing of a similar nature can be found" (*GW*, VIII, 324). Convinced of the uniqueness of his contributions and unwilling to see them rejected for formalistic reasons, he asked her advice: ". . . should I rewrite the whole project? Can I dare give it to Knopf in its present form?" Hannah Arendt must have answered promptly, for exactly one week after Broch's first letter he responds to her reactions. From this detailed answer (in the letter of February 21, 1949, in *GW*, VIII, 328–30) it is obvious that the Knopf proposal was similar if not identical with the fragment "Politik: Ein Kondensat" ("Politics: A Summary", *GW*, VII, 203–255). In agreement with his decision that "it would be better to write immediately the first part of the book" (*BBB*, 504), the fragment consists of a first part ("Anarchy and Enslavement") in two chapters ("The Earthly Absolute" and "Human Rights").

The problem around which the fragment "Politics" revolved, bore on a philosophy and the structure of law which would make concentration camps, and any acts of inhumanity of man against man, impossible. For this purpose, Broch developed the concept of the "earthly absolute" and defined it as the absolute barrier between what is human and subhuman. Man can remain human only if he abides by "absolute" boundaries against barbarism. He demanded that legislation must be proposed that would enforce "absolute" respect for human rights since "the 'earthly absolute' human rights are for politics the only chance perhaps still to alleviate the chaos of our times" (*GW*, VII, 219). The existence of the "earthly absolute" seemed to him self-evident when viewed in analogy to the natural sciences with their absolute limits (such as the speed of light) (*GW*, VII, 215–16). In this anology Broch saw the scientific irrefutability guaranteed which he so desired for his proposal.

The invention of the "earthly absolute" also shows a persistent pattern in Broch's thinking from his earliest days on. Ever since the impact of Kant and neo-Kantianism on the young Broch, Broch's thinking had focused on "boundary cases," that is, absolute limits, and on the realization that the perceptor of boundaries is part of the definition of these boundaries. His admiration for Kant and his "heroic skepticism" in view of the cognitive boundaries was documented in the "Ethics" essay. *The Sleepwalkers* showed the application of this principle to the narrative structure in the "narrator as idea." In his theory knowledge he spoke of "symbols per se," and in anology with the sciences of "the physical person per se," or "the mathematical person per se" (*GW*, VII, 173–83 passim). When Broch posited the "earthly absolute," he transferred a concept that he had used consistently during his intellectual life to his latest field of inquiry. The "earthly absolute" constitutes the absolute boundaries imposed by man on the definition of himself. Since the "earthly absolute" defines only the boundaries of humanness and humaneness, a great variety of manifestations of these qualities within these boundaries is possible.

Knopf insisted on the novel first and Broch started to rework the *Mountain Novel.* The "political book" remained a fragment.[18]

In the fall of 1948, he put together a list of "work in progress." In his letters to different friends the list varies slightly,[19] yet the overall impression remains the same. In each instance, he underestimated the time necessary to carry out the projects. A letter to Daniel Brody from September 29, 1948, is the most revealing, since here Broch alludes briefly to the motives for work on the project:

> Above all, I would like to put together a schedule for the completion of my work, in which I also include, for the time being, the *Mountain Novel:*
> 1) Hofmannsthal . . . . November 48
> 2) Theory of knowledge . . . . June 49 (inner necessity)
> 3) Mountain Novel . . . . March 50 (outer necessity)
> 4) Intern. University . . . . June 50 (vanity & career)
> 5) Third essay on mythology for Albae
>   Vig. . . . . August 50 (ambition)
> 6) Politics . . . . March 51 (debt to the
>   guilt of the world)
> 7) Mass psychology . . . . April 1, 1999
> The novellas, poems, essays, etc. are not included here since they do not require any real work. (*BBB*, 498)

Even with such a work schedule, Broch never admitted defeat and continued to write at an unremitting pace, while the horizons of his life grew constantly darker. There were inner obstacles to overcome and outer difficulties to be met, such as publishers' pressures or the unsettling move to New Haven. In addition, the Cold War and the atmosphere of incipient McCarthyism in the United States militated against the very ideals Broch hoped to propagate. The title of the last essay published during his lifetime sums up his untiring and defiant gesture: "Nevertheless: Humane Politics. The Realization of a Utopia" in the *Neue Rundschau* of January, 1950. The essay was a condensation of the "political book," proposed to Knopf and is the only document dealing with the institutionalizing of "total democracy" published during Broch's life time. It summarized his thoughts in an urgent voice: ". . . modern man in his insecurity needs totalitarian measures, and since these endanger human rights, democracy has to defend them with totalitarian means" (*NR*, 15). And he continued: "Totalitarian governments protect their regulative principles (*regulative Grundprinzipien*) through a severe penal code. The human rights as the regulative principles of democracy need the same protection." In order not to confuse "totalitarian democracy" with contemporary democracies, Broch replaced it with the term "totalitarian humanity" (*NR*, 16), and hoped that it would prove to be the rallying point for a new integration of values: "In former times, it was the task of religion to maintain the individual, partial value systems in an ethical balance: there is a faint glimmer of hope that today this could be accomplished, or at least initiated, by 'totalitarian humanity' which is built upon human rights; this hope alone justifies its formulation" (*NR*, 19).

Broch was not concerned about the exact methods or legal systems which would implement this vision. Since he insisted that each step on the long road toward this "concrete utopia" must be infused with the humanity of the goal, it seemed to him self-evident that the individual measures could never violate the dignity of man and the protection of the human rights. The absence of a single, definite formal structure even seemed of advantage: " 'Totalitarian humanity' is not bound to a specific form of government or state but is rather an 'attitude'; just because it is flexible in its formal solutions while adamant in these attitudes, it could truly form the basis for a world party . . ." (*NR*, 25).

Although Broch unswervingly insisted on the realization of this utopia, he was aware that the world situation made its advent unlikely. Yet to abandon belief in the feasibility of these theories would have been tantamount to declaring the bankruptcy of idealism as well as of the mission of the intellectual, and would have meant cancellation of his most deeply felt convictions. Thus, he continued to work stubbornly and at a hectic pace, and battled the contradictions between historical development and personal vision, between facts and desires with the single-minded affirmation of his beliefs.

This single-mindedness gained added weight under the impact of Stalinist Marxism, of which the Cold War and McCarthyism were two manifestations. On the one hand, Broch continued to view Marxism in the Austro-Marxist interpretation as a primarily ethical system with which he was largely in agreement; on the other hand, he saw it as a narrowly defined economic theory, atrociously enforced in Stalinist Communism, and in need of being defeated by a superior "ideology." Broch viewed his theory of democracy as exactly that philosophy which could offer a superior alternative to "Marxian ideology." On March 17, 1950, he sent an offprint of the *Neue Rundschau* essay to Alvin Johnson, with the following comments in English:

This paper is in fact the outline of my political book which is based on my *Mass Psychology*, on which I have worked for 5 years. What I try to do with it is no less than to find out whether there is a possibility for forming a democratic ideology which could take up the competition with the Marxian ideology. If such an ideology is possible, it would have to be, like the Marxian, a scientific one. Now the Marxian system would not have this convincing scientific aspect, if it had not been based on the Hegelian logic and theory of knowledge. I do not have to tell you that a good deal of the empirical facts on which Marx relies have proved untenable, but the whole system is logically knitted together so well that it still makes an irrefutable impression, which is one facet of its influence on the masses. The second one is even stronger: it is an appeal to social justice and the idea that only with this social justice the human rights may become reality. A democratic ideology therefore has to be based on a theory of human right . . . . (*GW*, VIII, 389)

A large fragment, written around 1948 and edited with the title "Zur politischen Situation unserer Zeit" ("On the Political Situation of our Times," *GW*, IX, 361–441), deals almost exclusively with the confrontation of Marxism and democracy. Broch admitted that the attractiveness of the Marxist *Heilslehre* is "structurally well suited to bring back to Western man the security of a uniform value system"

(*GW*, IX, 382), since the West lacked a specific, democratic ideology (*GW*, IX, 387). He agreed with Marx on the necessity of a scientific methodology that can predict and alter future events, and found in Marxism ethical, if not metaphysical, components. At the same time, however, he felt that the implementation of Marxism violated the very human rights and human dignity which he upheld as the cornerstones of democracy. This realization convinced him all the more of the need for *his* ideology. "Totalitarian humanity" would necessarily be superior to Marxism because it honored human rights and human dignity, and because it proposed to deal in the first instance, not with the material and economic laws of history, but with what Broch considered more pertinent factors: the psychological and metaphysical mechanisms, as they translated into historical value systems. A letter of June 10, 1950, shows in an almost offhanded manner, that for Broch economics is not the issue. It falls, quite simply, within the province of psychology.

> The mass psychology falls into three volumes, with the main accent, so far, on the falling apart. The first volume, a theory of knowledge and logic, is however finished in its basic concepts, but as long as it has not been published, nothing can be considered finished. The second volume contains the psychology proper, . . . also economics, demonstrating how all economic laws are simply psychological constructs; . . . and so I have put aside this project which is much too difficult for me and have started on the third volume which shall contain the political or rather metapolitical aspects of it all. . . . (*GW*, VIII, 394–95)

Yet such simple reductionism would not do. Broch did not have to become a Marxist economist to realize that his exclusive concentration on the cognitive-psychological aspects could not provide an effective approach to contemporary problems. He sensed the incongruities which existed between his concrete utopia and the historical development, and their awareness infiltrated even his manner of expression. "Nevertheless" became his battle cry, meant to build the bridge between ideal and reality. In the *Neue Rundschau* essay it assumed a most prominent position in the title.

It was also blatantly evident in Broch's last public statement, a written response to an invitation to participate in the "Congress for Cultural Freedom," held in Berlin in early 1950.[20] The invitation had been extended to him by Melvin J. Lasky, founder and editor of *Der Monat*, on the basis of Broch's recently published article in the *Neue Rundschau*. Broch did not accept the invitation since incomplete work pressed upon him, but he sent a reply which can be viewed as his last public credo. He stated:

The intellectual worker, actually the most unpolitical of human beings and therefore constantly forced to affirm and engage in politics, he, the most utopian of all men, proves in the end to be the realistic politician [*Realpolitiker*] *par excellence*. The instant initial successes of his political and intellectual revolutions have, irrespective of the most horrible reversals, become part of history in the form of progress of humanity, and of the realization of the rights of man. Progress is based upon immediate diminution of human suffering; and for the very reason that this suffering has grown to truly unimaginable proportions, the demand for immediate action must again be proclaimed. . . .[21]

The manner in which he saw these demands implemented bears striking resemblance to the approach envisioned in his proposals to the League of Nations twelve years earlier. In 1950, he hoped the United Nations would be the instrument to carry out the humanistic ideal. While implicitly acknowledging his earlier unsuccessful attempts to work through the United Nations, Broch still insisted:

Nevertheless: measured with the revolutionary yardstick, the turn to the UN may appear as a insignificant step, in fact, it may not even elicit a positive result. Yet it is a concrete step and it lies in the direction which soon will have to be followed. It leads toward reality and even though it is only a first attempt, it remains nevertheless significant, since only in this manner can the conscience of the world be awakened. Only visibly concrete actions can impress upon all people around the world the value and the need for the protection of each individual life, so that they shall awaken from their present indifference and demand the abolition of barbarism. And consider that without satisfaction of this fundamental prerequisite there is also no cultural freedom. [22]

Broch's ambition for the theory of democracy is obvious when he compares it with the "Marxian ideology." It is equally evident in his hopes that, as a rallying point for a reintegration of values, it would supersede the position which, in the novels, had been held by the Catholic Church. The theory of democracy agrees with the increasing secularization of our society and with the trend toward scientific formulations in the contemporary world. It ends the threat which loomed so large at the end of *The Sleepwalkers* in the concept of the "Anti-Christ," in the fear-infested demagogueries of the *Mountain Novel*, and in the apocalyptic devilries of *The Guiltless*.

Broch's democracy would convert the individual to a superior humanity and redeem him from the anguish of metaphysical uprootedness. Operating with the concepts of open versus closed systems, and the ethical-aesthetic value judgments accompanying them, Broch viewed his theory of democracy as an open system, forever in need of improvement, forever open because of the unattainability of its goal: the preservation and protection of human life, and the maximization of human happiness due to ethical and cognitive striving. Conversion to democracy, participation as an individual in a community of equally converted and convinced peers, full enjoyment of the human rights, and constant, militant alertness to the "human duties" seemed to him tasks that would challenge and satisfy the rational as well as the irrational components of the human psyche.

CHAPTER 8

Conclusion

WHEN Hannah Arendt called Broch a "poet despite himself"[1] and pointed to the fundamental conflict between his inclinations and what he conceived of as his responsibilities, she referred primarily to Broch's existence divided between active involvement in refugee organizations, the reluctant composition of novels, and the hectic research into ever widening areas of political and economic theory, mass psychology, and jurisprudence. Yet the conflict bore deeper than to the question of intellectual or artistic allegiance or to constantly shifting primary obligations. It was rooted in an idealism which saw itself increasingly at odds with the historical developments.

The designation "concrete utopia" emphasizes this double focus of Broch's vision. His view of a society safeguarded within the boundaries of the earthly absolute, enjoying the accomplishments of the "Bill of Rights" and called upon to defend them in the "Bill of Duties" aligns Broch's utopia with an enlightened, humanistic tradition and places him among the great utopists from Plato to the present. Yet the "concrete" manner in which Broch hoped to achieve such maximum humanity was more than wanting in practical efficacy. With the specter of the Russian Revolution and its bloodbaths before his eyes, Broch wanted at all cost to avoid cataclysmic changes which violated the principles of humanity even while they professed to institute them. He saw no alternatives to dictatorship on the one hand and the slow changes through the legislative and executive machinery on the other. It is moot to ponder whether passive resistance, protest marches, or economic pressure would have found his approval as opposed to petitions and proposals submitted to various institutions. On the basis of Broch's earlier positions one is inclined to disbelieve such "activism." Only the "Voices: 1933" of *The Guitless*, composed shortly before the essay in the *Neue Rundschau*, contains one prescription which goes far beyond any suggestions at political resistance

160

Broch had ever included in his work " . . . have the courage to say shit when someone/for the sake of so-called convictions incites/ others to murder his fellow . . ." (*GL*, 230). Yet even this statement cannot break the deadlock where strength of conviction finds no adequate outlet in action.

This predicament (for which Broch is by no means a unique example) is also connected with his methods of historical analysis. Broch had made cognitive advances one of the cornerstones of his philosophy. Consistent with it, he maintained that all historical phenomena express a specific *Zeitgeist*. With respect to his novels, Broch readily admitted that they were the product of, and responded to, a specific historical era. He did not see, however, that his insistence upon the individual as the carrier of historical advances, and his epistemology and ethics as propellent historical forces, were also the products of a specific historical thinking. Early in his life he had anchored his assumptions in idealism, and though he came to develop his own, rather idiosyncratic system, he never left this foundation. This rendered him myopic to other alternatives and made his theories less applicable in a rapidly changing world.

The gap that looms between his view of history as presented in the novels and in the political theory is a telling one. In the novels, the characters and events enact vividly and graphically what Broch was in a position to observe and to analyze. Yet his imagination was unable to project fictionally what a large section of his theory was about, namely, the design of a better future. The novels stop midway through an apocalypse when they might have portrayed feasible transitions into the "concrete utopia." The political theory, on the other hand, jumps into a utopian future and depicts a rational society based on unquestioned trust in the superiority of the ideals of "total democracy" and on the immediate effect of legislative action.

The Sleepwalkers and *The Death of Virgil* rank Hermann Broch among the novelists of world renown. No serious discussion of the major German language contributions to world literature in the twentieth century can afford to neglect these two novels. The *Mountain Novel* and *The Guiltless* are, for reasons discussed, not of the same caliber, but still respectable literary achievements. Above all, they are incisive documents of the rise of fascism or rather of those conditions, that made the advent of fascism possible. The *Mountain Novel* is one of the earliest novels dealing on the basis of first-hand observation with Hitler and fascist Germany. Because of their metaphysical orientation and historical overview, Broch's novels lack the specific vitriolic criticism that distinguishes, for example, the work of his younger compatriots Elias Canetti and Albert Drach. These authors, too, depict essentially similar petit bourgeois social strata in order to provide anatomies of the strongholds of totalitarian mentality.

While Broch's literary stature is assured, this is not true for his position as a philosopher. Despite the scientific intent of the theory of psychic cycles, Broch's philosophy of history is rooted in a static and basically irrational view of recurrent historical cycles. This is a common enough interpretation of history. With regard to his epistemology, the expertise of professional philosophers is necessary to determine whether Broch had broken new grounds. Are the absolute boundaries of cognition and the inclusion of "limiting factors" in all intellectual disciplines really the *novum* he maintained they were? Equally lacking is an evaluation of Broch's political theory. It may well be that his most original and unique contributions lie in this field. His concept of the "earthly absolute" and the program for a "total democracy" are as pertinent today as they were thirty years ago and should have continued theoretical appeal.

During his lifetime, Broch lacked the platform where his systems could be presented and discussed. This situation has not changed more than a quarter of a century after his death. Until Broch's theories are aired in the context of contemporary philosophy, it is moot to assign to the philosophical part of his *oeuvre* the same definite position of prominence that his novels enjoy.

Abbreviations

The following abbreviations have been used both in the text and in the notes:

B   *Der Bergroman*. Edited by F. Kress and H. A. Maier. Frankfurt: Suhrkamp, 1969.

BBB   *Hermann Broch–Daniel Brody Briefwechsel 1930 1951*. Frankfurt. Buchhandler-Vereinigung, 1971.

DV   *The Death of Virgil*. Translated by Jean Starr Untermeyer. New York: Universal Library, 1965.

E   "Ethik." *Der Brenner*, 4 (May, 1914), 684–90. Reprinted in st 375/1, 243-9.

GL   *The Guiltless*. Translated by Ralph Manheim. Boston: Little, Brown, 1974.

GW   *Gesammelte Werke in 10 Bänden*. Zurich: Rhein-Verlag, 1953 1961.

NR   "Trotzdem: Humane Politik. Verwirklichung einer Utopie." *Neue Rundschau*, 61 (1950), 1–31.

Re   *Völkerbund-Resolution*. Edited by Paul Michael Lützeler. Salzburg: Otto Müller, 1973.

st   *Kommentierte Werkausgabe in 13 Bänden*. Edited by Paul Michael Lützeler. Frankfurt: Suhrkamp, 1974–1980.

SW   *The Sleepwalkers*. Translated by Willa and Edwin Muir. New York: Universal Library, 1971.

YUL   Unpublished material in the Broch archives, Beinecke Rare Books Library of Yale University.

Notes and References

Preface

1. Theodore Ziolkowski, *Hermann Broch* (New York: Columbia University Press, 1964).

Chapter One

1. Carl Schorske as quoted in Harry Zohn, *Karl Kraus* (New York: Twayne, 1971), p. 31.
2. Allan Janik and Stephen Toulmin, *Wittgenstein's Vienna* (New York: Simon & Schuster, 1973), p. 61.
3. On the situation of the Austrian Jews in the professions and the arts, see C. A. Macartney, *The Habsburg Empire 1790-1918* (New York: Macmillan, 1969), pp. 517–20; William M. Johnston, *The Austrian Mind: An Intellectual and Social History* (Berkeley: University of California Press, 1972), pp. 23–29; and Karl R. Stadler, *Austria* (New York: Praeger, 1971), pp. 134–41.
4. Harry Zohn, *Karl Kraus*, p. 13.
5. Paul Michael Lützeler, *Hermann Broch—Ethik und Politik* (Munich: Winkler, 1973), pp. 33–4. Lützeler is the first one to have pointed out this slip in Broch's memory and its consequences for his intellectual biography.
6. The notebooks *Culture 1908–1909* are unpublished. They are located, with his other unpublished material, in the Beinecke Rare Books Library at Yale University.
7. Paul Michael Lützeler, *Hermann Broch—Ethik und Politik*, p. 15. See also Lützeler, "Die Kulturkritik des jungen Broch," *Deutsche Vierteljahrsschrift für Literaturwissenschaft und Geistesgeschichte*, 44 (1970), 208–28.
8. C. E. Williams, *The Broken Eagle: The Politics of Austrian Literature from Empire to Anschluss* (New York: Barnes & Noble, 1974), pp. xviii, xix.
9. Allan Janik and Stephen Toulmin, *Wittgenstein's Vienna*, p. 191.
10. On Broch's avid interest in journals and periodicals see Gisela Brude-Firnau, " 'Zufällig durch die Zeitung?' Die Bedeutung der Tageszeitung für Hermann Brochs 'Schlafwandler," *German Quarterly*, 49 (1976), 31–44.

11. On Weininger's influence see Janik and Toulmin, *Wittgenstein's Vienna*, pp. 71–74. The authors particularly mention Weininger's influence on Karl Kraus. In the introduction to this work, Weininger claims Plato, Kant, and Schopenhauer as his intellectual mentors, and these, in addition to Karl Kraus, are the very names that appear in Broch's essays of the pre–World War I years.

12. On Weininger's and Schopenhauer's influence see Manfred Durzak, "Hermann Brochs Anfänge: Zum Einfluss Weiningers und Schopenhauers," *Germanisch-romanische Monatsschrift*, 48 (1967), 293-306. Durzak discusses the same topic in a different version in *Hermann Broch: Der Dichter und seine Zeit* (Stuttgart: Kohlhammer, 1968), esp. pp. 11-34. One of the earliest discussions of influences upon the young Broch is Sidonie Cassirer's "Hermann Broch's Early Writings," *Publications of the Modern Language Association*, 75 (1960), 453-62.

13. On the Kant-Schopenhauer controversy in Broch's Vienna, see Janik and Toulmin, *Wittgenstein's Vienna*, pp. 146–57.

14. At this period, Broch was so convinced of the need for distinctive ornamentation that he even misinterpreted Adolf Loos. Loos states clearly: "Evolution of art is equivalent with the removal of the ornament from objects of daily use" ("Ornament und Verbrechen," in *Sämtliche Schriften*, I [Vienna: Herald Verlag, 1962], 277). Broch, however, could not accept this statement as a value judgment and maintained: "Adolf Loos' theory is only an affirmation, a most conscious affirmation of the incapacity of the moderns to create ornamentation, but therefore it cannot be taken as evaluation of the ornament in general . . ." (*GW*, X, 228).

15. Broch's list of library holdings indicates that he owned the collected works of Plato in the Schleiermacher translation, in addition to individual editions of *The Republic, Symposium, Lysis,* and *Phaedrus*. In Broch's novels the image of the Platonic cave appears frequently, recognizable by the setting only, without reference to Plato. On Broch's Platonism in general, see Hannah Arendt in her introduction to Broch's essays (*GW*, VI, 16-18).

16. This equation does not agree with Schopenhauer, who writes in Book 3, chapter 32 of *The World as Will and Idea:* "It follows from our consideration of the subject, that, for us, Idea and thing-in-itself are not entirely one and the same, in spite of the inner agreement between Kant and Plato, and the identity of the aim they had before them, or the conception of the world which roused them and led them to philosophise. The Idea is for us rather the direct, and therefore adequate, objectivity of the thing-in-itself, which is, however, itself the *will*—the will as not yet objectified, not yet become idea." *The World as Will and Idea*, trans. R. B. Haldane and J. Kemp (London: Routledge & Kegan Paul, 1964), I, 226.

17. Janik and Toulmin, *Wittgenstein's Vienna*, p. 146.

18. See *E*, 686.

19. Janik and Toulmin, *Wittgenstein's Vienna*, pp. 18, 26, 31.

Chapter Two

1. On Karl Kraus' persuasive influence upon Hermann Broch, see P. M. Lützeler, "Hermann Broch und Karl Kraus," *Modern Austrian Literature*, 8, No. 1 (1975), 211–39.

2. On the exact dating see Manfred Durzak, "Ein Frühwerk Hermann Brochs," *Neue Deutsche Hefte*, 13 (1966), 10–18; also Paul Michael Lützeler, *Hermann Broch—Ethik und Politik*, p. 145, n. 19.

3. Hermann Broch, "Cantos 1913," *Neue Deutsche Hefte*, 13 (1966), 9–10.

4. *Ibid.*, p. 8.

5. *Ibid.*, pp. 5, 6.

6. *Ibid.*, p. 7.

7. Particulars are given by Manfred Durzak, *Hermann Broch* (Stuttgart: Metzler, 1967), p. 17.

8. Broch had met Franz Blei around 1912. Blei, a rising critic and author on the Viennese literary scene and by fifteen years Broch's elder, introduced Broch to the literary life of the city. In 1917 he founded the magazine *Summa* and asked Broch to contribute to it. See Durzak, *Hermann Broch*, (Stuttgart: Metzler, 1967) pp. 17–18. During the two years of the magazine's existence, Broch published in almost every one of the quarterly issues.

9. Hermann Broch, "Konstitutionelle Diktatur als demokratisches Rätesystem," *Der Friede*, 3, No. 64 (April 11, 1919), 269–73; reprinted in *Gedanken zur Politik*, ed. Dieter Hildebrandt (Frankfurt: Suhrkamp, 1970), 11–23.

10. Hermann Broch, "Die Strasse," *Die Rettung*, 1, No. 3 (December 30, 1919), 25–28; reprinted in *GW*, X, 257–60.

11. On Broch and Austro-Marxism, see P. M. Lützeler, *Hermann Broch—Ethik und Politik*, pp. 43–59. On Austro-Marxism in general, see Norbert Leser, "Austro-Marxism: A Reappraisal," *Journal of Contemporary History*, 1, No. 2 (1966), 117–33.

12. Hermann Broch, "Rezension zu zwei Büchern von Max Adler: *Marx als Denker* [Vienna, 1921], *Engels als Denker* [Berlin, 1921]," *Kant-Studien*, 27 (1922), 184–86; reprinted in st 375/1, 264-7.

13. According to recent scholarship, philosophical connections between Kant and Marx do exist, but not along the line of the "neo-Kantianizing Austro-Marxists." Alfred Schmidt, ed., *Beiträge zur marxistischen Erkenntnistheorie* (Frankfurt: Suhrkamp, 1969), p. 15.

14. Thomas Masaryk, as quoted in Lützeler, *Hermann Broch—Ethik und Politik*, p. 48.

15. *Kant-Studien*, 27 (1922), p. 185; reprinted in st 375/1, p. 266.

16. *Gedanken zur Politik*, p. 12.

17. *Ibid.*, p. 23.

18. Manfred Durzak, *Hermann Broch* (Stuttgart: Metzler, 1967), p. 18. The original is in English since it was part of an application for a grant to the Rockefeller Foundation.

19. See my article "Hermann Broch and Modern Physics," *Germanic Review*, (forthcoming).

20. Manfred Durzak, *Hermann Broch* (Hamburg: Rowohlt, 1966), pp. 59–60, has the most detailed account on these transactions.

21. The *Vorlesungsverzeichnisse* (records of matriculation) of the courses Broch took at the University of Vienna are located at the Broch-Museum in Teesdorf near Vienna.

22. Ludwig Wittgenstein, *Tractatus logico-philosophicus* (Frankfurt: Suhrkamp, 1966). The *Tractatus* was completed in 1918 and published in 1921.

23. *Kant-Studien*, 27 (1922), p. 185; reprinted in st 375/1, p. 265.

Chapter Three

1. Parts 1 and 2 of the novel were published in the summer and fall of 1931, the last part in early 1932. On the genesis of the novel, see the divergent points of view of Theodore Ziolkowski, "Zur Entstehung und Struktur von Hermann Brochs 'Schlafwandlern,'" *Deutsch Vierteljahrsschrift für Literaturwissenschaft und Geistesgeschichte*, 38 (1964), 40–60, and Manfred Durzak, *Hermann Broch* (Hamburg, 1966), pp. 63–67. Ziolkowski replies to Durzak in *Dimensions of the Modern Novel: German Texts and European Contexts* (Princeton: Princeton University Press, 1969), p. 161, n. 27. A similar misconception, this time in reference to Broch's intellectual development and its manifestation in *The Sleepwalkers*, is cleared up by P. M. Lützeler in *Hermann Broch— Ethik und Politik*, p. 144, n. 23, where he takes issue with Heinz D. Osterle's statements in "Hermann Broch: *Die Schlafwandler*. Kritik der zentralen Metapher," *Deutsche Vierteljahrsschrift für Literaturwissenschaft und Geistesgeschichte*, 44 (1970), 229–68.

2. Compare also Manfred Durzak, "Hermann Brochs Auffassung des Lyrischen," *Publications of the Modern Language Association*, 82 (1967), 206 16, and my *Die Philosophie Hermann Brochs* (Bern: Francke, 1971), esp. pp. 78–104.

3. See the unpublished essay "Über Modelle," located at *YUL*.

4. Although Broch hardly ever refers to Wittgenstein, it stands to reason that he knew his work. He studied with Schlick while Schlick and Wittgenstein were acquainted and the *Tractatus* was being discussed. It is, however, unlikely that Broch realized how close Wittgenstein's position was to his own since Wittgenstein was appropriated by the Vienna Circle. The one mention of Wittgenstein in the Broch-Brody correspondence (*BBB*, 135; August 5, 1931) sees Wittgenstein, according to popular opinion, in the light of the Vienna Circle. Wittgenstein's biographer, Paul Engelmann, interprets Wittgenstein's philosophical intentions differently: "Positivism holds—and this is its essence—that what we can speak about is all that matters in life. Whereas Wittgenstein passionately believes that all that really matters in human life is precisely what, in his view, we must be silent about" (quoted in Janik and Toulmin, *Wittgenstein's Vienna*, p. 191). In the interpretation of Janik and Toulmin, Wittgenstein was concerned with delineating a field upon

whose exploration Broch had also embarked. In their opinion, Wittgenstein wanted to demonstrate "*both* that logic and science had a proper part to play within ordinary descriptive language . . . *and* that questions about 'ethics, value and the meaning of life,' by falling outside the limits of this descriptive language, become—at best—the objects of a kind of mystical insight, which can be conveyed by 'indirect' or poetical communication" (ibid.).

A further, amusing similarity between Wittgenstein and Broch is found in the description of Wittgenstein, which literally matches Broch: " . . . the two most important facts to remember about Wittgenstein were, firstly, that he was a Viennese and, secondly, that he was an engineer with a thorough knowledge of physics" (ibid., pp. 28–9). To add Musil to this duo might lead too far, though certainly not in the wrong direction.

5. The Muir translation chooses persons instead of period designations, thus "Pasenow the Romanticist" instead of "Pasenow or Romanticism." This practice individualizes events when, on the contrary, the protagonist should be viewed as an integral part of the period under investigation. The translation of "Huguenau oder die Sachlichkeit" as "Huguenau the Realist" is further misleading, since it ignores the matter-of-fact orientation and the thingness, that is, the nonhumaness, of the man and the period. With the exception of the titles, however, and unless otherwise stated, all page references in the text refer to the Muir translation (New York: Universal Library, 1964).

6. Richard Brinkmann, "Romanform und Werttheorie bei Hermann Broch: Strukturprobleme moderner Dichtung," *Deutsche Vierteljahrsschrift für Literaturwissenschaft und Geistesgeschichte*, 31 (1957), p. 172; and Henry Hatfield, *Modern German Literature: The Major Figures in Context* (Bloomington: Indiana University Press, 1968), p. 107. The Fontane resemblance of the first part was mentioned in the early correspondence on *The Sleepwalkers*, where Broch admitted to never having read Fontane (*GW*, VIII, 45).

7. Hartmut Steinecke, *Hermann Broch und der polyhistorische Roman* (Bonn: Bouvier, 1968), esp. pp. 88–92. Broch's own references can be found in many of the letters accompanying the genesis of *The Sleepwalkers*, for example, *GW*, VIII, 17–20 and 22.

8. Heinz Osterle subjects these dates to speculations concerning Broch's apocalyptic vision in "Hermann Broch, 'Die Schlafwandler:' Revolution and Apocalypse," *Publications of the Modern Language Association*, 86 (1971), esp. p. 948.

9. This technique of lifting moments out of the flux of history agrees with Broch's scientific approach to his subject. Like the scientist, he puts the period of investigation under the miscroscope. In his unpublished essay "Über Modelle" (*YUL*), he speaks of an illuminated screen on which selected events have to be projected in order to be analyzed.

10. Ziolkowski, *Dimensions of the Modern Novel*, p. 155.

11. To cite only a few examples which emphasize triviality experienced as

complexity: "Joachim's mother replied that it was both good and bad news, and this was a complicated response which he could not quite understand" (*SW*, 13). Or: "These weeks had been pregnant with trouble, and yet good" (*SW*, 14).

12. As a "Luxemburger [who] could not boast of military service" (*SW*, 175), he was *free* of the restrictions of the uniform, "was, so to speak, only a private official" (*SW*, 174). The lack of a military uniform indicates a "softening up" of the value system; it characterizes the succession Joachim—Esch or, in Broch's definition, romanticism—anarchy, and is anticipated early in the novel (*SW*, 20-24). When Esch regrets that he is "only" a private official, he shows that his personal desires are "romantic" and at odds with his "anarchic" situation. The ambivalence Joachim had earlier experienced focuses in Esch's case on the word "free." For example, working in the docks "was both a constricted and a *free* life that one led in this sanctuary" (*SW*, 173). The German original for "sanctuary" is *Frei*statt (*GW*, III, 186). "Free" is also part of *Frei*heitsstatue, *Frei*marke, *Frei*treppe—vocabulary that characterizes Esch. (All emphases are mine.)

13. For example: "With disgust she noticed that every time Hede, the waitress, passed the table, Esch could not help fondling her, and that finally he ordered her to sit down beside him, so that they might drink to each other. But the score [*die Rechnung*] was a high one, and when the gentlemen broke up after midnight, taking Hede with them, Frau Hentjen pushed a mark into her hand" (*SW*, 170).

14. Compare also Broch's comment in a letter of March 5, 1931, in *GW*, VIII, 47-8.

15. The character of Eduard von Bertrand has received the most divergent interpretations in Broch scholarship. For a survey and summary, see J. J. White, "The Identity and Function of Bertrand in Hermann Broch's 'Die Schlafwandler'" *German Life and Letters*, 24 (1970), 135-44.

16. On Eduard von Bertrand, see also *GW*, VIII, 18, 26.

17. Breon Mitchell, *James Joyce and the German Novel 1922-1933* (Athens, Ohio: Ohio University Press, 1976), esp. pp. 151-74.

18. On Broch's interest in the theory of relativity and its impact on his fiction, see Theodore Ziolkowski's article "Hermann Broch and Relativity in Fiction," *Wisconsin Studies in Contemporary Literature*, 8 (Summer 1967), pp. 365-76. After first assuming that the "ideal observer" is the reader (p. 370), Ziolkowski then infers that Bertrand Müller is the "narrator as idea" of the third part of the novel. And since the philosophical treatise of which Bertrand Müller is the author "refers to incidents in the narrative strands and thus embraces them, Bertrand Müller becomes, by extension, the author of the entire novel" (p. 374). Broch would not have chosen the term "narrator *as idea*" if he had meant to identify this concept with a fictional character. Ziolkowski realizes this when he says, in the same essay: "Although there is no personal narrator, every observation is tied somehow to an observing subject, to a 'narrator as idea.' The narrator, who enters the narrative field of

observation (as Broch puts it), has no existence outside the language of the novel" (p. 373). When Bertrand Müller becomes the author of the entire novel—a conjecture for which there is no basis in the text—the innovative function of the "narrator as idea" is lost. Breon Mitchell, *James Joyce and the German Novel 1922-1933*, p. 173, n. 44, offers the latest instance of this misinterpretation when he says: ". . . the author of the philosophical essay is also the author of the novel." The verbal link to which he refers (between one of the parallel stories and one segment of the theory of the disintegration of values) does not point to the same author, but rather to the same historical period in which, due to common experience, certain expressions become clichés. The frequent verbatim repetition of expressions in the manner of leitmotivs in apparently unconnected situations is one of Broch's many techniques to reveal the "narrator as idea." On Broch's acquaintance with the theory of relativity, see also my article "Hermann Broch and Modern Physics," *Germanic Review* (to be published).

19. Richard Brinkmann and Theodore Ziolkowski have used the opening passage of the novel to demonstrate the relativity of perception in "Romanform and Werttheorie bei Hermann Broch: Strukturprobleme moderner Dichtung," pp. 169-197 and "Hermann Broch and Relativity in Fiction," pp. 372–73 respectively. "In the year 1888 Herr von Pasenow was seventy, and *there were people* who felt an extraordinary and inexplicable repulsion when they saw him coming . . . Yet though Herr von Pasenow was not displeased with himself, *there were people* whom the looks of this man filled with discomfort . . . Whether this was true or not, *it was the belief of his two sons . . .*"(SW, 9). The italicized parts indicate the presence of the "subject of observation." Frequently, Broch switches to the conditional to indicate the presence of the "narrator as idea." For example: "Now Esch, who smoked cigars and drank wine and treated himself to huge portions of meat whenever he had a chance, *might not have been* so deeply *impressed . . . if he had not been struck . . .*" (SW, 190). On other occasions, a hypothesis reminds the reader that this novelistic universe is defined by a limited and typical range of possible actions. For example: ". . . yet the unasked question irritated him . . . and his irritation might, *for instance,* discharge itself in boxing his child on the ear for no reason at all . . ." (SW, 643). Leitmotivs, verbal and situational clichés, congruence of content and style (which appears in "Huguenau" as discontinuity bordering on chaos), and the historically exemplary quality of many events further indicate the "narrator as idea."

20. The most instructive essays on this topic are "Das Böse im Wertsystem der Kunst" ("The Evil within the Value System of Art") of August, 1933 (reprinted in *GW*, VI, 311-55 and in st 247, 119-57); and "Das System als Weltbewältigung" ("The System as Mastery of the World") of approximately ten years later (*GW*, VII, 111-149).

21. ". . . a still grosser reality" of the Muir translation is putting it mildly; "eine noch grössere Roheit" might better be translated as "a greater crudity yet."

22. The last sentence of the quotation is a literal translation of the German original and deviates considerably from the Muir translation. The German text reads: "Der ästhetische Mensch stellt innerhalb des Romantischen das böse Prinzip dar" (*GW*, II, 572).

23. This "vehemence" characterizes many protagonists and many scenes of the "Esch" part in particular. One is reminded of the impetuosity of Esch, of the rage of Mutter Hentjen, of Ilona's anger and jealousy, and one thinks of the violence inherent in the police breaking up the strike meeting, in the ladies' wrestling matches, in Teltscher-Teltini's knife-throwing. Esch's beating of Mutter Hentjen is echoed in Huguenau's slapping his child.

24. *SW*, 295, 335. The Muir translation of the German "den Kopf in den Nacken drehen" is less graphic than the original and less aware of the historical implications. It simply states that Esch "turned his head the wrong way."

25. "In the Sleepwalkers: Pasenow and Esch, both moral types, although subject to different moral dogmas. Moral dogmas, which in the period of disintegrating values are dying off, become 'romanticisms'" (*GW*, VIII, 26).

26. The adult male acting like a child, or wanting to be child to a mother figure, is a recurrent theme in Broch's novels. The two most prominent examples, Huguenau in *The Sleepwalkers* and A. in *The Guiltless*, are even physically similar. Only Virgil in *The Death of Virgil* is able to overcome that temptation. An interesting contrast to these males is provided in the presentation of female children. Marguerite (in *The Sleepwalkers*) and Rosa Wetchy (in the *Mountain Novel*) are most proficient adepts of matter-of-factness, junior editions of Mutter Hentjen and Ilona. A different interpretation of the problem of childhood along biographical-psychoanalytical lines is given by Peter Bruce Waldeck, *Die Kindheitsproblematik bei Hermann Broch* (Munich: Fink, 1968).

27. Paul Michael Lützeler briefly surveys the large variety of interpretations of the "sleepwalking" metaphor in *Hermann Broch–Ethik und Politik,* p. 168 n. 95. Bertrand Müller, as the most aware of the characters in the novel, is the only one who observes himself sleepwalking. He gives a description of his experience and offers explanations for this subjective state (*SW*, 574-5).

Chapter Four

1. C. E. Williams, *The Broken Eagle: The Politics of Austrian Literature from Empire to Anschluss* (New York: Barnes and Noble, 1974), p. 259.

2. Walter Lacquer, *Weimar: A Cultural History* (New York: Putnam, 1974), pp. 257–58.

3. The most important of these essays, written between 1933 and 1934, are "Das Weltbild des Romans," "Denkerische und dichterische Erkenntnis," "Das Böse im Wertsystem der Kunst," "Neue religiöse Dichtung," "Geist und Zeitgeist," "Gedanken zum Problem der Erkenntnis

in der Musik," and the two essays of 1936, "James Joyce und die Gegenwart," and "Erwägungen zum Problem des Kulturtodes."

4. The lecture "James Joyce und die Gegenwart" was delivered on April 22, 1932, at the *Volkshochschule* Ottakring in Vienna (*BBB*, 185). Broch's delivery was one of the earliest and most incisive appreciation of Joyce's work. The lecture was printed as a booklet in 1936. Breon Mitchell gives the history of the early Joyce reception in Germany in *James Joyce and the German Novel 1922-1933*. Pp. 151–174 deal exclusively with Joyce and Broch. See also Manfred Durzak, "Hermann Broch und James Joyce. Zur Ästhetik des modernen Roman," *Deutsche Vierteljahrsschrift für Literaturwissenschaft und Geistesgeschichte*, 40 (1966), 391–433; similarly in *Hermann Broch: Der Dichter und seine Zeit*, pp. 76–113.

5. On Broch's film plans, see Manfred Durzak, "Hermann Broch und der Film," *Der Monat*, 18 No. 212 (May, 1966), 68–75.

6. Two of them appeared in April, 1933: "Eine leichte Enttäuschung" in the *Neue Rundschau*, and "Vorüberziehende Wolke" in the *Frankfurter Zeitung*. In August, "Ein Abend Angst" was published in the *Berliner Börsen-Courier*. And in December of the same year, "Die Heimkehr" in the *Neue Rundschau*, and "Der Meeresspiegel" in *Welt im Wort*.

7. Contact with C. G. Jung and his work is repeatedly attested in the correspondence, esp. *BBB*, 195, 234, 238.

8. Never published in the *Neue Rundschau* at that period. Compare with *BBB*, 306; st 247, 288; *GW*, VIII, 101–2 and X, 288–310.

9. No exact dates are available as to when Broch started working on the *Mountain Novel*. On the difficulty of dating the inception of the novel see *BBB*, 401, n. On the stages of completing the different versions, see Frank Kress and Hans Albert Maier in the introduction to Volume 4 of the critical edition of the *Bergroman* (Frankfurt: Suhrkamp, 1969), p. 15. See also Manfred Durzak, "Zur Entstehungsgeschichte und den verschiedenen Fassungen von Hermann Brochs Nachlassroman," *Zeitschrift für deutsche Philologie*, 86 (1967), 594–627; Götz Wienold, "Hermann Brochs 'Bergroman' und seine Fassungen: Formprobleme der Überarbeitung (mit bisher ungedruckten Quellen)," *Deutsche Vierteljahrsschrift für Literaturwissenschaft und Geistesgeschichte*, Sonderheft 42 (1968), 773–804; and Timothy Casey, "Questioning Broch's 'Der Versucher,' " *Deutsche Vierteljahrsschrift für Literaturwissenschaft und Geistesgeschichte*, 47 (1973), esp. p. 499ff. In his correspondence, Broch referred to work in progress only as "the book," the "new book," the "religious novel," never by title. Since these terms were used in relation to the "Filsmann" material as well as the *Mountain Novel*, it is difficult to ascertain when he referred to which.

10. In the correspondence, Mösern occurs in three letters of April 20, May 7, and May 22, all to the same addressee, as the residence of the sender. Yet Broch wrote letters to other addressees during the same period from Laxenburg (*GW*, VIII, 115–27). *BBB*, 384, n. indicates that Broch was in Munich between July and early September. On September 7, 1935, he sent a

letter from Mösern, informing Daniel Brody: ". . . hence I arrived up here. It was not quite easy. Seefeld is awful, though now, in the off-season, I could have found royal lodgings for little money . . . after also having looked around in Reith, I have finally decided for Mösern, which is more primitive than Grundlsee and in no way as inexpensive, yet has the most enchanting location one can imagine . . ." (*BBB*, 385).

11. *BBB*, 405, n. traces Broch's residences in these years through his correspondence.

12. Paul Michael Lützeler has traced in detail all allusions to Hitler-Germany in "Hermann Brochs 'Die Verzauberung' als politischer Roman," *Neophilologus*, 61 (1977), 111-26.

13. Compare Michael Winkler, "Die Funktion der Erzählungen in Hermann Brochs 'Bergroman,' " in *Hermann Broch: Perspektiven der Forschung*, ed. Manfred Durzak (Munich: Fink, 1972), pp. 251–69.

14. This is Timothy Casey's view in "Questioning Broch's 'Der Versucher,' " pp. 481, 490. In fact, Broch never uses the term "anti-system," but speaks of opposition and imitation systems and points to the essential differences between them. See esp. st 247, 142–7.

15. See the article by Gundi Wachtler, "Der Archetypus der Grossen Mutter in Hermann Brochs Roman 'Der Versucher,' " in *Hermann Broch: Perspektiven der Forschung*, pp. 231–50.

16. In the essay "The Style of the Mythical Age" of 1947, Broch speaks of the development from myth to legend as manifestations of a closed system. "Thus, after the Dark Ages, the rigid grandeur of the myth became increasingly domestic and human, as it was swathed in the charms of legend; . . . in legend, the closed system representing the myth reaches a climax of humanization; but it is still a closed system . . ." (*GW*, VII, 254). The historical period, with which the country doctor is identified, extends from the late Gothic (*GW*, VII, 254) to the Counter Reformation (*SW*, 523). During this period, Catholicism attempted through various means to combat the onslaught of "progressive disintegration." All these efforts occur necessarily in a closed system.

17. Compare also *GW*, VIII, 151, 153, 155, 156. All these letters were written in 1936.

18. Though Broch recognized Kafka as the poet "whose primordial experience had remained intact" (*GW*, VIII, 282), he occasionally saw his achievements more critically, saying that Kafka had not yet found a completely adequate mode of expression (VIII, 266–67). While Kafka (further mentioned in VIII, 321; VI, 263) is ranked above and beyond Joyce (VIII, 373, 415; VI, 262), Thomas Mann, and Hermann Broch (VIII, 149, 155), where living on the mythical level is concerned, he is aligned with Joyce (VIII, 266–67) and even criticized, when the inadequacy of the "new vocabulary" is discussed (VIII, 386–87). Compare also Timothy Casey, "Questioning Hermann Broch's 'Der Versucher,' " p. 493, n. 85.

19. There is little information available on this period. Broch's friend and

publisher Daniel Brody had temporarily settled in Vienna after leaving Hitler Germany, thus eliminating a correspondence which provides one of the richest sources of information on Broch's plans and whereabouts. *BBB*, 274, n.

20. See also Paul Michael Lützeler's introduction to the "Resolution." He assigns to it a central position as point of departure for later work in the theory of law and politics and the studies in mass phenomena (*Re*, 10). In April, 1939, a few months after his arrival in the United States, Broch specified in a letter: ". . . in addition, I am working on a 'theory of humanity,' which continues on a broad basis the proposal for the League of Nations" (*GW*, VIII, 170). He again mentions the "Study for the League of Nations" in a letter to Daniel Brody, written at the conclusion of World War II. When Brody wonders whether historical events have not overtaken the reason for writing the "Resolution," Broch's answer of July 25, 1945, suggests the turn his research had taken during the war years: "*Völkerbundstudie:* this will be a book which should be completed in manuscript by fall. At this point, the first chapter is barely finished, and it has been read by half a faculty on government law. You can imagine how long it will take before the entire work is completed. . . . Revision followed revision. The result is quite acceptable and the legal scholars agree that a new principle has been introduced. It will hardly reach beyond academic excitement, though some attempts have already been made to translate it into practice . . ." (*BBB*, 456).

21. From "Autobiography as Work Program," which was written approximately in 1942 and provided Broch's retrospective evaluation of his own work. He continued the excerpted quotation of *GW*, IX, 47 by using the French Encyclopedists and Marx as examples to illustrate his point. Broch maintained his conviction in the decisive historical role of the intellectual through the years (compare *BBB*, 456 of 1945).

22. The unionist Geyring in the "Esch" part of *The Sleepwalkers* shows what Broch means by "compromise" as the more efficient road toward a social goal than radical polarization. In his theory, Broch formulates this opposition as one between realistic and unrealistic utopias. "Realistic utopias . . . have to take into account the logic of things; they are bound to facts" (*Literatur und Kritik*, 54–55 (1971), p. 194).

23. Broch's view was shaped in an Austria which, together with Hungary, was considered "Italy's satellite." See Francis P. Walters, *History of the League of Nations* (New York: Oxford University Press, 1952), II, 688.

24. James Joyce never met Broch, but knew of him. Both authors had their work published by the Rhein-Verlag, and Joyce had read Broch's essay "James Joyce and the Present." Since Joyce was Irish, he could not be of direct help but had a French friend obtain a visa for Broch. When the bureaucratic machinery broke down, he established connections with Stephen Hudson in London. For much of this information and details on the years in exile I am indebted to Paul Michael Lützeler, who allowed me the use of his unpublished manuscript "Hermann Broch in Exil." This informa-

tion will be available in the introduction to the forthcoming *Menschenrecht und Demokratie*, ed. P.M. Lützeler (Frankfurt: Suhrkamp, 1978).

Chapter Five

1. *The City of Man: A Declaration on World Democracy* (New York: Viking, 1941). The complete list of participants in this collective statement is most impressive. It includes, besides Broch, Thomas Mann and his son-in-law, the Italian scholar G. A. Borgese; the historians Lewis Mumford and Hans Kohn; the theologian Reinhold Niebuhr; Christian Gauss, dean of faculty at Princeton University; Alvin Johnson, director of the New School for Social Research in New York; Frank Aydelotte, director of the Institute of Advanced Studies in Princeton; Herbert Agar, writer and diplomat; the writers and critics Dorothy Canfield Fisher and Van Wyck Brooks; and Ada Comstock, president of Radcliffe College.

2. *BBB*, 463, 486, 495; *GW*, VIII, 257, 284, 289, 319.

3. *BBB*, 470.

4. See the letters of January 30, 1946 (*GW*, VIII, 240) and of February 27, 1946 (VIII, 248) from Broch to James Franck.

5. Broch described the circumstances of the accident in a letter excerpted in Lützeler, "Hermann Broch im Exil." Compare also *BBB*, 495, 496 n.

6. Broch gives an account of the inception of *The Death of Virgil* in a letter to Hermann Weigand of February 12, 1946. This account has been accepted by Manfred Durzak in "Hermann Brochs Vergil-Roman und seine Vorstufen," *Literaturwissenschaftliches Jahrbuch*, NF 9 (1968), esp. pp. 285–286. The factual information in the letter to Weigand is not always correct. Broch mentions Pentecost, 1935, as the date for which the Austrian radio network requested his reading. In "Autobiography as Work Program" (*GW*, IX, 51) he gives the date of 1937 as inception of the work, which is further substantiated by *BBB*, 274, n. A check of *Radio Wien*, the official publication of the Austrian radio network, indicates neither in 1935 nor in 1937 a reading by Broch. It does list on Pentecost Sunday, June 4, 1933, Broch's reading from *The Sleepwalkers*, which Broch had announced in a letter to Brody of June 2, 1933 (*BBB*, 274). In the correspondence of 1937, where Broch repeatedly refers to the early phases of composition of *Virgil*, he never mentions the radio broadcast. There is no evidence that the brief story was ever read over the network.

7. Jean Starr Untermeyer, the translator of *The Death of Virgil* into English, remembers Broch's account of that period in the following manner: "I know that [Huxley] realized the scope of the new work, appreciated it, and praised it, but advised Broch for the sake of the public to break the long, long sentences. Broch dictated to me his reply to this letter, telling Huxley that it was when he was in a Nazi prison, with the possibility of his own death not far off, that the germinal ideas of the work in question first came to him, and in just this form: long, wavelike sentences, mounting slowly to a peak and receding, their crescendos and diminuendos following each other like the

oceanic surge of an incoming tide. He must, he wrote, be true to his experience, and would prefer to break the public rather than break his long sentences." "Midwife to a Masterpiece," in *Private Collection* (New York: Knopf, 1965), p. 272.

8. On the organization of the novel, see also Götz Wienold, "Die Organisation eines Romans: Hermann Brochs 'Der Tod des Vergil,' " *Zeitschrift für deutsche Philologie*, 86 (1967), 571–93.

9. Aniela Jaffe, "Hermann Broch: 'Der Tod des Vergil:' Ein Beitrag zum Problem der Individuation," in *Studien zur analytischen Psychologie C. G. Jungs. Festschrift zum 80. Geburtstag von C. G. Jung* (Zurich: Rhein–Verlag, 1955), II, 288–43.

10. *GW*, VII, 73–74. Also "Skizze einer erkenntnistheoretischen Werttheorie" (*YUL*). The hypothetical epistemological "I"– core formalizes the concept of the cognitive drive in Broch's theory of knowledge.

11. The epistemological sphere of the unconscious is considered the reservoir of all possible knowledge (see the essay "Über syntaktische und kognitive Einheiten," *GW*, VII, 151–202). Implicitly reaffirming the concept of Platonic totality, Broch postulates fulness and totality in this sphere. However, the difference between the two realms, which in fact relegates them to the opposite ends of the cognitive hierarchy, is the difference in consciousness. Broch's theory of knowledge can be visualized as gains and losses on the ladder of cognition with both ends shrouded in inaccessibility. The ladder extends from the unfathomably vast epistemological sphere of the unconscious to the unattainable Platonic Idea. In *The Death of Virgil*, this hierarchical structure is symbolized in Virgil's ascent from the Vulcanic realm to the Apollonian sphere. The "enlightening" of this sphere of the unconscious through cognitive advances corresponds to Broch's early demand that the philosopher explore the "boundaries of reason." The visualization of cognitive explorations as lighting up hitherto dark areas on a screen is most vividly rendered in the unpublished essay "Über Modelle" (*YUL*). In the novels (particularly *The Sleepwalkers* and *The Death of Virgil*) the image of the Platonic cave is frequently used to embody these cognitive processes.

12. Compare also Manfred Durzak, "Hermann Brochs Auffassung des Lyrischen," *Publications of the Modern Language Association*, 82 (1967), 206–16.

13. See my essay on the triad "Hermann Broch's Theory of Symbols Examplified in a Scene from 'The Death of Virgil' ", *Neophilologus*, 54 (1970), 53–64.

14. At no point can insights gained be considered as permanently valid and fixed. In the light of new material, the entire complex of preceding information must be reevaluated.

15. ". . . the sphere of being" is my own translation, replacing Jean Starr Untermeyer's version, which uses "recognition" for the German *das Seiende*.

16. The continuity of this view throughout all the novels is most striking. *The Sleepwalkers* showed the helplessness and incapacity of the individuals

who experience disintegrative periods, and pointed to their susceptibility to leader–and redeemer promises. The *Mountain Novel* took the development further, showing how susceptibility leads to "conversion"; the villagers succumb to Marius's "magic." *The Death of Virgil* presents, as the next step, the mindless and calloused destructiveness and the cynical brutality pertaining to this realm. *The Guiltless* demythologizes the Vulcanic netherworld and locates hell concretely in the Germany of the incipient Nazi era.

17. An analysis of the fire and light imagery would provide an interesting interpretation of *The Death of Virgil*. The cognitive process can be traced from the Vulcanic, sweltering fires of the netherworld (which erupt in as uncontrolled a fashion as the irrational) to the Apollonian clarity where fire is distilled into pure light. In Broch's mythological scheme the Vulcanic realm deliberately denies cognition and concomitant creation; but denial—through perjury—implies knowledge. Prometheus, Vulcan's brother, took upon himself the humanizing task of stealing the "divine spark" (of cognition) from the highest deity. In many allusions to the Greek and Christian mythologies, Broch hints at the connection between cognition/crime, or cognition/sin and the incendiary spark. The political relevance of the "divine spark" of cognition, as it ignites revolutions, had been presented in *The Sleepwalkers*, particularly in the "Epilogue." Fire is always mutable. According to the context, it can carry cognitive-constructive or aesthetic-destructive connotations.

18. Although Virgil is *lying* in bed, he experiences this expectation as if he were *standing*.

19. Oskar Seyffert, *Dictionary of Classical Antiquities*, rev. and ed. Henry Nettleship and J. E. Sandys (New York: Meridian Books, 1959)

20. ". . . the Archer armed with his bow . . ." is my own translation, replacing the Untermeyer translation, ". . . the Archer defended by . . ." (*DV*, 266).

21. Broch used "ivory" and "horn" with direct reference to the Homeric gates of ivory and horn (*DV*, 184) through which the false and the true dreams are released. In the maze of the constantly changing meanings of Virgil's encounters, ivory offers one of the few reliable and unchanging identifications. It always points to temptation and illusion. The ivory and horn opposition is particularly stressed when both Lysanias and Plotius offer Virgil a drink. Lysanias offers wine in an ivory goblet (*DV*, 407), Plotius water in a beaker of brown horn (*DV*, 407). (Wine and ivory is a particularly noxious combination, since wine causes drunkenness and mocks the cognitive task.) The transformation of the ivory goblet into one of horn occurs in the last part of the novel (*DV*, 446) and points to Virgil's momentary release from illusion. Ivory associations accompany even the last phase of Virgil's journey (that is, *DV*, 454, 455, 456) to indicate that the earthly is never totally free from illusion. Ivory connotations also connect apparently disparate objects. In one instance, for example, Plotia's "softly shining skin" with "the tender veins which showed beneath it" (*DV*, 293) is like the paper on which Virgil's last

testament will be written. "And by holding it against the light one could see through its ivory color the [brownish] network of the grain" (*DV*, 411). ("Brownish" is not in the German original.)

22. It is interesting to note Broch's changed attitude toward "poetry as impatience for cognition." In the essays of the 1930s, this definition was viewed as a positive statement. *Dichtung* found its justification through the impatience which forced the poet to penetrate to the irrational in order to lift it through his art into consciousness. In the same manner in which the Orpheus myth and Aeneas' descent into the netherworld receive a negative interpretation in *The Death of Virgil*, almost fifteen years after the essays, the lofty goal of the poetic mission is rejected as illusory.

23. Virgil's position is the strongest statement Broch ever makes for an antimaterialistic interpretation of the world of phenomena. The theory of symbols here expounded stresses the importance of symbols, but insists that the symbol never be taken for the reality it only symbolizes. In a novel which almost defies translation, these passages are particularly difficult to comprehend without reference to the original German. When Virgil differentiates the *Abbild* from the *Urbild*, (*GW*, III, 527) he acknowledges that even the *Urbild* is still an image only, indicating that penetration to that of which the primordial image is an image, is impossible. Virgil's quest is, hence, by definition beyond attainment. The paradox of pursuing that which one knows by definition to be unreachable echoes the striving for the Platonic totality.

24. G. S. Kirk and J. E. Raven, *The Presocratic Philosophers* (Cambirdge: Cambridge University Press, 1957), p. 200. The context from which the quotation was excerpted adds still more meaning since it points to *aither* as "pure cosmic fire"—in terms of *The Death of Virgil* the realm of Apollonian clarity.

25. See Jean-Paul Bier, *Hermann Broch et 'la Mort de Virgile'* (Paris: Larousse, 1974), esp. pp. 145–49.

26. For example, laughter-smile; perjury-pledge; beauty-reality; life-death.

27. See Erich Neumann, *The Origins and History of Consciousness*, Bollingen Series 42 (Princeton: Princeton University Press, 1970), esp. chapter 1, "The Uroboros." Striking similarities exist between Neumann's presentation and Broch's mythology of cognitive processes. Neumann had studied with C. G. Jung in the 1930s. His book was originally published in 1949, four years after *The Death of Virgil*.

28. Chains and slaves are recurrent motifs in the novel (as well as a variation on the ring). They are historically appropriate to the Rome of Caesar Augustus, but they also express a cognitive function. In this life, man is chained to and slave of the earthly condition. All characters in the novel are at some point viewed in the slave or chain setting. In Caesar Augustus, this aspect is particularly stressed when Virgil meets him on the descent down the Misery Alley. ". . . on his neck-*ring* bobbed—as though he were the missing

erstwhile mate of the little Syrian—the end of a chain, of silver it is true . . ." (*DV*, 420) (emphasis is mine).

29. The English translation does not clarify the opposition between "cognition of life" and "cognition of death." *Erkenntnis des Lebens* (*GW*, III, 352) becomes "the store of knowledge" (*DV*, 321), and *Erkenntnis des Todes* (*GW*, III, 353) "the understanding of death" (*DV*, 321). Similarly, the nihilistic impact of Caesar Augustus's statement, which is characteristic for its noncognitive provenance, is lost in translation. ". . . das Leben ist so wenig wie der Tod; es führt zu ihm hin, und beide sind Nichts" (*GW*, III, 353), is quite different from " . . . and both amount to nothing" (*DV*, 322).

30. The English translation uses "true image" for *Abbild* and "arch-image" for *Urbild* (*DV*, 477 and *GW*, III, 527).

Chapter Six

1. On the genesis of the novel, see Richard Thieberger, "Hermann Brochs Novellenroman and seine Vorgeschichte," *Deutsche Vierteljahrsschrift für Literaturwissenschaft und Geistesgeschichte*, 36 (1962), 562–82; Manfred Durzak, "Die Entstehungsgeschichte von Hermann Brochs 'Die Schuldlosen.' Mit bisher ungedruckten Quellen," *Euphorion*, 63 (1969), 371–405; Hermann Weigand, " 'Die Schuldosen:' An Approach," *Publications of the Modern Language Association*, 68 (1953), 323–34. For a selective and updated bibliography on the novel, see *st* 209, 351.

2. The description of the square in front of the railroad station and the allusions to Goethe and Nietzsche identify this town as Weimar. Weimar provides a symbolic dimension as the residence of Goethe, who was, in Broch's opinion, the first "modern" poet, establishing secular claims for totality, and as the birthplace of the Weimar Constitution. As the locale for events taking place during the Weimar Republic, the choice of Weimar adds a clever touch. The geographical arrangement of the *Schlossplatz* and the *Schlosskirche* in Weimar does not quite agree, however, with that in the novel.

In the novel, two interpretative time schemes are connected with "Weimar." The first spans the period from the late Baroque (frequently alluded to in the novel) and Goethe to the Weimar Republic, testifying to the rise and demise of the most recent secular historical cycle. The second time frame spans the period of the Weimar Republic proper, where a minicycle of the rise and fall of democracy is acted out.

3. The ethically neutral A. and the aesthetically committed Zacharias represent two types of closed systems. This is obvious when A. identifies them as "brothers:" "You're Z. and I'm A. We're brothers, aren't we? So now we own all names between us, the whole lot from A to Z" (*GL*, 147). Zacharias reprimands A. for his neutrality: "Silly neutrality jokes. It is unworthy of a German man to take any note of them: 'Left or right; some are for Einstein, some are against, you can't be neutral . . .' " (*GL*, 139).

4. In a letter to Wilhelm Emrich of April 10, 1951, Broch points to music as a common bond between Thomas Mann's *Dr. Faustus* (published in 1947) and *The Guiltless*. He admits, however, that he did not by far approximate the depth of Mann's chapters on music (*GW*, VIII, 414). Broch must have seen the similarities in the use of music as a demonic element, and of the apocalypse as the appropriate reference system for pre-Nazi and Nazi Germany.

5. st 209, 255; translation and emphasis mine.

6. The apocalyptic connotations are further evident in a minor theme which runs in many variations through the novel: head gear and the complicated rhythm in which hats and caps are put on and taken off. Before the grandfather-Commandatore sits in judgment over A., he pulls a woolen cap out of his pocket and tugs it over his head. (The deliberately coarse language—"tug": *überstülpen*—reflects again the cheapness of the event.) A. wonders whether this woolen cap is perhaps the judge's "beret," necessary for handing down the sentence. In the entire novel, the word "beret" occurs only once before, when mention is made of Wagner "in a slanting beret" (*GL*, 136). The German original is more specific than the English translation, where the "beret" connection is not obvious. Compare: ". . . Wagner, dieser mit schiefem Barret . . ." (*GL*, 209) and ". . . da er eine Wollhaube aus der Tasche zog—oder war es doch das für die Urteilsverkündigung nötige Richterbarett?—und damit die weisse Mähne überstülpte" (*GL*, 259). Judge and judgment, a focus for divergent associations, allude to the Last Judgment and the apocalypse.

7. Alban Butler, *Lives of the Saints*, edited, revised and supplemented by Herbert Thurston and Donald Attwater (New York: Kenedy, 1962), entry under September 17th.

8. See also J. J. White, "Broch, Virgil, and the Cycle of History," *Germanic Review*, 42 (1966), 103–10.

9. On the same geometric constellation see Kimberley Sparks, "A Geometry of Time: A Study of Hermann Broch's Prose Imagery," Diss. Princeton University 1963.

10. On the epistemological level, this resistance to turn around reinforces Hildegard's "straightforward" characteristics; it supersedes the line of characters in Broch's novels extending from Esch, who "carried his head in his neck." to *The Death of Virgil* and Orpheus' disobedience to the command not to look behind him.

11. The similarities between Thomas Mann's *Dr. Faustus* and *The Guiltless*, to which Broch refers (*GW*, VIII, 414), lie only superficially in the use of music as a demonic force. The deeper similarities lie in both authors' view of history as theology/*Heilsgeschichte*, on the emphasis of methaphysics over physics, that is, on the spiritual and intellectual contributions, and the disregard for concrete, material phenomena shaping the course of history. In this respect, they are part of the tradition of which they show the disastrous end phase.

Chapter Seven

1. Letter to Hermann Salinger of September 29, 1950, *GW*, VIII, 404–6.
2. *The City of Man: A Declaration on World Democracy* (New York: Viking, 1941). For identification of the writers and scholars who drafted and signed the declaration, see chapter 5, note 1.
3. *The City of Man*, p. 87. In a letter to Alvin Johnson of March 17, 1950, written almost ten years after *The City of Man*, Broch uses almost identical phrases when he describes the attractiveness of Marxism to the masses: ". . . it is an appeal to social justice and the idea, that only with this social justice the human rights may become reality" (*GW*, VIII, 387).
4. *The City of Man*, pp. 27–28. This definition will be repeated in nearly identical vocabulary in the theory of democracy.
5. The view of America as an "endangered" democracy continues through the years. Compare letters of February and March, 1946 (*GW*, VIII, 252, 253.) As part of the political theory, this view is included, for example, in *GW*, IX, 390 and 403, of 1948.
6. See especially the "Epistemological Excursus" (*SW*, 559–65), where the connection is traced between values and history and the autonomy of the "I".
7. On conversion by irrational as opposed to rational means, see also *GW*, IX, 116-22. Although Broch does not deny the irrational element in "miraculous illuminations," as they occur in religious conversions, he insists on the rational-didactic approach in the political raising of the level of consciousness.
8. In his theory of cognitive advances Broch accounts for qualitative changes in history. But this view cannot be accommodated within the psychic cycles (unless one is prepared to see historical progress along a zigzag line or a spiral, something Broch does not do). The difficulty is intimately connected with Broch's understanding of dialectics, which he uses in the Platonic sense where "the task of dialectics is to separate and to mix" (Hugo Perls, *Lexikon der Platonischen Begriffe* [Bern: Francke Verlag, 1973], p. 57). Progress is possible only in Hegelian-Marxian dialectics, in which the triadic movement involves qualitative changes. Broch apparently did not see the difference between the two kinds of dialectics and applied Platonic dialectics to a dynamic field which had been shaped by Hegelian dialectics. (See Broch's use of "dialectic" in relation to the psychic cycles *GW*, IX, 95, 97.) Broch's *undialektischer Ansatz* is extensively discussed and criticized by Hermann Krapoth, *Dichtung und Philosophie. Eine Studie zum Werk Hermann Brochs* (Bonn: Bouvier, 1971), pp. 125–36.
9. In his correspondence he mentioned Sigmund Freud and Gustave Le Bon, also Wilhelm Reich and Franz Gabriel Alexander (*BBB*, 427); he knew C. G. Jung's work, as alluded to in *BBB*, 410; in *BBB*, 479 he also mentions Paul Reiwald. As early as June 19, 1943, he complained how difficult and vast the subject is (*BBB*, 425). Cursory references to the "New York Library" indicate that he did much of his research at the New York Public Library.

10. Compare on the same subject Wolfgang Rothe's introduction to Broch's mass psychology, esp. *GW*, IX, 19.

11. Among the published sources, the most concise rendition of the "Bill of Duties," though of a later date, is found in *GW*, IX, 414–16.

12. Attempted publication of the proposal in a journal likewise did not materialize due to its emphasis on legal-technical aspects. Compare Paul Michael Lützeler, "Hermann Broch im Exil."

13. Compare Hermann Broch, *Zur Universitätsreform*, ed. Götz Wienold (Frankfurt: Suhrkamp, 1969).

14. The expression occurs for instance in *GW*, VIII, 387.

15. See Paul Michael Lützeler, "Hermann Brochs Buch 'Hofmannsthal und seine Zeit' als kunstsoziologische Studie," *Literatur und Kritik*, 59 (1975), 537–52.

16. Broch's assignation of the "political book" into his *oeuvre* is not quite clear. Sometimes it is subsumed under mass psychology (for example, in the "Rockefeller Outline" or a letter of June 10, 1950, in *GW*, VIII, 394–95), sometimes it is presented, as in the Knopf proposal, as an additional field of inquiry. In a letter of November 2, 1948, he explains that the "political book" presents "the psychological foundations of democracy" (*GW*, VIII, 305).

17. 1936 marks the beginning of Broch's research for the "Resolution." He discontinued these studies when he returned from Vienna to Alt-Aussee in late 1937.

18. Compare also the letter of June 12, 1949, to Brody in *BBB*, 513.

19. Compare *BBB*, 498 of September 28, 1948, and *GW*, VIII, 304 of November 2, 1948.

20. The address bore the title *"Die Intellektuellen und der Kampf um die Menschenrechte"* ("The Intellectuals and the Fight for the Human Rights"). It is reprinted in *Literatur und Kritik*, 54–55 (1971), 193–97. The essay is followed by Paul Michael Lützeler's article on Broch's political pamphlets, 198–206. On the cultural politics of the congress, see the article by Christopher Lasch," The Cultural Cold War: A Short History of the Congress for Cultural Freedom," in *Towards a New Past: Dissenting Essays in American History*, ed. Barton J. Bernstein (New York: Vintage Books, 1969), esp. pp. 322–332.

21. *Ibid.*, p. 194.

22. *Ibid.*, p. 197.

Chapter Eight

1. *Dichter wider Willen: Einführung in das Werk von Hermann Broch* (Zurich: Rhein Verlag, 1958), p. 41.

Selected Bibliography

BIBLIOGRAPHIES

HACK, BERTOLD, and KLOSS, MARIETTA, eds. *Hermann Broch—Daniel Brody Briefwechsel 1930–1951*. Bibliography by Klaus Jonas. Frankfurt: Buchhändler-Vereinigung, 1971. This volume contains the most complete bibliography of Broch's *oeuvre* and of the secondary literature published through 1970.

Updated bibliographies on individual subjects are found in the new edition of Broch's collected work, now in progress. (See separate entries in the *Werkausgabe*.)

PRIMARY SOURCES

1. Collected Editions

Gesammelte Werke. 10 vols. Zurich: Rhein-Verlag, 1953–1961. Until the new revised edition, published by Suhrkamp, has been completed, this is still the standard edition of Broch's work in German. (1) *Gedichte*. Edited by Erich Kahler; (2) *Die Schlafwandler*; (3) *Der Tod des Vergil*; (4) *Der Versucher*; (5) *Die Schuldlosen*; (6) *Dichten und Erkennen: Essays*. Vol. 1. Edited by Hannah Arendt; (7) *Erkennen und Handeln: Essays*. Vol. 2. Edited by Hannah Arendt; (8) *Briefe*; (9) *Massenpsychologie*. Edited by Wolfgang Rothe; (10) *Die unbekannte Grösse und frühe Schriften. Mit den Briefen an Willa Muir*. Edited by Ernst Schönwiese.

Werkausgabe. 13 vols. Edited by Paul Michael Lützeler. Frankfurt: Suhrkamp. Since the individual volumes appear in the suhrkamp taschenbuch series, they are not numbered consecutively but in accordance with the series. To date, the following volumes have been published: st 209 *Die Schuldlosen*, 1974; st 246 *Schriften zur Literatur 1: Kritik*, 1975; st 247 *Schriften zur Literatur 2: Theorie*, 1975; st 296 *Der Tod des Vergil*, 1976; st 350 *Die Verzauberung*, 1976; st 375 *Philosophische Schriften 1: Kritik*, 1977; *Philosophische Schriften 2: Theorie*, 1977; st 393 *Die Unbekannte Grösse*, 1977. Forthcoming: *Politische Schriften*, 1978; *Massenwahntheorie*, 1978.

2. Prose
Die Heimkehr. Edited by Harald Binde. Frankfurt: Fischer, 1962.
Der Bergroman. 4 vols. Edited by Frank Kress and Hans Albert Maier.
   Frankfurt: Suhrkamp, 1969. The four volumes comprise the three
   versions of the novel and one volume of variants and commentaries.
Barbara und andere Novellen. Suhrkamp taschenbuch 151. Edited with a
   postscript by Paul Michael Lützeler. Frankfurt: Suhrkamp, 1973.

3. Works in Philosophy
The City of Man: A Declaration on World Democracy. New York: Viking,
   1941.
Zur Universitätsreform. edition suhrkamp. Edited by Götz Wienold.
   Frankfurt: Suhrkamp, 1969.
Gedanken zur Politik. Bibliothek Suhrkamp. Edited by Dieter Hildebrandt.
   Frankfurt: Suhrkamp, 1970.
Völkerbund-Resolution. Edited by Paul Michael Lützeler. Salzburg: Otto
   Müller, 1973.
Menschenrecht und Demokratic. Edited by Paul Michael Lützeler. Frank-
   furt: Suhrkamp, 1978.

4. Essays
   Only those essays are listed that have not been published in the *Gesammelte Werke.*

"Cantos 1913." *Neue Deutsche Hefte,* 13, No. 2 (1966), 3–10. Introduction by
   Manfred Durzak
"Ethik." *Der Brenner,* 4, No. 16 (May, 1914), 684–90. Reprinted in 375/1,
   243-9.
"Konstruktion der historischen Wirklichkeit." *Summa, IV (1918),* i–xvi.
   Reprinted as part of "Zur Erkenntnis dieser Zeit" in st 375/2, 23-39.
"Rezension der Bücher Max Adlers über Marx und Engels." *Kant–Studien,*
   27 (1922), 184–86. Reprinted in st 375/1, 264–7.
"Die erkenntnistheoretische Bedeutung des Begriffes 'Revolution' und die
   Wiederbelebung der Hegelschen Dialektik. (Zu den Büchern Arthur
   Lieberts)." *Prager Presse,* 2, No. 206 (July 30, 1922) iii–iv. Reprinted in
   st 375/1, 257–63.
"Trotzdem: Humane Politik. Verwirklichung einer Utopie." *Neue
   Rundschau,* 61, No. 1 (1950), 1–31.
"Die Intellektuellen und der Kampf um die Menschenrechte." *Literatur und
   Kritik,* 54–55 (1971), 193–97.

5. English Translations
The Sleepwalkers. Translated by Willa and Edwin Muir. Boston: Little,
   Brown, 1932. Reprint, New York: Universal Library, 1971.
The Unknown Quantity. Translated by Willa and Edwin Muir. New York:
   Viking, 1935.
The Death of Virgil: Translated by Jean Starr Untermeyer. New York:
   Pantheon, 1945. Reprint, New York: Universal Library, 1965.

The Guiltless. Translated by Ralph Manheim. Boston: Little, Brown, 1974.
Short Stories. Edited by Eric Herd. London: Oxford University Press, 1966.

SECONDARY SOURCES

1. General Background

JANIK, ALLAN, and TOULMIN, STEPHEN. *Wittgenstein's Vienna*. New York: Simon and Schuster, 1973.

JOHNSTON, WILLIAM M. *The Austrian Mind: An Intellectual and Social History 1848–1938*. Berkeley: University of California Press, 1972.

LESER, NORBERT. "Austro-Marxism: A Reappraisal." *Journal of Contemporary History*, 1, No. 2 (April, 1966), 117–33.

MACARTNEY, C. A. *The Habsburg Empire 1790–1918*. New York: Macmillan, 1969.

STADLER, KARL A. *Austria*. New York: Praeger, 1971.

WILLIAMS, C. E. *The Broken Eagle: The Politics of Austrian Literature from Empire to Anschluss*. New York: Harper and Row, 1974.

2. Books

BIER, JEAN-PAUL. *Hermann Broch et "la Mort de Virgile."* Paris: Larousse, 1974.

BLANCHOT, MAURICE. *Le Livre à venir*. Paris: Gallimard, 1959. Pp. 136–54.

BOYER, JEAN. *Hermann Broch et le Problème de la Solitude*. Paris: Presses Universitaires de la France, 1954.

Broch heute. Edited by Joseph Strelka. Frankfurt: Suhrkamp, 1977.

COHN, DORRIT C. *The Sleepwalkers: Elucidations of Hermann Broch's Trilogy*. The Hague: Mouton, 1966.

COLLMAN, TIMM. *Zeit und Geschichte in Hermann Brochs "Der Tod des Vergil."* Bonn: Bouvier. 1967.

DURZAK, MANFRED. *Hermann Broch*. Hamburg: Rowohlt, 1966.

———*Herman Broch*. Stuttgart: Metzler, 1967.

———*Hermann Broch: Der Dichter und seine Zeit*. Stuttgart: Kohlhammer, 1968. Contains chapters on Broch's relation to Weininger, Schopenhauer, Goethe, Thomas Mann, James Joyce, Robert Musil, and Hugo von Hofmannsthal.

———, ed. *Hermann Broch: Perspektiven der Forschung*. Munich: Fink, 1972. Contains reprints of some of the most seminal essays in Broch scholarship. A selection of them is listed separately under each author's name.

KAHLER, ERICH. *Die Philosophie von Hermann Broch*. Tübingen: Mohr, 1962.

———, ed. *Dichter wider Willen*. Zurich: Rhein-Verlag, 1958.

KOEBNER, THOMAS. *Hermann Broch*. Bern: Francke, 1965.

KRAPOTH, HERMANN. *Dichtung und Philosophie. Eine Studie zum Werk Hermann Brochs*. Bonn: Bouvier, 1971.

KREUTZER, LEO. *Erkenntnistheorie und Prophetie: Hermann Brochs Romantrilogie "Die Schlafwandler."* Tübingen: Niemeyer, 1966.

LOOS, BEATE. *Zeit und Tod: Der Bergroman Hermann Brochs und seine dichtungstheoretischen Voraussetzungen.* Frankfurt: Athenäum, 1971.

LÜTZELER, PAUL MICHAEL. *Hermann Broch—Ethik und Politik. Studien zum Frühwerk und zur Romantrilogie "Die Schlafwandler."* Munich: Winkler, 1973. Contains authoritative information of the young Broch.

MANDELKOW, KARL ROBERT. *Hermann Brochs Romantrilogie "Die Schlafwandler": Gestalt und Reflexion im modernen deutschen Roman.* 2d ed. Heidelberg: C. Winter, 1975.

MEINERT, DIETRICH. *Die Darstellung der Dimensionen menschlicher Existenz in Brochs "Der Tod des Vergil."* Bern: Francke, 1962.

MENGES, KARL. *Kritsche Studien zur Wertphilosophie Hermann Brochs.* Tübingen: Niemeyer, 1970.

REINHARDT, HARTMUT. *Erweiterter Naturalismus: Zu Hermann Brochs Schlafwandlern.* Cologne: Bölau, 1972.

SAVIANE, RENATO. *Apocalissi e Messianismo nei Romanzi di Hermann Broch.* Padua: Universita de Padova, 1971.

SCHLANT, ERNESTINE. *Die Philosophie Hermann Brochs.* Bern: Francke, 1971.

STEINECKE, HARTMUT. *Hermann Broch und der polyhistorische Roman.* Bonn: Bouvier, 1968.

WALDECK, PETER BRUCE. *Die Kindheitsproblematik bei Hermann Broch.* Munich: Fink, 1968.

ZIOLKOWSKI, THEODORE. *Hermann Broch.* Columbia Essays on Modern Writers. New York: Columbia University Press, 1964.

3. Articles

ANSTETT, JEAN-JACQUES. "Le Romantisme de Hermann Broch." *Etudes Germaniques*, 11 (1956), 224–39.

ARENDT HANNAH. "The Achievement of Hermann Broch." *Kenyon Review*, 11 (1949), 476–83.

BIER, JEAN-PAUL. "Le double problème de la demarche creatrice dans les théories esthétiques de Hermann Broch." *Revue Belge de Philologie et d'Histoire*, 48 (1970), 822–49.

BRINKMANN, RICHARD. "Romanform und Werttheorie bei Hermann Broch," *In Hermann Broch: Perspektiven der Forschung.* Edited by Manfred Durzak. Munich: Fink, 1972. Pp. 35–68.

BRUDE-FIRNAU, GISELA. " 'Zufällig durch die Zeitung'? Die Bedeutung der Tageszeitung für Hermann Brochs 'Die Schalfwandler.' " *German Quarterly*, 49 (1976), 31–44.

CASEY, TIMOTHY J. "Questioning Broch's 'Der Versucher.'" *Deutsche Vierteljahrsschrift für Literaturwissenschaft und Geistesgeschichte,* 47 (1973), 467–507.

CASSIRER, SIDONIE. "Hermann Broch's Early Writings." *Publications of the Modern Language Association,* 75 (1960), 453–62.

DURZAK, MANFRED. "Apokalypse oder Utopie? Bemerkungen zu Hermann Brochs 'Schlafwandlern.'" *Etudes Germaniques,* 24 (1969), 16–35.

———. "Hermann Brochs 'Der Tod des Vergil:' Echo und Wirkung. Ein Forschungsbericht." *Literaturwissenschaftliches Jahrbuch im Auftrag der Görres-Gesellschaft,* N.S. 10 (1969), 273–348.

———. "Hermann Brochs Auffassung des Lyrischen." In *Hermann Broch: Perspektiven der Forschung.* Edited by Manfred Durzak. Pp. 293–313.

FABER DU FAUR, CURT VON. "Der Seelenführer in Hermann Brochs 'Tod des Vergil.'" In *Hermann Broch: Perspektiven der Forschung.* Edited by Manfred Durzak. pp. 77–92.

FUCHS, ALBERT. "Hermann Broch. 'Der Tod des Vergil.'" In *Der deutsche Roman vom Barock bis zur Gegenwart.* Edited by Benno von Wiese. Düsseldorf: Bagel, 1963. II, 326–60.

HARDIN, JAMES. "'Der Versucher' and Hermann Broch's Attitude toward Positivism." *German Quarterly,* 39 (1966), 29–41.

HARDIN, JAMES. "The Theme of Salvation in the Novels of Hermann Broch." *Publications of the Modern Language Association,* 85 (1970), 219–77.

———. "Hermann Broch's Theories on Mass Psychology and 'Der Versucher.'" *German Quarterly,* 47 (1974), 24–33.

HERD, ERIC. "Hermann Broch and the Legitimacy of the Novel." *German Life and Letters,* 13 (1960), 262–70.

———. "The Guilt of the Hero in the Novels of Hermann Broch." *German Life and Letters,* 18 (1964), 30–39.

HINDERER, WALTER. "Grundzüge des 'Tod des Vergil.'" In *Hermann Broch: Perspektiven der Forschung.* Edited by Manfred Durzak. Pp 89–134.

JAFFE, ANIELA. "Hermann Broch: 'Der Tod des Vergil.' Ein Beitrag zum Problem der Individuation." In *Hermann Broch: Perspektiven der Forschung.* Edited by Manfred Durzak. Pp. 135–76.

KAHLER, ERICH. "The Epochal Innovations in Hermann Broch's Narrative." In *The Legacy of the German Refugee Intellectuals.* Edited by Robert Boyers. New York: Schocken, 1972. Pp. 186–92.

KIEL, ANNA. "Hermann Brochs theorie over de massawaan." *Mens en Kosmos,* 18 (1962), 1–16.

———. "De romans van Hermann Broch en zijn massawaantheorie." *Mens en Kosmos,* 18 (1962), 49–65.

————. "Das Begriffspaar 'Offen' und 'Geschlossen' im philosophischen Werk Hermann Brochs und in seinem Roman 'Der Tod des Vergil.' " *Duitse Kroniek*, 15 (1963), 18–28 and 53–69.

Literatur und Kritik, 54–55 (May–June, 1971). The entire issue of this journal is dedicated to Broch in memory of the twentieth anniversary of his death and contains a number of articles on Broch.

LÜTZELER, PAUL MICHAEL. "Die Kulturkritik des jungen Broch. Zur Entwicklung von Hermann Brochs Geschichts–und Werttheorie." In *Hermann Broch: Perspektiven der Forschung*. Edited by Manfred Durzak. Pp. 329–51.

————. "Erweiterter Naturalismus. Hermann Broch und Emile Zola." *Zeitschrift für deutsche Philologie*, 93 (1974), 214–38.

————. "Hermann Broch und Karl Kraus." *Modern Austrian Literature*, 8 No. 1 (1975), 211–39.

————. "Hermann Brochs Buch 'Hofmannsthal und seine Zeit' als kunstsoziologische Studie." *Literatur und Kritik*, 59 (1975), 537–52.

————"Hermann Brochs 'Die Verzauberung' als politischer Roman." *Neophilologus*, 61 (1977), 111–26.

OSTERLE, HEINZ. "Hermann Brochs 'Die Schlafwandler.' Kritik der zentralen Metapher." *Deutsche Vierteljahrsschrift für Literaturwissenschaft und Geistesgeschichte*, 44 (1970), 229–68.

————. "Hermann Broch's 'Die Schlafwandler': Revolution and Apocalypse." *Publications of the Modern Language Association*, 86 (1971), 946–57.

ROTHE, WOLFGANG. "Hermann Broch als politischer Denker." In *Hermann Broch: Perspektiven der Forschung*. Edited by Manfred Durzak. Pp. 399–416.

SAMMONS, CHRISTA. "Hermann Broch Archive—Yale University Library." *Modern Austrian Literature*, 5 (1972), 18–69.

SCHLANT, ERNESTINE. "Hermann Broch's Theory of Symbols Exemplified in a Scene from 'The Death of Virgil.' " *Neophilologus* 54 (1970) 53–64.

————. "Hermann Broch als politischer Utopist Zwischen 'Geschichtsgesetz und Willensfreiheit.' *Literatur und* Kritik, 54/55 (1971), 207–13.

————. "Zur Ästhetik von Hermann Broch." In *Hermann Broch: Perspektiven der Forschung*. Edited by Manfred Durzak. Pp. 371–84.

————. "Hermann Broch and Modern Physics." *Germanic Review*. Forthcoming.

SCHOOLFIELD, GEORGE. "Notes on Hermann Broch's 'Der Versucher.' " *Monatshefte*, 48 (1956), 1–16.

STEINECKE, HARTMUT. "Hermann Broch." In *Deutsche Dichter der Moderne. Ihr Leben und Werk*. Edited by Benno von Wiese. Pp. 454–78. Berlin: Erich Schmidt, 1965.

————. "Hermann Broch als politischer Dichter." In *Deutsche Beiträge zur geistigen Überlieferung. Ein Jahrbuch.* Edited by George J. Metcalf and H. Stefan Schultz. Pp. 140–83. Heidelberg: Stiehm, 1970.

STRELKA, JOSEPH. "Hermann Broch. Comparatist and Humanist." *Comparative Literature Studies,* 12 (1975), 67–79.

WACHTLER, GUNDI. "Der Ich-Erzähler in Hermann Brochs Roman 'Der Versucher.' " In *Germanistische Studien.* Edited by Johannes Erben and Eugene Thurnher. Innsbruck: Institut für vergleichende Sprachwissenschaften, 1969. Pp. 277–94.

―――. "Der Archetyp der Grossen Mutter in Hermann Brochs Roman 'Der Versucher.' " In *Hermann Broch: Perspektiven der Forschung.* Edited by Manfred Durzak. Pp. 231–50.

WEIGAND, HERMANN J. "Broch's 'Death of Virgil': Program Notes." *Publications of the Modern Language Association,* 62 (1947), 525–54.

―――. 'Die Schuldlosen': An Approach." *Publication of the Modern Language Association,* 68 (1953), 323–34.

WHITE, J. J. "The Identity and Function of Bertrand in Hermann Broch's 'Die Schlafwandler.' " *German Life and Letters,* 24 (1970–1971), 135–44.

WINKLER, MICHAEL. "Die Funktion der Erzählungen in Hermann Brochs 'Bergroman.' " In *Hermann Broch: Perspektiven der Forschung.* Edited by Manfred Durzak. Pp. 251–69.

―――. "The Wanderer in Search of a System." *German Quarterly,* 48 (1975), 234–43.

ZIOLKOWSKI, THEODORE. "Hermann Broch: 'The Sleepwalkers.' " In *Dimensions of the Modern Novel. German Texts and European Contexts.* Princeton: Princeton University Press, 1969. Pp. 138–80.

―――. "Hermann Broch and Relativity in Fiction." *Wisconsin Studies in Comparative Literature,* 3 (1967), 365–76. Reprinted in German in *Hermann Broch: Perspektiven der Forschung.* Edited by Manfred Durzak. Pp. 315–27.

ŽMEGAC, VIKTOR. "Realitätsvokabeln: Ästhetik and Romantheorie bei Hermann Broch." In *Kunst und Wirklichkeit.* Bad Homburg: Gehlen, 1969. Pp. 43–85.

Index

190

DATE DUE

DEMCO 38-297